The Explanation for Everything

SEXUAL CULTURES: New Directions from the Center for
Lesbian and Gay Studies
General Editors: José Esteban Muñoz and Ann Pellegrini

Times Square Red, Times Square Blue
Samuel R. Delany

Private Affairs
Critical Ventures in the Culture of Social Relations
Phillip Brian Harper

In Your Face
9 Sexual Studies
Mandy Merck

Tropics of Desire
Interventions from Queer Latino America
José Quiroga

Murdering Masculinities
Fantasies of Gender and Violence in the American Crime Novel
Greg Forter

Our Monica, Ourselves
The Clinton Affair and the National Interest
Edited by Lauren Berlant and Lisa Duggan

Passing
Identity and Interpretation in Sexuality, Race, and Religion
Edited by María C. Sánchez and Linda Schlossberg

The Explanation for Everything
Essays on Sexual Subjectivity
Paul Morrison

The Explanation for Everything
Essays on Sexual Subjectivity

PAUL MORRISON

NEW YORK UNIVERSITY PRESS

New York and London

NEW YORK UNIVERSITY PRESS
New York and London

© 2001 by New York University

Earlier versions of chapters 3 and 4 appeared in *GLQ: A Journal of Lesbian and Gay Studies* 1, no. 1 (1993) and *Genders* 11 (fall 1991) respectively.

Library of Congress Cataloging-in-Publication Data
Morrison, Paul (Paul A.)
The explanation for everything : essays on sexual subjectivity /
Paul Morrison.
p.   cm. — (Sexual cultures)
Includes bibliographical references and index.
ISBN 0-8147-5673-5 (cloth : alk. paper)
ISBN 0-8147-5674-3 (pbk. : alk. paper)
1. Homosexuality. 2. Homosexuality in literature. 3. Homosexuality
in art. 4. Heterosexuality. I. Title. II. Series.
HQ76.25 M667 2001
306.76'6—dc21   2001003800

New York University Press books are printed on acid-free paper,
and their binding materials are chosen for strength and durability.

Manufactured in the United States of America

10 9 8 7 6 5 4 3 2 1

For Catherine, Georgia, and Grace
and in loving memory of Tom

Contents

Acknowledgments

Of the many hands involved in the writing of this book, it gives me particular pleasure to recall those of Stuart Blackley, John Burt, Mary Campbell, John Jay Crickett, Scott Derrick, Lee Edelman, William Flesch, Eugene Goodheart, David M. Halperin, Thomas A. King, Alan Levitan, Joseph Litvak, Richard Meyer, Helena Michie, Frank Nye, Ann Pellegrini, Henry Schaffer, and Susan Staves.

1 The Explanation for Everything (Bad)

The claim "I'm straight" is the psychosexual analogue of "The check is in the mail": if you need to say it, your credit or credibility is already in doubt. But such was not always the case. Up until the end of the eighteenth century, Foucault argues, the regulation of sexuality focused primarily on legitimate alliances. The right to privacy (as we now call it) did not extend even to a law-abiding bedroom; the married couple, much more so than the pervert, was the object of anxious scrutiny and control, and the normative were routinely obliged to justify themselves as such:

The sex of husband and wife was beset by rules and recommendations. The marriage relation was the most intense focus of constraints; it was spoken of more than anything else; more than any other relation, it was required to give a detailed accounting of itself. It was under constant surveillance: if it was found to be lacking, it had to come forward and plead its cause before a witness.[1]

The modern world exactly reverses this "incitement to discourse." The pervert comes to occupy center stage, endlessly declaring that he-is-what-he-is, even as the "legitimate couple" withdraws discreetly to the wings:

The legitimate couple, with its regular sexuality, had a right to more discretion [than in the past]. It tended to function as a norm, one that was stricter, perhaps, but quieter. On the other hand, what came under scrutiny was the sexuality of children, mad men and women, and criminals; the sensuality of those who did not like the opposite sex. . . . It was time for all these figures, scarcely noticed in the past, to step forward and speak, to make the difficult confession of what they were. (38–39)

Exclusion from representation is conventionally held to be the unhappy fate of the socially marginal or the sexually aberrant. Exemption from representation, Foucault counters, is the singular privilege of the normative. To occupy center stage, to declare one's heterosexual credentials, is already to protest too much. The only compelling proof of sexual "legitimacy" is the subject's felt knowledge that no proof is necessary. "Don't ask, don't tell": the policy of compulsory discretion that now governs gays in the U.S. military has long been the informing (if thoroughly internalized) decorum of normativity. Heterosexuality is the love that dare not speak its name.

Conventional wisdom has it otherwise. Homosexuality is the proverbially innominate love, although if it too is not to be named, it is for reasons that have little to do with gay reticence. Heterosexuality speaks the name of its demonized other only at some peril to itself. As Eve Sedgwick has shown, the dreary game of "find-that-faggot," the ferreting out of latent or repressed or closeted homosexuality, is always troubled by the logic of "it takes one to know one"; too deft a hand at the game easily betrays a limp wrist.[2] But as Foucault suggests, silence is not "the absolute limit of discourse," and it is easy enough to invoke the specter of homosexuality without ever once risking the word:

Silence itself—the things one declines to say, or is forbidden to name, the discretion that is required between different speakers—is less the absolute limit of discourse, the other side from which it is separated by a strict boundary, than an element that functions alongside the things said, with them and in relation to them within over-all strategies. (27)

It requires but little ingenuity to speak of what one nevertheless declines to say: when denotation proves perilous, connotation can be relied upon to do its work.[3] I am sometimes told, for example, that my prose is too mannered, but surely that is not all I'm being told. (Or perhaps it is. I am hardly in a position to argue otherwise, which is precisely the point.) By the same token, however, what one declines to say can be equally compromising. Speak of last night's partner in gender-neutral terms, for instance, and your sexual proclivities are immediately apparent to everyone. A sexuality that falls too conspicuously below the level of representation is as suspect as one that rises too eagerly to it. Hence, the paradox: if heterosexual credentials are to prove convincing, they must never be offered or demanded, yet the subject's felt knowledge that no proof is necessary must never feel like exclusion from representation. When imposed on gays in the military, the policy of "Don't ask, don't tell" merely guarantees the normative the triumphalism of their knowingness. (To be entirely pleasurable, sexual knowledge must be extracted from, not freely given by, the perverse subject.) When internalized by heterosexuals themselves, however, the same policy underwrites the strategic silence that envelops the norm. In the modern world, the norm is "stricter" but "quieter"—so quiet, in fact, that the very attempt to formulate it (one of the ambitions of the present study) presupposes a failure to attain to it.

The normative subject would thus seem to be in a highly vexed relation to what Foucault terms "the truth of sex":

Between each of us and our sex, the West has placed a never-ending demand for truth; it is up to us to extract the truth of sex, since this truth is beyond its grasp, it is up to sex to tell us our truth, since sex is what holds it in darkness. (77)

But sex speaks (or remains eloquently dumb) only when the subject is in distress, and only the deviant or the dubiously normal seek out the ear of the doctor, the official custodian of the truth of sex. No one, of course, is obliged to do so. Between the subject and its sex the West has placed a never-ending demand for truth, but it compels no interventions. If we find ourselves on the head-doctor's couch, it is only because we have gone looking for help. The social worker comes knocking at our door; the head-doctor simply receives us when we arrive (money in hand) and dismisses us when we go. The triangulation of the subject's relation to the truth of its sex is occasioned solely by the subject's felt need for it—there is never any question of involving the authorities—and the doctor intervenes only in the role of amanuensis, the translator of the opaque discourse of sex.[4] Yet a subject in need of the ear of the doctor is by definition a subject out of touch with its needs and desires, which renders such voluntarism highly problematic. How is it possible to know what I don't know, that I don't know? How am I to decipher sex speaking when its language is opaque both to it and to me?

The genius of psychoanalysis is to insist that we never can know, at least with any certainty, although not to know has potentially devastating consequences for the subject. Heterosexuality remains the goal of all psychosexual development and much anxious social engineering, yet the Freudian premise of a universal bi-sexuality renders all sexual categories, heterosexuality included, problematic at best. Apologists for "the new bisexuality" argue that this is as it should be: "The new bisexuality, which is to say, the old bisexuality—bisexuality as eroticism, 'un-pigeonholed sexual identity,' *not* bisexuality as the 'third' choice between, or be-yond, hetero- or homosex."[5] Precisely: the new/old dispensation, the Freudian construction of sexuality, places bisexuality within, rather than between or be-yond, the hetero/homo binary, which is thus no binary at all. But again, such was not always the case. The German Homosexual Emancipation Movement of Freud's own day tended to construe homosexuality as a "special variety of the human species—a 'third sex,'" but psychoanalysis would have none of it. *Three Es-says on the Theory of Sexuality* explicitly opposes any attempt to separate "homo-sexuals from the rest of mankind as a group of a special character," and the Freudian premise of a universal bisexuality carried the day.[6] But why? Surely a "third sex" model of sexual difference, which preserves the integrity of the het-ero/homo divide, would seem the logical corollary of our culture's commitment to compulsory heterosexuality. For gays and lesbians, the choice of models may be academic: as David Halperin argues, both the psychoanalytic premise of a univer-sal bisexuality and "third sex" models of homosexual deviance have proven ef-fective arguments against the extension of basic civil liberties to the perverse.[7] For the normative, however, the choice would seem to be of some consequence, and the normative seem to have chosen unwisely. Why did the psychoanalytic prem-ise of a universal bisexuality, so apparently threatening to the regime of compul-sory heterosexuality, nevertheless emerge triumphant?

Freud offers the paradoxical assurance that there is no form of heterosexuality sufficiently coincident with itself that it cannot be shown, when need arises or convenience dictates, to be inhabited by its demonized "other." The procedure is not, however, reversible:

Rather than naming an invisible, undernoticed minority now finding its place in the sun, "bisexual" turns out to be, like bisexuals themselves, everywhere and nowhere. There is, in short, no "really" about it. The question of whether someone was "really" straight or "really" gay misrecognizes the nature of sexuality, which is fluid, not fixed, a narrative that changes over time rather than a fixed identity, however complex. The erotic discov-ery of bisexuality is the fact that it reveals sexuality to be a process of growth, transfor-mation, and surprise, not a stable and knowable state of being.[8]

The new sexual fluidity has little patience with what it takes to be the old identity categories of hetero and homo, but even given "the erotic [re]discovery of bisexuality," a crucial asymmetry obtains: for all practical purposes, homosexuality is an achievable identity; heterosexuality isn't. The question "Was Shakespeare really gay?" is "really" (and only) the question "Was Shakespeare really straight?" This may seem a distinction without a difference, but to conflate the two is to misconstrue the practical politics of sexual knowingness, if not "the nature of sexuality" itself. (Claims to normativity are characteristically met with skepticism. Only parents doubt confessions of deviance.) Oscar Wilde, to cite an obvious example, was the married father of two children, yet he is now received as virtually the Platonic Essence of Homosexuality, and his identity seems secure enough. Certainly no one feels compelled to ask whether he was "really" gay. Or, for that matter, "really" bisexual. True, he is sometimes celebrated as sexually "fluid" or "ambiguous," but as Lee Edelman notes, nothing is more punitively "known" in our culture than sexual ambiguity.[9] (Sexual ambiguity isn't.) Sedgwick argues that the very "insecurity"—I would say impossibility—of heterosexual identity allows for the effective regulation of the many by the specific oppression of the few:

Not only must homosexual men be unable to ascertain whether they are to be the objects of "random" homophobic violence, but no man must be able to ascertain that he is not (that his bonds are not) homosexual. In this way, a relatively small exertion of physical or legal compulsion potentially rules great reaches of behavior and filiation.[10]

Even better, at least from the perspective of all things normative: the criminal or merely reprehensible behavior and filiations of the many can be explained—again, when need arises or convenience dictates—as a latent or repressed form of the sexual perversions of the few. When no man is able to ascertain that he is not (that his bonds are not) homosexual, there is no atrocity that homosexuality cannot be made to explain (away).

No man, but what of women? The claim "I'm lesbian"—at least when the speaker is sufficiently femme—is routinely taken to mean "I have yet to meet the right man." Our culture is wonderfully adept at ferreting out male homosexuality anywhere and everywhere; it remains willfully blind, however, to all but the butchest manifestations of female deviance. Hence, the curious asymmetry: no man must be able to ascertain that he is not (that his bonds are not) homosexual, but no lesbian, no matter how homosexual her bonds, must ever be received as irredeemably lesbian. Gender trumps sexuality. A lesbian is, after all, a woman, and a woman is defined by her sexual availability to men. The Pussy Galore of James Bond fame is typical. James to Pussy: "They told me you only like women." The newly heterosexualized Pussy to James: "I never met a man before." Our culture's paradigmatic (non)lesbian is a heterosexual-in-waiting.[11]

Yet if actual lesbians are nowhere to be found, the charge of lesbianism remains generally available. Thus military women who bring sexual harassment suits against their male counterparts are frequently met with the countercharge of sexual deviance. "Don't ask, don't tell," but to resist normal male heterosexual flirtation—and only a man-hating dyke would mistake innocent flirtation for sexual harassment—is itself highly telling. (How else to explain the otherwise inexplicable? She has no sexual interest in *me*.) Janet Halley suggests that the Clinton "compromise" on gays in the military may be fueling incidents of sexual harassment against women, which, in its own way, is hardly surprising.[12] The legally acknowledged tolerance of closeted homosexuals necessarily calls into question the heterosexual credentials of all military men, who thus feel compelled (or so I imagine) to seek conspicuous re-accreditation. Boys are under immense social pressure to be boys, and what better way to become one, to be publicly acknowledged as one, than to act under the compulsion of an allegedly irresistible biological imperative? ("Don't ask, don't tell" raised either testosterone levels or anxieties about the nature of male homosocial bonding. I suspect the latter, although the former does have a certain pornographic appeal.) An unwelcome sexual advance always risks legal action, but even a failed assault succeeds in ferreting out a closeted lesbian. Male sexual predators of whatever variety tend to be construed as homosexual, actual or latent. (Is he "a homosexual or a necrophilic," Freud blithely speculates, as if the difference were both academic and difficult to negotiate.)[13] Female resistance to routine sexual harassment is received as evidence of lesbianism, actual or latent. In either case, heterosexuality can't lose.

Can't lose, moreover, even when all bonds are exposed as homosexual. Queens are everywhere, Luce Irigaray cautions, and queens rule: "Reigning everywhere, although prohibited in practice, hom(m)o-sexuality is played out through the bodies of women, matter, or sign, and heterosexuality has been up to now just an alibi for the smooth working of man's relation with himself, of relations among men."[14] A hundred-odd years of compulsory heterosexuality—who would have known?—turn out to be little more than a beard for the smooth workings of relations among men. The antidote to the patriarchal oppression of women is thus an authentic heterosexuality (and, presumably, a more thorough oppression of de facto as well as de jure homosexuality). The exculpatory appeal of the argument is obvious—with enemies like Irigaray, heterosexual patriarchy hardly needs friends —and it has the added advantage of being universally applicable. The admission of a little (theoretical) bisexuality is a small price to pay for a grant of unlimited political immunity, and when homosexuality is construed as internal to heterosexuality, everything else unsavory can be dismissed as external to it. As Edelman notes,

The field of sexuality—which is always, under patriarchy, implicated in, and productive of, though by no means identical with, the field of power relations—is not . . . merely bifurcated by the awareness of homosexual possibilities; it is not simply divided into the separate but unequal arenas of hetero- and homo-sexual relations. Instead, homosexuality comes to signify the potential permeability of every sexual signifier—and by extension, of every signifier as such—by an "alien" signification. Once sexuality may be read and interpreted in light of homosexuality, all sexuality is subject to a hermeneutics of suspicion.[15]

All sexuality is subject to a hermeneutics of suspicion, but there is only one (the usual) suspect.

Consider, in this context, Freud's most explicit excursion into the realm of social psychology, his reading of the two "great artificial groups, the Church and the army":

The love relation between men and women remains outside these organizations. Even when groups are formed which are composed of both men and women the distinction between the sexes plays no part. There is scarcely any sense in asking whether the libido which keeps groups together is of a homosexual or a heterosexual nature.[16]

Psychoanalytic readings of fascism characteristically take their theoretical bearings from Freud's analysis of these two "artificial"—and, tellingly, all-male— groups, which he initially construes as innocent of the hetero/homo divide. But exactly one paragraph later:

Love for women breaks through the group ties of race, of national divisions, and of the social class system, and it thus produces important effects as a factor in civilization. It seems certain that homosexual love is far more compatible with group ties, even when it takes the shape of uninhibited sexual impulses—a remarkable fact, the explanation of which might carry us far. (141)

A remarkable fact indeed, although the explanation that underwrites the political innocence of the regime of compulsory heterosexuality is never in fact given. (If normative sexuality "breaks through the group ties of race, of national divisions, and of the social class system," heterosexuality can hardly be implicated in racism, nationalism, or classism. And fascism was, of course, given to extreme forms of all three.) Elsewhere, Freud characterizes homosexuality as an innately antisocial form of narcissism, which renders the very notion of a gay group or collectivity a contradiction in terms;[17] in *Group Psychology*, he construes homosexuality as the logic of the social itself. All in all, he credits deviance with a wildly promiscuous, if logically dubious, explanatory power. Opponents of gays in the military can thus point to the incompatibility of homosexuality and any group tie; liberal opponents of the military can counter by triumphantly outing the de facto homosexuality of all military ties. And both can invoke the authority of Freud. True, the debate over gays in the military was not distinguished by its careful analysis of rival passages in Freud, but such is the historical good fortune of psychoanalysis, which becomes all the more powerful for its vulgarization. (The obvious explanation for the historic success of psychoanalysis, the immense intellectual power of its founding texts, does not strike me as compelling. I readily acknowledge that power, but I'm not convinced that the marketplace of ideas is a meritocracy. Were such the case, the state of my own career would be too distressing to contemplate.) What begins as a therapeutic practice is quickly liberated from the specific context of its exercise; what emerges is a general hermeneutic only tenuously bound to its theoretical premises; what triumphs is a ubiquitous, exculpatory, and quasi-instinctual form of sexual knowingness.

There is a growing consensus, of course, that Freud is no longer relevant. Cognitive scientists and the like routinely assure us that we have moved beyond him, that we now know better. But as D. A. Miller says of another Victorian curiosity, "the traditional novel," the past can have a strange afterlife: "The office that the traditional novel once performed has not disappeared along with it. The 'death of the novel' . . . has really meant the explosion everywhere of the novelistic, no longer bound in three-deckers, but freely scattered across a far greater range of cultural experience."[18] Freud (or even Freudianism) may no longer be with us, but a general sexual knowingness, freely scattered across a broad range of cultural experience and practices, is. The game of find-that-faggot can be enjoyed by anyone, anywhere. The sport might logically presuppose a commitment to the premise of a universal bisexuality, including the homophobe's own. In practice, however, no theoretical self-consciousness, no such commitment, is required.

Yet it is precisely the "ideal" of a universal bisexuality that underwrites the political innocence of the regime of compulsory heterosexuality. Bisexuality is "everywhere and nowhere," as Marjorie Garber puts it, which is exactly right: bisexuality everywhere inhabits an "always already" compromised heterosexuality, but when forced to appear, it goes by the name of latent or repressed or open homosexuality, which is uniquely privileged with explanatory power. (To my knowledge, no shrink, Freud included, has ever once diagnosed "repressed heterosexuality.")[19] This is not, I hasten to add, to criticize anyone's choice of erotic objects, straight, gay, bi, or otherwise, which I am hardly in a position to do; nor is it to deny the particular social and political pressures facing practicing bisexuals. It is to insist, however, that the regime of compulsory heterosexuality has good reasons for embracing a deconstructive, destabilizing premise that, as luck would have it, is anything but threatening to it. Barbara Johnson defines the aim of deconstructive criticism as the elaboration of "a discourse that says *neither* 'either/or,' *nor* 'both/and,' not even 'neither/nor,' while at the same time not totally abandoning these logics either."[20] As a description of the formal project of deconstruction, this is at once elegant and accurate. But the formal project is routinely credited with political efficacy—the more melodramatic of Johnson's theoretical cohorts speak of deconstruction and "the end of Western metaphysics" as coextensive—and the political claims seem to me dubious at best. The promised ontological apocalypse is, in any case, already at hand, and all signs point to heterosexism as usual: without ever once abandoning a pragmatic commitment to the logic of the hetero/homo divide, psychoanalysis nevertheless renders any "either/orism" or "neither/norism," any structuring binarism, theoretically untenable. In *Ulysses*, Stephen Dedalus offers a seemingly counterintuitive explanation for the historic success of the One, Holy, Catholic, and Apostolic Church: "The church is founded and founded irremovably because founded, like the world, macro and microcosm, upon the void. Upon incertitude, upon unlikelihood."[21] Psychoanalysis, the new custodian of the soul, is equally catholic in its aspirations, and it too is founded upon "incertitude," "unlikelihood." (Whether or not it proves "irremovable" will depend, at least in part, on our ability to distinguish an inaugurating and sustaining instability from a deconstructive undoing.) Foucault argues that sex is now received as "the explanation for everything" (78), but the nonbinary premise that is the non-bedrock of psychoanalysis renders the formulation too broad by half. Between each of us and his or her sex, the West has placed an asymmetrical demand and capacity for truth. Heterosexuality explains nothing, including the crimes committed in its name. Homosexuality explains everything in need of explanation, including the crimes committed against it in the name of compulsory heterosexuality.

9

Sexuality is not, of course, the only explanatory axis available to us. Race, gender, and class constitute "the holy trinity of contemporary criticism"; sexuality is not named, although its exclusion from the triumvirate may well bear paradoxical testimony to its explanatory power. Early feminists had to establish the validity of the analytical axis of gender; lesbian and gay critics, by contrast, inherited a culture in which (homo)sexuality was already too meaningful. The Father, Son, and Holy Spirit are three parts of the same Godhead. Race, gender, and class are mutually inflecting but nonidentical categories of social positioning, and the introduction (or open acknowledgment) of sexuality only further complicates the mix. Attempts to construe sexual "minorities" on the basis of the racialized subject, for example, tend to be received with a certain skepticism by the latter—recall the debate over gays in the military, in which "middle class careerists and sexual adolescents" were accused of "hijacking the freedom train"—which is as Freud would have wished.[22] Footnote 4 to *United States v. Carolene Products*, the seminal 1938 Supreme Court decision, accords protection only to groups that are "discrete and insular," and Freud insists that homosexuals are neither.[23] (The woeful inadequacy of the Supreme Court decision—in effect, racial "minorities" are reduced to their visual legibility and geographic ghettoization—in no way impinges on its cultural power.) "We are everywhere," as the old activist slogan has it, and Freud concurs. But homosexuality does not thereby escape detection and/or localization. In the passage from *Group Psychology* quoted above, for example, Freud invokes his own version of "the holy trinity of contemporary criticism"—"the group ties of race, of national divisions, and of the social class system," but only to insist that the "[heterosexual] love of women" "breaks through" all three. The logic of apartheid, the racist desire to maintain race relations that are "discrete" and "insular," thus intersects with sexuality only in the form of repressed or flagrant homosexuality, which effectively renders (homo)sexuality itself "discrete" and "insular." Scratch a racist, find a faggot.

Or so Frantz Fanon contends: "The Negrophobic man is a repressed homosexual."[24] The formulation, which is obviously indebted to psychoanalytic premises, explains a normative racial and racist politics by an exculpatory psychologism. What thus elude analysis—and political responsibility—are both heterosexuality and whiteness. (The homophobic contention that homosexuality is "a white man's disease," which is sometimes heard in the African American community, functions in much the same way. If white racism is repressed homosexuality, black homosexuality is race capitulation or collusion.) Critical Race Theory seeks, among other things, to render whiteness visible, but so long as homosexuality continues to "enjoy" virtually unlimited explanatory power, whiteness, no less than heterosexuality, will remain in the hermeneutic closet. Fanon calls for a seemingly radical expansion of the reach of psychoanalysis:

Reacting against the constitutionalist tendency of the late nineteenth century, Freud insisted that the individual factor be taken into account through psychoanalysis. He substituted for a phylogenetic theory the ontogenetic perspective. It will be seen that the black man's alienation is not an individual question. Beside phylogeny and ontogeny stands sociogeny. (11)

The alienation of gays and lesbians is likewise irreducible to the ontogenetic perspective, and gay activists and theorists have in fact reiterated Fanon's call for a move beyond "the individual factor."[25] A text-based, psychoanalytically inflected criticism has had its day; what is now needed (or so the argument usually goes) is an analysis of the social dimension of the sexual. The ambition is admirable, but the opposition is specious: psychoanalysis has always been a theory of the social. True, the new science of the soul encourages subjective reflection on the nature of sexuality (like the old, it emphasizes the confessional) and Freud's own practice obviously privileged individual psychology. But psychoanalysis is no less a theory of the social for its strategic insistence on the priority of the individual. Or, more to the point, psychoanalysis is no less a theory of the social for its highly selective insistence on the imbrication of the sexual and the social. Freud is only too eager to position homosexuality within the field of the social, the better to render heterosexuality a hermeneutically empty category of the same.

If, then, sociogeny is to issue in anything other than an exculpatory psychologism, it must involve more than a simple renegotiation of the relation between "group" and "individual" psychology—a little more of the former, a little less of the latter. Such is Fanon's strategy, and his sociogeny merely rehearses the alibi of heterosexual innocence, which is also an alibi of race innocence, that psychoanalysis "always already" affords. Certainly cultural conservatives understand the advantages of explaining the racial by the (homo)sexual, which is not to say they commit Freudianism. (On the contrary, they tend to be overtly hostile to any secular science of the soul. But again, the historical good fortunes of psychoanalysis are in no way contingent on anyone's conscious commitment to it.) The Civil Rights Act of 1964, which affords various legal protections to racial/ethnic minorities and women, is precisely that: a civil rights act. For cultural conservatives, however, the extension of the same protections to gays and lesbians instantly metamorphoses civil rights into "special rights," and special rights for "middle class careerists and sexual adolescents" mean fewer rights for blacks. Only minorities that are "discrete" and "insular" deserve protection under the law; "behavior-based" identities, like homosexuality, cannot be equated with biological dispensations. (Cultural conservatives obviously dispute Foucault's contention that the modern "homosexual," unlike the "sodomite," is a category of being rather than behavior.) But once civil rights are (re)defined as "special rights," all civil rights, including those already granted racial/ethnic minorities and women, are imperiled, which was no doubt the ambition all along.[26] Divide and conquer, and what emerges triumphant from the fray is the cause that need never speak its name: straight, white masculinity.

The contention that heterosexuality is somehow exempt from representation—the perhaps dubious bedrock of my own thesis—might seem as patently counterintuitive (not to say counterfactual) as anything psychoanalysis itself has to offer. Certainly it is not meant to deny the obvious: heterosexual culture is all about itself, which is why heterosexual culture construes homosexuality as narcissism. Freud, for one, would be surprised to learn that the normative elude representation; if anything, he holds rather specific views as to the mode of representation proper to heterosexual genitality. "Dora: An Analysis of a Case of Hysteria" is perfectly explicit: the goal of psychoanalysis is both therapeutic and narrative. The deviant or dubiously normal are incapable of giving "an ordered history of their life," but those newly restored to health produce an "intelligible, consistent, and unbroken case history."[27] In effect, the normative is the narrative, and perversion is but a qualitatively early and fixated moment in a developmental trajectory that both infolds and supersedes it.

Freud privileges narrative, however, only to preserve the "discretion" that the legitimate couple, with its regular sexuality, traditionally enjoys. In the modern world, the pervert comes to occupy center stage, endlessly declaring that he-is-what-he-is, but heterosexuality wisely refrains from so tautological an assertion: a psychosexual dispensation that understands itself as a chronologically and qualitatively later form of the stable and knowable state of being that is homosexuality is strategically unknowable in its own terms. (All identity categories, it will be objected, are relational, and thus unknowable in their own terms. True enough, but some categories are clearly more relational than others.) Partisans of the new bisexuality universalize Freud's commitment to narrative: all sexuality is held to be "fluid . . . a narrative that changes over time rather than a fixed identity." The extension of the (to my mind) dubious virtue of "fluidity" to the sexually perverse renders the psychoanalytic paradigm more accommodating—you too can claim sexual "ambiguity," if only at academic conferences—but a structuring opposition survives intact: narrative is what fixity is not.

Freud considers literary production to be little more than culturally ambitious day dreaming, and day dreaming is impelled by one of two gender-specific plots:

These motivating wishes vary according to the sex, character and circumstances of the person who is having the phantasy; but they fall naturally into two main groups. They are either ambitious wishes, which serve to elevate the subject's personality; or they are erotic ones. In young women the erotic wishes predominate almost exclusively, for their ambition is as a rule absorbed by erotic trends. In young men egoistic and ambitious wishes come to the fore clearly enough alongside of erotic ones.[28]

The novel is characteristically celebrated for its heterogeneity or heteroglossia, but Freud insists on a distinctly heterosexual division of labor: young man takes Paris, the plot of "ambitious wishes," and/or young woman marries young man who takes Paris, the plot of "erotic wishes." What might be considered a "third sex" alternative to the gendered pairing—young man discovers that he likes men, young woman discovers that she likes women—has no heterosexual counterpart whatsoever. The traditional novel simply assumes an already given, infinitely renewable reserve of heterosexual desire; it schools women in the choice of the right man, but offers no reason for choosing men. Normativity is thus spared the indignity of explanation, but like the vision granted Adam and Eve at the end of *Paradise Lost*—a seminal moment for nineteenth-century novelistic closure—its prospects seem so vast and various only because they are strategically unspecified. Readers of *Three Essays*, for instance, might reasonably expect a fourth: Freud takes us to the threshold of normativity, "The Transformations of Puberty," but stops short of a full discussion of a fully realized heterosexuality. A similar discretion structures explicitly fictional renderings of the trajectory of erotic ambition: betrothal, not marriage, is the conventional fulfillment of the thus misnamed marriage plot. So long as the norm remains definitionally bound to what it is not, but which it nevertheless infolds and supersedes—"The Sexual Aberrations," which is, perversely, where Freud begins *Three Essays*—it need never make the difficult confession of what it is. Oblige it to speak its name, however, and the heterosexual reproduction of the same, which is intimately bound to the narrative return of the same, no longer passes as "hetero." (Am I alone in taking some comfort from the passage of the "Defense of Marriage Act," the seemingly disastrous repercussion of the ill-conceived campaign for same-sex unions? For the first time in modern history, marriage has been officially acknowledged for what it is: exclusively heterosexual. Claims for the theoretical inclusiveness and fluidity of the institu-tion should now be more difficult to maintain.) Sedgwick holds that homosexu-ality as "we know it today" is too "destructively presumable."[29] Heterosexuality, I want to suggest, is not presumable enough. This is not to advocate a rear guard re-turn to identity politics, although the unfashionable truth be told, virtually every significant advance in post-Stonewall gay civil rights is indebted to those politics. (The allegedly "discrete and insular" model of black civil rights activism is the in-forming paradigm.) Cindy Patton argues that identity "functions deontologically in a field of power," and it is not my intention to claim for heterosexuality a spe-cious ontological coherence.[30] But I do mean to insist that heterosexuality is a hermeneutically meaningful category of the social. The love that dare not speak its name has good reasons not to. There is no reason, however, why the project of outing need restrict itself to the deviant.

A book that purports to explain (rather than confirm or augment) a virtually unlimited explanatory power has a singular advantage: it can be about more or less anything. The chapters that follow are thus various in subject matter and largely occasional in their origins, and I have made only a perfunctory effort to bring them into conversation with each other. But owing, no doubt, to the bane-ful influence of my early education, I find that they do in fact cohere, if only in a set of shared obsessions. ("Totalizing" ambitions are now considered politically suspect, and introductions routinely declare their innocence of them. But if my own reading of heterosexuality is less than totalizing, it is for reasons of intellec-tual laziness rather than theoretical or political scruple. Resistance to totalization has always been part of the P.R. of heterosexuality, the self-proclaimed dispensa-tion of difference, and heterosexuality hardly requires another apologist.) I begin, in any case, with Oscar Wilde, although not Oscar-the-Essence-of-Homosexuality of much recent biographical and critical work. "Revenge Oscar" was once a famil-iar slogan of gay activism (or, less happily, gay "consciousness raising"), and the best revenge may well be a continuation of the paradoxical project of Wilde's only novel: resistance to narrative—which is to say, normative—technologies of sexual self-fashioning and self-knowledge. Chapter 2 is thus a study of the adventure of genre in Wilde's oeuvre, which is also the adventure of subjectivity; much of what follows is an attempt to tease out the implications of Dorian's resistance to all things novelistic. ("A little formalism," as Roland Barthes notes, "turns one away from History but . . . a lot brings one back to it.")[31] *The Picture of Dorian Gray* is roughly contemporary with the discursive birth of the modern "homosexual," but its relation to that less-than-blessed event is one of systematic opposition. Freud construes perversion as a failure of narrative teleology; Dorian resists the developmental logic of his generic dispensation. Freud maintains that pathology registers somatically; Dorian refuses the conventional—that is, psychoanalytic—wisdom that holds a man (or at least those of us of "a certain age") responsible for his face.

Life imitates art, as Wilde was fond of noting, and chapter 3, which addresses the cultural construction and reception of AIDS, provides unwelcome confirmation of life's mimetic proclivities. The "novelistic," if not the nineteenth-century novel of psychological depth, is still very much with us, and its conventions continue to structure the lives and deaths of gay men. Between every pervert and his or her sex, the West has placed a never-ending demand for truth, which the pandemic realizes: AIDS is the narrative revelation of the hitherto occluded truth of homosexuality; homosexuality is the deep truth of AIDS. Dorian can temporarily elude, but not finally escape, the narrative logic that renders his face a somatic judgment on the state of his soul, and every gay man living with AIDS is Dorian come again.

Chapters 4 and 5, which focus on the work of Robert Mapplethorpe and the practice of bodybuilding respectively, explore two instances of perverse (although not necessarily "gay" or "homosexual") resistance to the ubiquitous sexual knowingness that purports to know the sexual subject better than it knows itself. Photography is an aggressively nonnarrative art, and the various moments in *The Perfect Moment,* the aptly named Mapplethorpe retrospective, reject the narrative logic that would render AIDS the belatedly revealed truth of the pervert's life. The always perilous, easily deconstructed binarism of same- or cross-gender object choice is the condition of sexual knowingness in the modern West, but the perverts who populate Mapplethorpe's photographs are innocent of its categories. Bodybuilders figure prominently among them, for the simple reason that they too are committed to an *ars erotica* rather than a *scientia sexualis*.[32] The narrative logic that saturates Dorian's body with meaning is the logical corollary of a hermeneutics of the gaze; the irreducible density and bulk of the muscled body, however, resist irradiation by the spirit. It thus solicits carnal knowledge, an erotics of the gaze. The musclehead "revenges Oscar" by remaining wholly body, by refusing the narrativizing, psychologizing energies that would render the flesh a window unto the soul.

My sixth and final chapter, "Lavender Fascists," most explicitly addresses the concerns adumbrated in these opening remarks. Nazism remains our century's defining image of evil, radically inexplicable in its horror, and the Holocaust purportedly tests the limits of thought. Yet for all its posturing, our culture has little difficulty in thinking the Unthinkable in (homo)sexual terms. Narrative conventions, which tend to figure structural violence as individual villainy, determine the conditions under which genocide can be "legitimately" thought, and what can be "legitimately" thought guarantees the political innocence of the "authentically" heterosexual. The ease with which a crime of compulsory, state-sponsored heterosexuality—for Nazism was, among other things, precisely that—is construed as an implicitly gay atrocity constitutes the obscene limit of my own contention. Homosexuality, the explanation for everything politically and ethically aberrant. Determination, in the last instance, by the deviant.

2 Motion Pictures

Dorian Gray is a character in search of a different generic dispensation:

"How sad it is!" murmured Dorian Gray with his eyes still fixed upon his own portrait. "How sad it is! I shall grow old, and horrible, and dreadful. But this picture will remain always young. It will never be older than this particular day of June. . . . If it were only the other way! If it were I who was to be always young, and the picture that was to grow old! For that—for that—I would give everything! Yes, there is nothing in the whole world I would not give! I would give my soul for that!"[1]

Dorian enters the novel that bears his name only to tell Basil and Lord Henry that he will not grow to maturity, will not be a character in a *Bildungsroman*, will not suffer his face to become a somatic judgment on the state of his soul. Dorian would be a beautiful object. The novel will insist, however, that he become a morally intelligible—which is to say, a somatically legible—subject. We are all familiar by now (altogether too familiar perhaps) with the famous passage in the first volume of Foucault's *History of Sexuality*:

The nineteenth-century homosexual became a personage, a past, a case history, and a childhood, in addition to being a type of life, a life form, and a morphology, with an indiscreet anatomy. . . . Nothing that went into his total composition was unaffected by his sexuality. It was everywhere present in him: at the root of all his actions because it was their insidious and indefinitely active principle; written immodestly on his face and body because it was a secret that always gave itself away.[2]

Wilde himself was to emerge as the century's most spectacularly legible homosexual, but what of his characters? Homosexuality is presumed to be at the root of all Dorian's actions, but how do we know what we all think we know, even if that knowledge characteristically goes under the gentlemanly decorum of "it goes without saying"? The Marquess of Queensberry thought he knew: his Plea of Justification held that *Dorian Gray* "was designed and intended by Wilde" and "was understood by the readers thereof to describe the relations, intimacies, and passions of sodomitical and unnatural habits, tastes, and practices." But when pressed by Wilde's counsel, the prosecution could cite no specifically "sodomitical" passages.[3] (Heterosexual passages were there for the asking, although no one saw fit to ask. Apparently the affair with Sibyl Vane does not convincingly describe relations, intimacies, and passions of a normative kind.) Foucault directs us to the homosexual's past, his childhood, but the novel offers us little in the way of the usual proto-gay traumas (i.e., mothers, fathers). *The Picture of Dorian Gray* effectively elides its central character's past, and Dorian himself denies his future, or at least the future as it is conventionally understood. Hence, the defining paradox of Wilde's only novel (or reluctant novel or non-novel or anti-novel): Dorian is motivated by a desire for a perpetual present, a discrete series of perfect moments, yet a perpetual present is an intolerable motive for narrative. In *The Importance of Being Earnest*, Miss Prism maintains that the "good ended happily, and the bad unhappily. That is what Fiction means" (341). The narrative fulfillment of the ethical distinction, she might have added, is ultimately written on the face. Dorian knows of what he speaks, of what he rejects: if you don't want the face you will learn to think you deserve, don't get caught up in the logic of the novelistic.

But it is a logic not easily eluded. "If it were only the other way! If it were I who was to be always young, and the picture that was to grow old!": narrative energy is displaced, not destroyed; the developmental discipline to which Dorian will not subject his living body is translated onto his painted image. And as the displacement has the effect of rendering kinetic a static image, it uncannily anticipates a technology of meaning production—the motion picture—that was historically unavailable to Wilde. Walter Benjamin argues that "one of the foremost tasks of art has always been the creation of a demand which could be fully satisfied only later":

The history of every art form shows critical epochs in which a certain art form aspires to effects which could be fully obtained only with a changed technical standard, which is to say, in a new art form. The extravagances and crudities of art which thus appear, particularly in the so-called decadent epochs, actually arise from the nucleus of its richest historical energies.[4]

Motion pictures were to make their debut in Britain a few years after the publication of *Dorian Gray*, and Wilde's novel has been filmed a number of times: most memorably, in a 1945 production directed by Albert Lewin and with the unlikely cast of George Sanders, Hurd Hatfield, Donna Reed, and Angela Lansbury. Wilde is innocent, however, of Benjamin's myth of technological progress and determination.[5] *The Picture of Dorian Gray* does not aspire to effects that can be fully attained only with a changed technological standard: the novel about a motion picture has no desire to become one. Rather, *Dorian Gray* explores, and subjects to proleptic critique, a technology of meaning production that will find its most efficient—and so mystified—fulfillment in the moralized visual economy of classic narrative cinema. Benjamin posits an unbridgeable technological divide between the dominant art forms of the nineteenth and twentieth centuries, the novel of psychological depth and the motion picture. I argue for their continuity. Novel and film evince a well-nigh ontological affinity; it is an unembarrassed, unapologetic theatricality that conventionally troubles both.

The Picture of Dorian Gray is an exception: the novel that proleptically critiques what was to come, the new technology of the motion picture, actively works to recover what has been left behind, the residual (although not therefore moribund) art of the theater.[6] The novel of psychological depth was the definitive cultural accomplishment and dominant spiritual discipline of the nineteenth century, but Wilde's one apparent concession to it actually concedes very little. *The Picture of Dorian Gray* is less a novel than a staging ground for the clash between and among generic dispensations: drama, novel, and (pre-posterously) film. The agon is never simply formal. At issue are the modes of human subjectivity and somatic organization—perverse or otherwise—that any given aesthetic form presupposes and promotes.

i. Generic Bodies

The Picture of Dorian Gray opens, appropriately enough, with a meditation on the relation between the stasis of pictorial representation and the temporality of the content it labors to represent: embroidered draperies put Lord Henry in mind "of those pallid jade-faced painters of Tokio who, through the medium of an art that is necessarily immobile, seek to convey the sense of swiftness and motion" (18). Lord Henry thinks of Japanese art; what Wilde seems to have in mind is Lessing's distinction between the stasis of the plastic or the pictorial arts and the temporality of the linguistic:

I reason thus: if it is true that painting and poetry in their imitations make use of entirely different means or symbols—the first, namely, of form and colour in space, the second of articulated sounds in time—if these symbols indisputably require a suitable relation to the thing symbolized, then it is clear that symbols arranged in juxtaposition can only express subjects of which the wholes or parts exist in juxtaposition; while consecutive symbols can only express subjects of which the wholes or parts are themselves consecutive.

Subjects whose wholes or parts exist in juxtaposition are called bodies. Consequently, bodies with their visible properties are the peculiar subjects of painting.

Subjects whose wholes or parts are consecutive are called actions. Consequently, actions are the peculiar subject of poetry.[7]

Wilde queers Lessing's binarism: *The Picture of Dorian Gray* is literally about a motion picture, the static rendered temporal, and a still-life narrative, the temporal rendered static. Lessing's distinction, the logical fulfillment of the classical concept of decorum, is predicated on the notion that signs must have a "suitable" or proper relation to the thing signified. Wilde's queering of the distinction is, then, an impropriety, a violation of a decorum that is at once formal and ideological. "Sin is a thing that writes itself across a man's face," Basil tells Dorian. "It cannot be concealed" (117). In seeking to elude the developmental logic of narrative, however, Dorian also seeks to deny any "proper" or naturalized relation between his body and the meanings it would otherwise be obliged to express. Dorian is confronted with the problem of what to do with Basil's corpse, which, as he tells Campbell, is the "only piece of evidence" linking him to the crime (130). But what should properly bear evidence against Dorian—and what eventually will, when *Dorian Gray* the novel capitulates to the logic of the novelistic—is Dorian's own face. Campbell, reluctantly acquiescing to Dorian's blackmail, dissolves Basil's body into nothingness, but moral turpitude is not thereby deprived of somatic inscription. The portrait, the body ideological, sweats meaning:

He held the light up again to the canvas, and examined it. The surface seemed to be quite undisturbed, and as he had left it. It was from within, apparently, that the foulness and horror had come. Through some strange quickening of inner life the leprosies of sin were slowly eating the thing away. (122)

The workings of the inner life are indeed strange, stranger, in fact, than even Wilde's quasi-biologizing, quasi-naturalizing trope of moral leprosy allows. As D. A. Miller observes,

All the deployments of the "bio-power" that characterize our modernity depend on the supposition that the most effective take on the subject is rooted in its body, insinuated within this body's "naturally given" imperatives. Metaphorizing the body begins and ends with literalizing the meanings the body is thus made to bear.[8]

Wilde's only novel is a remarkably demystified exploration of this, perhaps the defining mystification of our modernity. *The Picture of Dorian Gray* insists that what takes "root" in the flesh was first, as Foucault puts it, "implanted" from without.[9] In "The Decay of Lying," Vivian says of Wordsworth that he "found in stones the sermons he had already hidden there" (977–78). Much the same might be said of our relation to the human body, particularly to the face. "Does flesh mean conscience?" an exasperated Count Fosco asks in *The Woman in White*.[10] Wilde's question is rather more pragmatic: "How is flesh made to mean conscience?"

The linguistic arts may be given to the representation of actions in time rather than bodies in space, but as Lessing concedes, actions imply agents and agents imply bodies: "Actions cannot exist by themselves, they must depend on certain beings. So far, therefore, as these beings are bodies, or are regarded as such, poetry paints bodies, but only indicatively, by means of action (91)." Hamlet, the character who haunts nineteenth-century novelistic characterization (as he himself is haunted), regrets his dependence on "certain being" or somatic existence. Embodiment is the most fundamental condition of theatrical existence, yet Hamlet experiences his flesh as "too too solid" (or "sullied"). An exquisite Renaissance sensibility trapped in a hoary revenge plot, he too seeks a different generic dispensation, which the nineteenth century was only too pleased to grant him. From the *Stage*, January 13, 1845:

Yes, Hamlet is truly a man of these present times. It is thou Werther, thou Lara, thou Obermann, it is, above all, thou immortal René, in whom we see the sons and daughters of Hamlet. . . . It is to our age that Hamlet belongs; it is our age that has discovered him . . . and Hamlet himself has grown to maturity in the midst of the psychological literature in which we have all been nourished.[11]

21

But as Wilde was willing to concede his century very little, least of all its unwholesome diet of psychological literature, he utterly rejects its psychologizing embrace of Hamlet. "The world has become sad," Vivian quips in "The Decay of Lying," "because a puppet was once melancholy" (983). We may owe our unhappy interiorities to Shakespeare's Prince, or to the Prince as mediated by the novel of psychological depth, but Wilde's Hamlet is only so much theatrical artifice. And everything the Prince devoutly wishes for—a world in which it is *not* possible to smile and smile and be a villain—Dorian Gray utterly rejects.

Hamlet denies that flesh can ever mean conscience:

Seemes Maddam, nay it is, I know not seemes,
Tis not alone my incky cloake good mother
Nor customary suites of solembe blacke
Nor windie suspiration of forst breath
No, nor the fruitfull riuer in the eye,
Nor the deiected hauior of the visage
Together with all formes, moodes, shewes of griefe
That can denote me truely, these indeede seeme,
For they are actions that a man might play
But I haue that within which passeth showe
These but the trappings and the suites of woe.[12]

In "The Decay of Lying," Vivian traces "the beginning of the end" of English drama—or the beginning of the hegemony of the culture of the book—to "the overimportance" Shakespeare assigns to characterization (978). But for the Shakespearean character perhaps most invested in the priority of character, there can be no such thing. Hamlet conceives himself—and there is a sense in which the fatherless son is literally attempting to "conceive himself," to originate his own existence—in opposition to the corporeal, the external, the visual, which is also the order of the spectacle, the theatrical. Not for Hamlet the kinetic consummations, the being-through-action, of theatrical self-definition. Not for Hamlet the publicly accessible surfaces, the "incky cloakes" and "customary suites," of theatrical appearances.

Not for Hamlet and, as Harold Bloom suggests, not for us. The Prince who would originate his own existence also originates ours:

With Falstaff as with Hamlet (and perhaps with Cleopatra) Shakespearean representation is so self-begotten and so influential that we can apprehend it only by seeing that it originates us. We cannot judge a mode of representation [or, in the case of the passage cited above, a sweeping dismissal of a mode of representation] that has overdetermined our ideas of representation.[13]

Hamlet has few rivals (and even these, as Bloom notes, would be Shakespearean) in determining our position in what Foucault terms "l'aventure de l'individual-ité": "from the early Middle Ages to the present day the 'adventure' is an account of individuality, the passage from the epic to the novel, from the noble deed to the secret singularity, from long exiles to the internal search for childhood, from combat to phantasies."[14] The passage from the epic to the novel might also read from drama to the novel, as drama, at least in its Aristotelian form, is predicated on the priority of action to character, praxis to ethos:

For Tragedy is an imitation, not of men, but of an action and of life, and life consists in action, and its end is a mode of action, not a quality. Now character determines men's qualities, but it is by their actions that they are happy or the reverse. Dramatic action, therefore, is not with a view to the representation of character: character comes in as subsidiary to the action. Hence the incidents and the plot are the end of a tragedy; and the end is the chief thing of all. (Poetics 1450a 48–58)

Hamlet rejects these Aristotelian priorities, and so anticipates, literally *avant la lettre*, a novelistic or discursive mode of subjectivity. Against the depraved spectacle of the world's "seemings," Hamlet lays claim to a theatrically inaccessible interiority, the implicitly novelistic mode of subjectivity that would soon come "to dominate and organize bourgeois culture."[15]

Hamlet's rejection of any role that a man might play is itself, however, radically self-dramatizing: his "incky" cloak may gesture toward discursivity, the novelistic dispensation that the nineteenth century was to grant him, but it also registers visually, in the explicitly theatrical mode of spectacle. Clothes declare the man, as Polonius styles it, including the man who implicitly declares they don't. Yet if the novel, like the drama, remains dependent on "certain beings" or somatic agents, it is spared the embarrassment, at least from the perspective of all things modern, that is the actor's body. Metaphorizing the body may begin and end with literalizing the meanings it is made to bear, but it is infinitely easier, although not necessarily ideologically more efficacious, to begin with a body that is made of words.

Consider one of the great operatic fiascos of the nineteenth century, the March 6, 1853, premiere of *La Traviata* at the Teatro la Fenice in Venice. The role of Violetta was sung by "a full figure gal," as the TV commercials used to say, one Mme. Salvini-Donatelli, the wife of the famous actor. Verdi apparently thought her voice adequate; the audience, however, found her flesh too too abundant. The patrons at the Teatro la Fenice required a seamless mesh of soma and significance; Shakespeare's contemporaries accepted their productive non-coincidence:

We need to confront both the gaps and the links between representation and existence in the theater [of Shakespeare]. In particular, it seems important to explore the relation (which I do not hesitate to call central) between the representation of fictive meaning and the actual circumstances of performing practice. . . . The rich cultural semiotics of this diversity existed because there were particularly vital and consequential gaps as well as links between actors and roles, between the performing agents and the performed agenda of representation itself.[16]

If it requires a considerable leap of the historical imagination to recover these consequential gaps, the noncoincidence of performing agents and performed agendas, it is because we have long been nourished on the culture of the book, on flesh so purely discursive, so utterly subservient to the demands of the soul, that all such fissures are moot.

Hegel maintains that it is precisely the destiny of art to overcome all such fissures, to subject the meaningless exteriority of the flesh to irradiation by the spirit:

The external element [of a work of art] has no value for us simply as it stands; we assume something further behind it, something inward, a significance, by which the external semblance has a soul breathed into it. . . . Just so the human eye, a man's face, flesh, skin, his whole figure, are a revelation of mind and soul, and in this case the meaning is always something other than what shows itself within the immediate appearance. This is the way a work of art should have its meaning, and not appear as exhausted in these mere particular lines, curves, surfaces, borings, reliefs in the stone, in these colours, tones, sounds, of words, or whatever other medium is employed.[17]

Hegel is speaking of the destiny of all art, but not all mediums or genres are equally receptive to irradiation by the spirit. "How has Shakespeare drawn his Hamlet?" Serlio asks in Goethe's *Wilhelm Meister*:

"In the first place," answered Wilhelm, "he is fair-haired."

"That I call far-fetched," observed Aurelia. "How do you infer that?"

"As a Dane, as a Northman, he is fair-haired and blue-eyed by descent."

"And you think Shakespeare had this in view?"

"I do not find it specially expressed; but, by comparison of passages, I think it in-contestable. The fencing tires him; the sweat is running from his brow; and the Queen remarks, He's fat and scant of breath. *Can you conceive him to be otherwise than plump and fair-haired? Brown complexioned people, in their youth, are seldom plump. And does not his wavering melancholy, his soft lamenting, his irresolute activity, ac-cord with such a figure? From a dark-haired young man, you would look for more deci-sion and impetuosity."*

"You are spoiling my imagination," cried Aurelia: *"away with your fat Hamlets! Do not set your well-fed Prince before us!"*[18]

The paradigmatic *Bildungsroman* of the nineteenth century engages in a process of bodybuilding that works from the inside out: Hamlet's physique may be surmised in part from his nationality, but the bulk of his body (in effect, the conspicuous absence thereof) is imagined as the outward sign of an inward grace.[19] The dis-cussion of Hamlet's physique is occasioned by a projected performance of *Hamlet* the play. It is everywhere informed, however, by a sense of the explicitly literary (as opposed to theatrical) qualities of the text (as opposed to script) under consid-eration. Wilhelm distinguishes between drama and the novel in terms that echo Aristotle's distinction between tragedy and the epic:

In the novel it is chiefly sentiments *and* events *that are exhibited; in the drama, it is* characters *and* deeds. *The novel must go slowly forward; and the sentiments of the hero, by some means or another, must restrain the tendency of the whole to unfold itself and to conclude. The drama, on the other hand, must hasten, and the character of the hero must press forward to the end; it does not restrain, but is restrained. The novel-hero must be suffering; at least he must not in a high degree be active; in the dramatic one, we look for activity and deeds. (288–89)*

For Wilhelm, *Hamlet* is given to a "novelistic" expansiveness that is for Aristotle both a defining characteristic of the epic and a mark of its inferiority to the tragic. Hamlet himself, moreover, has only *Gesinnungen,* sentiments. In a direct reversal of Aristotelian priorities, ethos, not praxis, defines the essence of novelistic "being." Gertrude, who should know, calls Hamlet "fat," but Aurelia's text-based speculation—"You are spoiling my imagination . . . away with your fat Hamlets"— has taken precedence over the Queen's dramatic observation.[20] And even today, a fat Hamlet remains a cultural impossibility. Or, to translate all this into Hegelese: the novel is better equipped than the drama to overcome the meaningless exteri-ority of the flesh, for it alone can create in such a way that "the human eye, a

25

man's face, flesh, skin, his whole figure, are a revelation of mind and soul." Drama is bound to the "solidity" of the actor's body; the novel makes the flesh word.

Hamlet is never fully granted this novelistic translucency: the character in search of a different generic dispensation is ultimately reclaimed for and by the theatrical. In the closet scene, for example, he recommends a role that a Queen might play, an explicitly theatrical construction of identity:

> Assume a vertue if you haue it not,
> That monster custome, who all sence doth eate
> Of habits deuillish, is angell yet in this
> That to vse of actions faire and good,
> He likewise giues a frock or Liuery
> That aptly is put on. (11. 2366–71)

Hamlet's parting advice to his mother recalls his earlier polemic against "seems," but only to reject its metaphysics of depth, its conflation of being and interiority. An earlier Hamlet would have demanded a transformation of consciousness; here he argues for the public deployment of the body, the fashioning of a virtue that is "aptly," indeed only, "put on" in the theater of the world. "To act" is to construct, rather than to manifest, character; in Aristotelian terms, praxis is productive of ethos. There is, however, no saving reversal for Dorian Gray. In the concluding moments of the novel, Lord Henry inquires after the fatal portrait, which he believes to be lost. Dorian responds with an allusion to some "curious lines" in *Hamlet*:

> "I forget," said Dorian. "I suppose I did [lose the portrait]. But I never really liked it. I am sorry I sat for it. The memory of the thing is hateful to me. Why do you talk of it? It used to remind me of those curious lines in some play—Hamlet I think—how do they run?—
> 'Like the painting of a sorrow,
> 'A face without a heart.'
> Yes: that is what it was like." (161)

But in a genre given to the irradiation of the phenomenal by the spirit, a face without a heart is a contradiction in terms. The Hegelian dream of somatic translucency finds its nightmare realization, and Dorian's inner self is rendered obscenely visible in his flesh. One of Dorian's final acts is to assume a virtue that he has not; he refrains from seducing a simple country girl "wonderfully like Sibyl Vane" (158) in the desperate hope that praxis might beget ethos. But to no avail. Lord Henry translates "the noble deed" back into Dorian's "secret singularity"—"I should think the novelty of the emotion must have given you a thrill of real pleasure" (158)—and the portrait confirms his interiorizing, psychologizing wisdom:

He [Dorian] went in quietly, locking the door behind him, as was his custom, and dragged the purple hanging from the portrait. . . . The thing was still loathsome—more loathsome, if possible, than before—and the scarlet dew that spotted the hand seemed brighter, and more like blood newly spilt. Then he trembled. Had it been merely vanity that had made him do this one good deed? Or the desire for a new sensation, as Lord Henry had hinted, with his mocking laugh? Or that passion to act a part that sometimes makes us do things finer than we are ourselves? (166)

Unlike Gertrude, Dorian is not afforded the opportunity to act a part discontinuous with his "secret self." In the novelistic conclusion of *Dorian Gray*, good behavior is but the exquisitely perverse manifestation of an inner depravity, the ultimate refinement in the pursuit of novel sensations. ("Had it been merely vanity that had made him do this one good deed? Or the desire for a new sensation?") Dorian questions whether it is possible "that one could never change" (164), the answer to which may well be specific to the genre in which it is asked. The *Bildungsroman* is always the promise of an essential sameness deployed along a chronological axis; apparent discontinuities in the self are only that, apparent, and all is ultimately assimilable to the logic of the developmental. The climactic revelation of a body that is "withered, wrinkled, and loathsome of visage" (167) is not, then, a change in Dorian, but the final coming into somatic intelligibility of what he always already was. It is the theatrical, the world of Sibyl Vane, that affords the opportunity for existence without essence, for acting parts discontinuous with the "secret self."

That Hamlet should be construed as the presiding genius of this discourse of psychological continuity is patently counterintuitive. How, for example, are we to account for the much-noted caesura between the figure who is deported and the figure who returns, a fissure that troubles precisely because it lacks obvious psychological—which is to say, novelistic—explanation or motivation? "Rather than the maturation or development of 'character' that we have been taught to look for in Shakespeare," Francis Barker argues, "there is a quasi-Brechtian discretion" between the pre- and post-England Hamlets.[21] Hamlet himself, moreover, schools Ophelia in the logic of psychosexual discontinuity:

Ophelia: My lord, I haue remembrances of yours
That I haue longed long to redeliuer.
I pray you now receiue them.
Hamlet: *No, no, I, neuer gaue you ought.*
Ophelia: My honor'd lord, you know right well you did.
. . .
Hamlet: *. . . this was sometime a paradox, but now the time giues it proofe, I did loue*
you once.
Ophelia: Indeed my lord you made me belieue so.
Hamlet: *You should not haue beleeu'd me . . . I loued you not. (8. 1631–56)*

"I, I, I," or "I. I. I.," as Stephen Dedalus engagingly puts it: Ophelia is committed to the logic of the comma, the continuity of the self in time; Hamlet is of the party of the full stop. For Ophelia, the lapse into radical particularity, "quasi-Brechtian discretions," heralds the ruin of love; for Dorian Gray, it is its precondition:

"To-night she is Imogen," he [Dorian] answered, "and to-morrow she will be Juliet."
"When is she Sibyl Vane?"
"Never."
"I congratulate you." (53)

Sibyl Vane bodies forth that most utopian of erotic fantasies: promiscuity without the tedium of searching out a new partner every night. The "only thing worth loving," Dorian tells Lord Henry, "is an actress" (51), and so long as Sibyl remains a creature of the theater, she is a series of discontinuous roles, the whole being less interesting than the individual parts. But when she is awakened to what she terms "the hollowness, the sham, the silliness of the empty pageant" in which she has always played (75), the roles coalesce into a coherent self, and Sibyl threatens to become the same person every night. Like Dorian, she attempts to negotiate a transition between generic dispensations: having discovered that it is not possible to "be in love and [to] play Juliet" (62), she trades theatrical artifice for what she takes to be the genuine, novelistic article. Sibyl is denied, however, the happy combination of class mobility and realized desire that is a staple of the romance novel. Her tragedy is to have made herself over into a novelistic being, a coherent self, for the sake of a man who refuses all commerce with the novelistic.

That the transition between generic dispensations proves both violent and abortive suggests that the novel is not, as Bakhtin would have it, infinitely open, endlessly generous:

The novel parodies other genres (precisely in their role as genres); it exposes the conven-
tionality of their forms and their language; it squeezes out some genres and incorporates
others into its own peculiar structure, re-formulating and re-accentuating them. . . . In an
era when the novel reigns supreme, almost all the remaining genres are to a greater or less
extent "novelized"; drama . . . epic poetry . . . even lyric poetry. . . . Those genres that
stubbornly preserve their canonic nature begin to appear stylized.[22]

Other genres, like Narcissus, may desire only that which they resemble, but the
novel is apparently all generosity and accommodation, definable only in its resistance to definition. Bakhtin explicitly asserts that there is no experience, meaning, or value that cannot be verified or expressed in the heteroglossia of the novel,
but his own argument implicitly suggests otherwise: a genre that parodies other
genres in their role as genres can never acknowledge its own existence as such. In
the context in which Bakhtin's work was originally written and circulated (if not
always published), the subversive power it attributes to the novel is plausible
enough. Translated into the very different milieu of the liberal West, however, it
quickly devolves into an apology for business as usual. It is difficult to know, for
example, how the celebration of the novel as a polyphonic play of voices can do
anything to disrupt the parliamentarianism—Marx terms it a form of "cretinism"
—that is at the heart of the liberal settlement. Indeed, the contention that the
novel is somehow extrageneric is itself the most compelling evidence of its bourgeois investments, of its collusion with the class that does not want to be named.
The celebration of open form underwrites a perfectly closed economy: the genre-
that-is-not-one, the aesthetic dispensation that eludes ideological determination,
merely returns to the-class-that-is-not-one, the political settlement that embraces
and infolds all, an idealized image of its own infinitely plastic, endlessly plural
self.[23] But where Bakhtin maintains that the novel seamlessly incorporates other
genres into its own peculiar structure, which is thus released from the constraints
of structurality itself, *Dorian Gray* insists on a fundamental incompatibility. For
Sibyl Vane, there is finally no entry into the novelistic, and for Dorian, there is no
escape from it. The contention that "Hamlet . . . has grown to maturity amidst the
psychological literature in which we have all been nourished" posits literary history itself as a kind of *Bildungsroman*, a process of organic, developmental maturation in which content labors toward adequate form. Wilde refuses, however, so
thoroughly naturalized a version of literary history. *Dorian Gray* stages the clash
between generic dispensations as a clash, and although the novelistic emerges triumphant, the theatrical does not concede the field without a struggle. Wilde does

29

Bakhtin one better. His only novel opposes the unification of the verbal-ideological world in and as the novel.

Raymond Williams suggests that the historical hegemony of any given aesthetic form is not as absolute as Bakhtin insists. Even in an era when the novel reigns supreme—an imperial image curiously at odds with the celebration of novelistic heteroglossia—"residual" cultural practices survive:

By "residual" I mean that some experiences, meanings, and values, which cannot be verified or cannot be expressed in terms of the dominant culture, are nevertheless lived and practised on the basis of the residue—cultural as well as social—of some previous social formation.[24]

To risk a tautology: the experiences, meanings, and values that can be expressed in the heteroglossia of the novel are themselves necessarily novelistic, a point of some significance to, among others, the sexually perverse. There is considerable thematic continuity, for example, between *The Picture of Dorian Gray* and *The Importance of Being Earnest*—both deal with "Bunburying," the pleasures and perils of "a double life"—yet the novelistic rendition of the theme, unlike the dramatic, issues in tragedy. Why? Joel Fineman argues that *Earnest* "precisely figures" that now most familiar of critical concerns, the problem of "The Self in Writing":

Jack-Ernest, the hero of the play, discovers the unity of his duplicity when he learns that as an infant he was quite literally exchanged for writing in the cloak-room of Victoria Station, his absent-minded governess having substituted for his person the manuscript of a three-volume novel which is described as being "of more than usually repulsive sentimentality." As a result, because Jack-Ernest is in this way so uniquely and definitively committed to literature, with literature thus registered as his alter-ego, he is one of those few selfs or subjects whose very existence, as it is given to us, is specifically literary, an ego-ideal of literature.[25]

The unity of Jack-Ernest's duplicity may be an ego-ideal of literature, but not the duplicity of his unity: Jack-Ernest's existence as a Bunburyist is predicated on the strategic misplacement—from the perspective of the play if not Miss Prism—of a novel "of more than usually repulsive sentimentality," and hence on his distance from all things "textual" or "literary."[26] True, Bunbury is "quite exploded" by the end of the play, and it is through the mediation of another text that Jack comes to learn that he always was earnest, that his identity has remained unwittingly continuous through time:

Jack: M. Generals . . . Malam—what ghastly names they have—Markby, Migsby, Mobbs, Moncrieff. Moncrieff! Lieutenant 1840, Captain, Lieutenant-Colonel, Colonel, General 1860, Christian names, Ernest John. (Puts book quietly down and speaks quite calmly.) I always told you Gwendolen, my name was Ernest, didn't I? Well, it is Ernest after all. I mean it naturally is Ernest. (382–83)

The text fixes identity with military precision, and where identity is fixed and continuous, Bunbury is not.

But exactly how exploded is he? As with Oakland, so too with Bunbury: there is no there there, and thus nothing to explode. "Bunbury" is a proper name that designates a practice rather than an identity, and *Earnest* is a world of Bunburying to the end of it. The play defers to the conventional teleology of the comic plot, but what should be the final expression of a hitherto thwarted heterosexual desire becomes, in Wilde's wildly improbable every-Jack-shall-have-his-Jill conclusion, the imposition of a heterosexual and heterosexualizing "machinery."[27] Plot produces heterosexuality; heterosexual desire does not subtend the unfolding of plot. The "possibility" that the machinery occludes, moreover, is not "homosexuality," the symmetrical obverse of heterosexuality, but an entire *ars erotica*, a reserve against sensual impoverishment: "A man who marries without knowing Bunbury has a very tedious time of it" (327). For Wilde as for Aristotle, plot enjoys priority over character. For Aristotle, however, plot is the imitation of "an action that is whole and complete"; for Wilde, it is the imitation of an imitation, a miming of the technologies of self-fashioning and self-knowledge that produce the sexual subjects that purport to subtend them. *The Importance of Being Earnest* exactly reverses the ontological priorities of *The Picture of Dorian Gray*. Dorian cannot finally assume or "perform" a virtue that he has not. The "character" of Jack or Gwendolen is nothing but an occasion for a gesture and a pose.[28]

The irreducible theatricality of *Earnest* guarantees the survival of the ostensibly "exploded" Bunbury, but it is perhaps *Salomé* that best takes the measure of Wilde's distance from the primary aesthetic and spiritual discipline of his age. The reception of the play has been dominated by the charge of sensationalism, but *Salomé* already anticipates the terms of its critical denigration: Wilde's drama is, among other things, a quasi-historical allegory of the displacement of a culture of spectacle by the dispensation of the Word. The ruin of the pagan truths—"The son of man hath come. The centaurs have hidden themselves in the rivers" (555)—is also the eclipse of theater as a culturally significant experience.

Salomé figures spectatorship as erotic danger:

The Young Syrian: *How beautiful is the Princess Salome tonight!*
The Page of Herodias: *You are always looking at her. You look at her too much. It is dangerous to look at people in such fashion. Something terrible may happen. (553)*

For Aristotle, there is no real need to look: "the power of Tragedy, we may be sure, is felt even apart from representation and actors." Aristotle does concede that spectacle possesses "an emotional attraction of its own," but of all the components of a well-made play, "it is the least artistic, and connected least with the art of poetry" (*Poetics* 1450b 104–10). For Wilde, however, there was no opportunity to look: the Lord Chamberlain's office closed a production of *Salomé* already in rehearsal, and the play was not staged in England until long after its author's death. But if Wilde was thus restricted to a purely textual appreciation of his own genius, it was not due to any distrust of the phenomenal properties of his art. *Salomé* is less a closet drama than an exploration of the historical forces that would relegate it—and the theatrical in general—to the closet.

The spectacular physicality of Salomé, gendered as female and historicized as pagan, is opposed to the verbal proclivities of the Jews:

First Soldier: *What an uproar! Who are those wild beasts howling!*
Second Soldier: *The Jews. They are always like that. They are disputing about their religion.*
First Soldier: *Why do they dispute about their religion?*
Second Soldier: *I cannot tell. They are always doing it. (552)*

Salomé's openness to visual consumption and fetishization, which her veils only augment, is opposed to the Jewish worship of an unseen God:

First Soldier: *The Jews worship a God that you cannot see.*
The Cappadocian: *I cannot understand that.*
First Soldier: *In fact, they only believe in things that you cannot see.*
The Cappadocian: *That seems to me altogether ridiculous. (553)*

What seems altogether ridiculous to the Cappadocian is, however, a significant "step forward in culture" for Freud: "Turning from the mother to the father points . . . to a victory of intellectuality over sensuality—that is, an advance in civilization, since maternity is proved by the evidence of the senses while paternity is a hypothesis, based on an inference and a premiss."[29] Salomé is the least maternal of figures, yet she too occupies a superseded position in a gender-specific, quasi-Hegelian Progress of the Spirit: the feminine physicality of paganism is prelude to the verbal homosociality of Judaism. (Freud distinguishes between "thing-representation," which is gendered as female, and "word-representation," which he celebrates as male.) The dominance of the patriarchal principle, the ideality of deduction and premise, presupposes the noncoincidence of the cognitive and the phenomenal, and hence a limited escape from what Hegel construed as the ontological inadequacy of art, its dependence on the materiality of signs. (Religion and philosophy, not the aesthetic, are the highest manifestations of the Idea.) The "pagan" world tended to posit an analogy between the verbal and the pictorial: *ut pictura poesis*, "poetry is like painting," in Horace's influential formulation. For Jokanaan, however, pictures speak only to the lust of the eyes:

The Voice of Jokanaan: Where is she who, having seen the images of men painted on walls, the images of the Chaldeans limned in colours, gave herself up unto the lust of her eyes, and sent ambassadors into Chaldea? (557)

Jewish iconoclasm represents an advance over pagan idolatry, yet Judaism is itself but prelude, and what Salomé and the Jews divide between them Christianity allegedly fuses. *Salomé* is posited on the threshold of a new dispensation, the perfect reconciliation of matter and spirit that is the God/man Jesus.

From the perspective of all things dramatic, however, the Word made Flesh isn't: like Bunbury, Christ remains theatrically inaccessible, forever offstage. Even Jokanaan, His herald and dramatic surrogate, is introduced as voice rather than body:

The Voice of Jokanaan: After me shall come another mightier than I. I am not worthy so much as to unloose the latchet of his shoes. When he cometh, the solitary places shall be glad. They shall blossom like the lily. The eyes of the blind shall see the day, and the ears of the deaf shall be opened. (553–54)

The body natural is unredeemed, unregenerative, but Christ is the promise of a radical restructuring of sensuous perception. Jokanaan is thus in the paradoxical (and distinctly Hegelian) position of embodying a disavowal of the body. Like Hamlet, he can only dramatize his desire to be released from the condition of dramatic existence:

Jokanaan: Who is this woman who is looking at me? I will not have her look at me. Wherefore does she look at me with her golden eyes, under her gilded eyelids? I know not who she is. I do not wish to know who she is. Bid her begone. It is not to her that I would speak. (558)

Jokanaan would be pure voice. His openness before Salomé's gaze, however, returns him to his flesh. Jokanaan stands surrogate for the Word that cannot be rendered dramatically in the flesh. Salomé renders the body itself eloquent. The Princess remains convinced that had the Baptist looked with his human eyes he would have known human love:

Well, thou hast seen thy God, Jokanaan, but me, me, thou didst never see. If thou hadst seen me thou wouldst have loved me. I saw thee, Jokanaan, and I loved thee. Oh, how I loved thee! I love thee yet, Jokanaan, I love thee only . . . I am athirst for thy beauty; I am hungry for thy body. (574)

But Jokanaan refuses the explicitly theatrical condition of seeing and being seen. Salomé triumphs over the body natural by de-idealizing the source of voice: she kisses the mouth of the Baptist's severed head. The woman who would return Jokanaan to his body is herself, however, subsumed into the ideality of voice:

The slaves put out the torches. The stars disappear. The great black cloud crosses the moon and conceals it completely. The stage becomes very dark.
The Voice of Salomé: *Ah! I have kissed thy mouth, Jokanaan. I have kissed thy mouth. There was a bitter taste on thy lips. Was it the taste of blood. . . ? But perchance it is the taste of love. (574–75)*

Salomé exits the stage as Jokanaan entered it, a symmetry that suggests, as Herod seems dimly to intuit, that a new dispensation is at hand:

Herod: *I will not stay here. Come, I tell thee. Surely some terrible thing will befall. Manasseth, Issachar, Ozias, put out the torches. I will not look at things, I will not suffer things to look at me. Put out the torches! Hide the moon! Hide the stars! Let us hide ourselves in our palace, Herodias. I begin to be afraid. (574)*

The world of pagan spectacle has run its historical course. Like Jokanaan before him, Herod will neither look at things nor suffer things to look at him. His final act is thus to order the execution of Salomé, the play's central object of visual consumption and fetishization.

In *De Profundis*, Wilde professes a certain weariness with "the articulate utterances of men and things"; like Hegel, he would seem to abandon the ontological unfreedom of art, its dependence on the materiality of signs, for a more perfect relation to the Idea:

I am conscious now that behind all this Beauty, satisfying though it be, there is some Spirit hidden of which the painted forms and shapes are but modes of manifestation, and it is with this Spirit that I desire to become in harmony. I have grown tired of the articulate utterances of men and things. (955).

This more or less conventional Christianity—a de-Catholicized Protestantism— suggests the redeemed counterpart to the hermeneutics of *Dorian Gray*, in which beauty disguises moral depravity. Like Dorian himself, however, Wilde has been accused of doing the right thing, or at least the pious thing, for the wrong reason. Lord Henry insists that Dorian's eleventh-hour exercise in erotic restraint is but an exquisite refinement in the pursuit of novel sensation. T. S. Eliot dismisses Wilde's prison-house embrace of orthodox Christianity as an exercise in emotional auto-eroticism.[30] (Charges of closet Catholicism dogged Wilde during his lifetime and beyond.) Eliot, unlike Lord Henry, does not intend a compliment, but the point is well taken: the man who professes weariness with "the articulate utterances of men and things" is nevertheless fully invested in the phenomenal properties of his work: "I cannot reconstruct my letter, or rewrite it. You must take it as it stands, blotted in many places with tears, in some with the signs of passion or pain, and make it out as best you can, blots, corrections and all" (948). Far from abandoning the sensible "signs of passion or pain," Wilde renders them spectacularly, embarrassingly visible.[31] In *Salomé*, Christ remains visually inaccessible; in *De Profundis*, He subtends a perverse physicality. Hegel maintains that the Word is made flesh, but is never fully of it:

The Greek god is not abstract but individual, and is closely akin to the natural human shape; the Christian God is equally a concrete personality, but in the mode of pure spiritual existence, and is to be known as mind *and in mind. His medium of existence is therefore essentially inward knowledge and not external natural form, by means of which He can only be represented imperfectly, and not in the whole depth of His idea. (78)*

But even when Wilde was forced to speak "from the depths"—his original title was the properly political *Epistola: In Carcere et Vinculis*, not the sacramental *De Profundis*—there is no capitulation to this "essentially inward knowledge." Christ remains relentlessly embodied and His Passion the occasion for so much theatrical artifice:

One cannot but be grateful that the supreme office of the Church should be the playing of the tragedy without the shedding of blood, the mystical presentation by means of dialogue and costume and gesture even of the Passion of her Lord, and it is always a source of pleasure and awe to me to remember that the ultimate survival of the Greek Chorus, lost elsewhere to art, is to be found in the servitor answering the priest at Mass. (924–25)

The ritual reenactment of Christ's Passion preserves the otherwise lost conventions of "pagan" theater. *De Profundis* thus reverses the trajectory adumbrated in, but never endorsed by, *Salomé*. Wilde's relation to his generic dispensation rivals the perversity of Dorian's: convention dictates that he make a discursive spectacle of his soul; he responds by displaying the beautiful body of the God/man Jesus.

ii. Novel Sensation

In "Private Property and Communism," Marx speaks of the absolute sensuous poverty to which humankind had to be reduced in order to give birth to all its "inner wealth":

Private property has made us so stupid and partial *that an object is only* ours *when we have it, when it exists for us as capital or when it is directly eaten, drunk, worn, inhabited, etc. in short,* utilized *in some way. But private property itself only conceives these various forms of possession as* means *of life, and the life for which they serve as means is the* life *of* private property—*labor and the creation of capital.*

Thus all *physical and intellectual senses have been replaced by the simple alienation of* all *these senses; the sense of* having. *The human being had to be reduced to this absolute poverty in order to be able to give birth to all its inner wealth.*[32]

For Marx, perception is itself historical; for Walter Benjamin, historically specific modes of perception presuppose the dominance of historically specific aesthetic forms: "During long periods of history, the mode of human sense perception changes with humanity's entire mode of existence. The manner in which human sense perception is organized, the medium in which it is accomplished, is determined not only by nature but by historical circumstances as well" (222). No genre has ever been more invested in the creation of private subjects or in the accumulation of inner capital than the nineteenth-century novel of psychological depth. In the archaic art of storytelling, "words, soul, eye, and hand are brought into connection," and their interaction "determines a practice."[33] In typographic culture, however, the oral-aural-tactile bond gives way to the privatized, silent assimilation of meaning through the visual perusal of black marks on a white page. Robert Sherard dismisses the sensational marketing of Wilde's body for his British lecture tour as a "degradation."[34] Would, however, that all lectures were equally degraded, and one man's degradation is, in any case, another man's performance art. (Why suffer through the tedium of yet another academic conference, that most archaic of all rituals, were it not for the hope that the speaker's body, the grain of her voice or the choreography of her gestures, will register differently, more perversely, than her words?) During his American lecture tour, Wilde was under contractual obligation to sport his aesthetic drag, and his willingness to perform the complex cultural semiotics of his body, to embrace the role of Oscar Wilde, evinces his distance from all things typographical. The archaic art of storytelling was not, after all, so very archaic in Ireland.

By definition (or generic dispensation), Dorian does not enjoy the same distance, yet he too resists the sensuous deprivations that the novel, in the conditions of both its production and consumption, presupposes and promotes. Much of *Dorian Gray* is given over to catalogues of perverse sensory experiences, which, if released from the teleology of plot, are also outside normative hierarchies of sensuous organization. Characters in novels seem particularly sensitive to the influence of them, and Dorian is no exception. His life, we are told, is "poisoned by a book" (115), specifically a book "without a plot" (101), and the protagonist of what may well be that book—Huysmans's *À Rebours*—maintains that it is "no more abnormal to have an art that consisted in picking out odorous fluids than it was to have other arts based on a selection of sound waves or the impact of various coloured rays on the retina."[35] An art of the olfactory can be thought normal, however, only if thought itself can escape the tyranny of visualist metaphors.[36] *À la recherche du temps perdu* might be considered a narrative art of the nose, but Wilde has little interest in substituting olfactory "revelation" (itself a visualist metaphor) for scopic intelligibility. *The Picture of Dorian Gray* opens with an appeal to the nose:

The studio was filled with the rich odour of roses, and when the light summer wind stirred amidst the trees of the garden, there came through the open door the heavy scent of the lilac, or the more delicate perfume of the pink-flowering thorn. (18)

Before queering Lessing's distinction between bodies-in-space and actions-in-time, the novel discriminates between perfumes. The riff on Lessing, however perverse, rehearses the terms of an aesthetic that, in privileging abstraction and formalization, privileges sight. The discrimination between perfumes serves only to expand the sensuous resources of the novel itself.

Nietzsche claimed that his genius resided in his nostrils: "I perceive physiologically—*smell*—the proximity or—what am I saying?—the innermost parts, the 'entrails,' of every soul."[37] But if this is to challenge the traditional supremacy afforded the eyes, it is otherwise meaning-mongering as usual: to smell out the entrails of every soul is to pursue psychological truth even unto its innermost parts. Dorian's nose is less gainfully employed: he contemplates writing "a psychology of perfumes" (106) not in order to smell out what anyone is, but the better to refine the body's pursuit of novel sensation. In Wilde, smell is an erotics, not a hermeneutics, although an erotics opposed to the increasing objectification and visualization of the sexual field. The construction of the hetero-homo binary, in which Wilde was to play a seminal if unwitting role, presupposes a logic of gender difference grounded in the visual evidence of the body itself. Men (even gay men) have one; women don't, which is for Freud both the most self-evident and significant of facts. But if it is possible to have an art that consists in picking out odorous fluids rather than visual images, why not a sexual field structured by the diacritics of smell rather than sight?[38]

Freud argues for a thoroughly deodorized sexual life: man's upright posture, his perpetual erection, expands his visual field and releases his sexuality from dependence on the nose.[39] Hegel argues for a thoroughly deodorized aesthetic life:

The sensuous aspect of art only refers to the two theoretical senses of sight and hearing, while smell, taste, and feeling remain excluded from being sources of artistic enjoyment. For smell, taste, and feeling have to do with matter as such, and with its immediate sensuous qualities. . . . On this account these senses cannot have to do with the objects of art, which are destined to maintain themselves in their actual independent existence, and admit of no purely sensuous relation. (43–44)

Wilde willingly permits no such exclusions. In *Degeneration*, Max Nordau poses a series of rhetorical questions—"Why should the sense of smell be neglected in poetry? Has it not the same rights as all other senses?"—the answer to which is already implicit in his title:

The underdeveloped or insufficiently developed senses help the brain little or not at all, to know and understand the world. . . . Smellers among degenerates represent an atavism going back, not only to the primeval period of man, but infinitely more remote still, to an epoch anterior to man.[40]

That Dorian Gray should prove himself a "smeller," as Nordau terms it, is hardly surprising. His perversion is precisely his resistance to the logic of the developmental:

The worship of the senses has often, and with much justice, been decried, men feeling a natural instinct of terror about passions and sensations that seem stronger than themselves, and that they are conscious of sharing with the less highly organised forms of existence. But it appeared to Dorian Gray that the true nature of the senses had never been understood, and that they had remained savage and animal merely because the world had sought to starve them into submission or to kill them by pain. . . . As he looked back upon man moving through History, he was haunted by a feeling of loss. (104)

A more conventional retrospective might celebrate the social triumph over stench. *The Picture of Dorian Gray* is written at a time when the great bourgeois dream of a universal deodorization had begun to colonize all but the most marginal of bodies, and Dorian's erotic life, like Wilde's own, involves considerable interclass contact. (A spectator at Wilde's trial unfamiliar with the term "gross indecency" might have taken it to mean a sexual life released from the obligations of class solidarity.) Nocturnal slumming provides Dorian access to forbidden smells and, for a time, he emerges from London's underbelly "smelling like a rose." But only for a time. The olfactory metaphor implies a failure of scopic intelligibility, the traditional promise of narrative, and *The Picture of Dorian Gray* is finally true to its title: the man who would not suffer his beautiful face to become a somatic judgment on the state of his soul is ultimately revealed as "withered, wrinkled, and loathsome of visage" (167). (Which no doubt accounts for the novel's enduring popularity. If the current pandemic teaches us anything, it is that our culture takes solace in making the perverse body bear somatic witness to its own perversions.) Yet if *Dorian Gray* allows us (or forces us) "to see what it means," it also insists on how unnecessarily impoverished an exclusive taste for scopic intelligibility can be. Unlike sight, which is generally considered a distributive and limiting sensory mode, smell is experienced as associative and expansive. The binarism may confuse the physiology of perception with its cultural construction—there are "osmologies," worlds structured by the diacritics of smell, as well as cosmologies—yet visual difference clearly underwrites the modern sexual regime.[41] That Wilde should have proved seminal to the construction of that regime is thus doubly ironic: his own sexual life (of which more presently) failed to conform to the categorizations demanded by it and he was opposed to the hegemony of the scopic that subtends it.

The omniscient narrators of nineteenth-century novelistic fame are allegedly only that: omniscient, not omnipotent; they cop to seeing all, not to constructing all.[42] Narrative can thus pretend simply to register the distinction between the good and the bad, the healthy and the sick. Any ideologically effective use of the body requires the body's own felt self-evidence, its willingness, as it were, to write its own pathologies across its face. Having tortured the body into meaning, the omniscient narrator purports merely to record a confession spontaneously given. Yet if only through the fantastic conceit of a motion picture, *Dorian Gray* foregrounds the weird technology of meaning production itself. "I keep a diary of my life from day to day," Dorian tells Basil, "and it never leaves the room in which it is written" (120). By diary he means portrait, but the confessional impulse that the diary-picture embodies clearly has its origins outside Dorian. Lord Henry, for example, advances a philosophy of radical individualism and self-realization, which occasions an epiphany in Dorian, who becomes "dimly conscious that entirely fresh influences were at work within him. Yet they seemed to him to have come really from himself" (29). Lord Henry's diatribe against belatedness and influence influences Dorian, and in adopting a philosophy of perfect self-realization he becomes the perfectly colonized subject.[43] Foucault argues that "the obligation to confess is now relayed through so many different points, is so deeply ingrained in us, that we no longer perceive it as the effect of a power that constrains us; on the contrary, it seems to us that truth, lodged in our most secret nature, 'demands' only to surface" (60). To us, certainly, but not to Cecily in *The Importance of Being Earnest*:

Algernon: *Do you really keep a diary? I'd give anything to look at it? May I?*
Cecily: *Oh, no. (*Puts her hand over it.*) You see, it is simply a very young girl's record of her own thoughts and impressions, and consequently meant for publication. When it appears in volume form I hope you will order a copy. (357)*

What is this but a parody of a genre that has its origins in the rendering public of private correspondence or discourse? Jürgen Habermas argues that the "directly or indirectly audience-oriented subjectivity of the letter exchange or diary explained the origin of the typical genre and authentic literary achievement" of the eighteenth century: "the domestic novel, the psychological description in autobiographical form."[44] Cecily concurs, but radicalizes the contention. The public sphere wholly determines—although determines, as it were, from within—the structure and content of every ex-pressive utterance.

In *The Importance of Being Earnest*, Jack considers inscriptions in cigarette cases private discourse. Algernon suffers from no such scruples:

Oh! it is absurd to have a hard and fast rule about what one should read and what one shouldn't. One should read everything. More than half of modern culture depends on what one shouldn't read. (324)

The authorities at the Old Bailey—and for a brief period of time, both shows, *The Importance of Being Earnest* and "The Trial of Oscar Wilde," ran concurrently—were of the party of Algernon. The cigarette cases Wilde lavished on his lower-class tricks were introduced as evidence against him, the meaning of which was apparently obvious to everyone. In his not-quite open letter to Lord Alfred Douglas—until his death in 1945, Douglas's fabled litigiousness effectively governed the dissemination of Wilde's correspondence—Wilde reflects on the de facto openness of an earlier letter:

You send me a very nice poem, of the undergraduate school of verse, for my approval: I reply by a letter of fantastic literary conceits. . . . Look at the history of that letter! It passes from you into the hands of a loathsome companion; from him to a gang of blackmailers: copies of it are sent about London to my friends, and to the manager of the theatre where my work is being performed. . . . Society is thrilled with the absurd rumours that I have had to pay a huge sum of money for having written an infamous letter to you: this forms the basis of your father's worst attack; I produce the original letter myself in Court to show what it really is: it is denounced by your father's Counsel as a revolting and insidious attempt to corrupt Innocence; ultimately it forms part of a criminal charge: the Crown takes it up: the Judge sums up on it with little learning and much morality; I go to prison for it at last. That is the result of writing you a charming letter. (889–90)

The term "open letter" is here a redundancy and "private correspondence" a contradiction in terms: Wilde's incarceration, his withdrawal from visibility, is the direct result of his general legibility. In a famous reading of Poe's "The Purloined Letter," Lacan maintains that the letter "always arrives at its destination." Derrida counters:

A letter does not always arrive at its destination, and since this belongs to its structure, it can be said that it never really arrives there, that when it arrives, its possibly-not-arriving [son pouvoir-ne-pas-arriver], torments it with an internal divergence.[45]

To which the author of *De Profundis* might have added: the letter is always legible to, interceptible by, the-powers-that-be. Wilde imagines preempting the authority of the law by internalizing its operations:

I remember as I was sitting in the dock on the occasion of my last trial listening to Lock-wood's appalling denunciation of me—like a thing out of Tacitus, like a passage in Dante, like one of Savonarola's indictments of the Popes of Rome—and being sickened with horror at what I heard. Suddenly it occurred to me, "How splendid it would be, if I was saying all this about myself!" *I saw then at once that what is said of a man is nothing. The point is, who says it. A man's very highest moment is, I have no doubt at all, when he kneels in the dust, and beats his breast, and tells all the sins of his life. (947)*

But to what is Wilde to confess? To a homosexual identity that, homophobically imposed from without, will henceforth be the truth of his nature? (Although I came under the influence of Wilde at a young and impressionable age, which doubtless explains a great deal, the one text I always refused to read was *The Soul of Man under Socialism*, which I assumed to be an antisocialist tract. Homosexuality seemed more than enough identity for one man to bear; it never occurred to me that it was possible to be both a pervert and a socialist.) Far from eluding the violence of the law, Wilde's "splendid" scenario is but the most insidious manifestation of a power that, now lodged firmly within the psyche's own imperatives, demands only to surface.

The Picture of Dorian Gray is rather more skeptical about the liberatory power of confession. The novel ultimately inscribes the confessional impulse in the flesh, but to "perceive physiologically," as Nietzsche puts it, is to perceive no less ideologically for that. In "The Decay of Lying," Vivian denies the possibility of perception as such:

At present, people see fogs, not because there are fogs, but because poets and painters have taught them the mysterious loveliness of such effects. . . . They did not exist till Art had invented them. Now, it must be admitted, fogs are carried to excess. They have become the mere mannerism of a clique, and the exaggerated realism of their method gives dull people bronchitis. Where the cultured catch an effect, the uncultured catch cold. (986)

Scopic knowledge is grounded not in the self-evidence of somatic experience, but in the ideological insinuation of the same, in making the body speak naturally the meanings it has been taught to bear. Jonathan Crary argues that the disembodied, interiorizing paradigm of vision promoted by the *camera obscura*, the privileged metaphor for sight in the seventeenth and eighteenth centuries, was radically transformed in the nineteenth. The invention of photography dramatized the productive role played by the body in vision; physiology replaced Cartesian mental privacy as the model for subjective action and response, and vision was henceforth thinkable only in relation to the "opacity and carnal density" of the observer.[46] Wilde, however, thinks carnal density only in relation to ideology. Where the cultured catch an effect, the uncultured catch cold, which renders health, no less than perception, an ideological and class-specific construct. ("I am glad," Lady Bracknell says of the recently exploded Bunbury, "that he made up his mind at the last to some definite course of action, and acted under proper medical advice" [372–73].) The portrait that proves fatal to Dorian is not the first Basil paints. It is unique only in that it abandons classicizing visual conventions:

"I [Basil] had drawn you [Dorian] as Paris in dainty armour, and as Adonis with huntsman's cloak and polished boar-spear. . . . One day, a fatal day I sometimes think, I determined to paint a wonderful portrait of you as you actually are, not in the costume of dead ages, but in your own dress and in your own time. Whether it was the Realism of the method, or the mere wonder of your own personality, thus directly presented to me without mist or veil, I cannot tell. But I know that as I worked at it, every flake and film of colour seemed to me to reveal my secret." (94)

The pictorial arts might seem exempt from the arbitrary order of the signified, and Basil's portrait perpetuates the dream of direct visual contact with the thing-in-itself. But in the most familiar of Wildean paradoxes, the extreme realism of the method proves patently counternatural: the painting assumes an inner life of its own. Basil fears that the portrait reveals more about its creator than its subject matter, but in actuality it reveals neither. *The Picture of Dorian Gray* has no interest in the game of find-that-faggot: what is outed here is not a psychosexual aberration—Basil's or Dorian's or anyone's "homosexuality"—but a ubiquitous cultural logic, of which AIDS is only a particularly devastating instance, that decrees homosexuality to be legible in the process of its own decomposition. Basil declares there is a "fatality" about physical "distinction" (19), but if anatomy is indeed destiny, it is first and foremost a rhetoric, a murderous typology of signs.

To return, then, to the question with which I began: how do we know what we all think we know, that homosexuality is at the root of all Dorian's actions? Seeing may be believing, pictures may be worth a thousand words, but in the context of a novel in which a portrait is figured as a diary, the evidence of sight and the order of the signified, somatic perception and cultural inscriptions, are functionally indistinguishable. "The Portrait of Mr. W.H." insists on the point. A forged painting substantiates a perverse reading of Shakespeare's sonnets, which reduces visual evidence to little more than a mystified extrapolation from rhetorical experience. But even if visual certainty were possible, a troubling question still remains: is it safe to look? The homosexual must be visually legible if the diacritics of gender, understood as the visual self-evidence of the body, are to command the sexual field; the homosexual must not gain access to representation, however, for precisely the same reason. Here the lunatic Right is right: the prohibition against the representation of gay bodies can only be predicated on the knowledge that to see one is to risk wanting one, to risk becoming one. If homosexuality were to prove resistant to visual delineation and categorization, anatomical difference could not be said to determine essence; if homosexuals were allowed to flaunt their difference—and any form of gay visibility is inevitably construed as flaunting—compulsory heterosexuality, the self-proclaimed dispensation of difference, would be threatened with different forms of difference. The question "How do we know what we all think we know" becomes, then, "How do we see what we dare not look on?" And if this is to construct an impossible epistemological quandary, so much the better: the impasse is meant to underwrite the ontological incoherence, the essential nonbeing, of its object. To gaze upon a beautiful male body offering itself up for visual consumption and fetishization is perilous. To gaze upon that same body decomposing "through some strange quickening of the inner life" is morally instructive.

Or, should looking prove too perilous, one can always smell the rot. From the *St. James Gazette*, June 20, 1890: "Not being curious in ordure, and not wishing to offend the nostrils of decent persons, we do not propose to analyse 'The Picture of Dorian Gray.'" From the *Daily Chronicle,* June 30 of the same year: *The Picture of Dorian Gray* is "a poisonous book, the atmosphere of which is heavy with the mephitic odours of moral and spiritual putrefaction."[47] Like Nietzsche, the reviewers busy themselves with sniffing out the decadent, the unwholesome, the perverse. *Dorian Gray* would recover the nostrils for what Lord Henry terms "a new hedonism," but our culture engages in such pleasures only disingenuously:

Anyone who seeks out "bad" smells, in order to destroy them, may imitate sniffing to his heart's content, taking unrationalized pleasure in the experience. The civilized man "disinfects" the forbidden impulse by his unconditional identification with the authority which has prohibited it; in this way the action is made acceptable.[48]

The olfactory form of the game of find-that-faggot allows for sniffing in good conscience.

iii. Cut/Uncut

As Basil completes the portrait of Dorian in the 1945 film version of Wilde's novel, Lord Henry captures, kills, and mounts "a rare and beautiful butterfly." The immobilized eroticism of Lord Henry's prey serves as an image for the Dorian who gives himself over to the beauty of images. So long as the portrait figures a beautiful male body offering itself up for visual consumption and fetishization, it is necessarily demonized. Only when the portrait assumes a life of its own—only when it becomes a window unto the soul, the outward sign of an inward depravity—does it qualify as a figure for the technology of cinematic inscription itself. The pictorial arts are best suited to the representation of bodies in space; the linguistic arts, to the representation of actions (or psychosexual development) in time. Motion pictures amalgamate the two: the portrait of Dorian figures film's ability to grant the appearance of motion to bodies frozen within a frame.

The Dorian who gives himself over to the eroticism of images functions within an economy of pederastic love that, even in Wilde's own lifetime, the hetero/homo binarism was in the process of displacing. And this too the novel seems uncannily to anticipate:

The suppression of the original defining differences between Dorian and his male admirers—differences of age and initiatedness, in the first place—in favor of the problematic of Dorian's similarity to the painted male image that is and isn't himself, seems to reenact the discursive eclipse in this period, by the "homo"-sexual model, of the Classically based pederastic assumption that male-male bonds of any duration must be structured around some diacritical difference—old/young, for example, initiator/initiate, or insertive/receptive—whose binarizing cultural power would be at least comparable to that of gender.[49]

Dorian Gray adumbrates both the historical coming-into-being of this new psychosexual dispensation, the unprecedented cultural power afforded the diacritics of gender, and the visual economy presupposed and promoted by it. Dorian initially commands the visual field; sight is an erotics, not yet a hermeneutics in the fully modern sense. Vision enthralls. Dorian solicits the gaze, which is thus rendered receptive, passive, before the spectacle of his beauty. Any structure of representation that flirts with homosexuality—and the flirtation, as Edelman suggests, may be endemic to representation[50]—will meet with cultural success only to the extent that it rigorously distinguishes between a hermeneutics and an erotics of the gaze. I watch Dorian, but I also watch Lord Henry and Basil watching Dorian.

45

How, then, am I to distinguish my own properly heterosexual hermeneutic—my will-to-see-through, to know the (non)truth of, the homosexual—from Lord Henry's and Basil's erotic investment in the same? So long as Dorian remains what he longs to be, a beautiful object, the film is panicked. Only when narrative begins to torture him into moral intelligibility—which is to say, somatic legibility—does it become comfortable with a body whose very beauty is thus rendered morally suspect. The organ of sight is re-phallicized. Penetrate beneath the beauty that is, after all, only skin deep and see the faggot for what he is.

All of which issues in a curious paradox: the straight male gaze can dwell with impunity on the gay male body only by getting into it, by penetrating it, by fucking it over. Sight is conventionally held to be the most objectifying of all modes of perception. Blanchot, for instance, speaks of it as "the power not to be in contact and to avoid the confusion of contact."[51] Objectification is, however, precisely what the film will not risk. It is through an inappropriate (because de-eroticized) penetration with an inappropriate (because de-eroticized) organ that one avoids the confusion of contact with a beautiful male body. Subjectification defines the homophobic response to the homosexual body. Carnal knowledge without the bother of touching, tasting, or smelling.

There is, of course, no touching, tasting, or smelling in motion pictures. The sensuous aspects of the art refer only to "the two theoretical senses of sight and hearing," despite its reputation for what, following Wilde, might be termed "the exaggerated realism" of its representational modality. Benjamin speaks of "the equipment-free aspect of [filmic] reality," which, as he also notes, is "the height of artifice." "The sight of immediate reality"—the formulation is almost worthy of Wilde—"has become an orchid in the land of technology" (233). It is the equipment-dependent aspect of reality, however, that the making into a motion picture of a novel about a motion picture necessarily foregrounds. As Lord Henry enters Basil's studio where he first sees Dorian's portrait, he conspicuously discards a book—Baudelaire's *Fleurs du mal*—as if he were crossing a threshold into a new technological dispensation: from text to film, from the archaic order of the word to the new art of the motion picture. In one sense, the "film" (as opposed to the "motion picture") remains relentlessly literary, and its (albeit less-than-faithful) relation to Wilde's novel, like the Ivan Allbright portrait of Dorian commissioned for it, is meant to guarantee its high art credentials. At the same time, however, the film is uncomfortable with the sexually suspect aestheticism of Lord Henry and company, and it is eager to establish its technological superiority over the anachronistic art of easel portraiture.

46

Curiously, however, the film saves its most conspicuous technological effect for the portrait. It alone is in color, which suggests that it is of a different and higher ontological order than the black and white motion picture that contains it. Unlike the movie, moreover, the portrait betrays its origins in human productivity. We witness the process of its completion and it is conspicuously signed by both Basil and his niece. (The film introduces the character of Gladys, Basil's niece, in order to provide a properly heterosexual love interest for Dorian after the death of Sibyl. She succeeds, however, only in exacerbating the homosexual panic she is meant to quiet.) The novel distinguishes between the fatal portrait and Basil's earlier sketches of Dorian in terms of the superior realism of its method. Cinema characteristically distinguishes itself from older forms of visual expression in precisely the same terms. In the film version of *Dorian Gray*, however, it is the movie that aspires to the condition of somatic intelligibility that only the portrait enjoys. When Dorian stabs the canvas, he assumes the physical properties of his image, which returns to its pristine state. In effect, Dorian Gray the character, Dorian Gray in black and white, becomes his reproduction, Dorian Gray in color. Stanley Cavell holds that the "inherent drama of black and white film," like Wilde's Salomé, belongs to an innately theatrical, and thus superseded, aesthetic order:

When dramatic explanations cease to be our natural mode of understanding one another's behavior—whether because we tell ourselves human behavior is inexplicable, or that only salvation (now political) will save us, or that the human personality must be sought more deeply than dramatic religions or sociologies or psychologies or histories or ideologies are prepared for—black and white ceases to be the mode in which our lives are convincingly portrayed.[52]

But Wilde will have none of this: the entire burden of *The Picture of Dorian Gray* is to denaturalize our "mode of understanding one another's behavior." The film satisfies a taste for explanations that seem to arise "de profundis," but what Cavell terms the "mode in which our lives are convincingly portrayed" Wilde renders as a wildly improbable conceit. Cavell rehearses Hamlet's metaphysic of depth. *Dorian Gray* explores how that metaphysic comes to be naturalized as the logic of the human itself.

Cavell once again: "It is an incontestable fact that in a motion picture no live human being is up there. But a human *something* is, and something unlike anything else we know" (26). Benjamin, following Pirandello, suggests what that curious something might be:

What matters is that the part is acted not for an audience but for a mechanical con-
trivance. . . . "The film actor," wrote Pirandello, "feels as if in exile—exiled not only from
the stage but also from himself. With a vague sense of discomfort he feels inexplicable
emptiness: his body loses its corporeality, it evaporates, it is deprived of reality, life, voice,
and the noises caused by his moving about, in order to be changed into a mute image,
flickering an instant on the screen, then vanishing into silence." (229)

The film version of *Dorian Gray* performs a perverse riff on this estrangement: Dorian lives all the more fully in his flesh for being exiled from his image, from the
meanings his body would otherwise be made to bear. Unlike theater, film is not
bound to the specific materialities of an actor's body; unlike the novel, however,
film can insinuate its meanings in what is nevertheless experienced as the somatic. That curious "something" on the screen thus differs from both the corporeality of theatrical representation and the discursivity of novelistic, yet however
different, it may not be so very curious after all. Hegel on the traditional art forms,
for example, might also be Hegel on film:

What it [the work of art] requires is sensuous presence, which, while not ceasing to be
sensuous, is to be liberated from the apparatus of its merely material nature. And thus
the sensuous in works of art is exalted to the rank of a mere semblance *in comparison*
with the immediate existence of things in nature. (43)

Sensuous presence, which, while not ceasing to be sensuous, is yet liberated from
its dependence on the grossly material: the paradox anticipates perhaps the definitive accomplishment of motion pictures, the production of radically demate-
rialized images that nevertheless issue in the experience of sensuous plenitude and
immediacy.

It is this paradoxical relation to the somatic, to materiality, that accounts for
the ideological efficacy of film. Recall the 1890 review of *Dorian Gray* from the *St.*
James Gazette: "Not being curious in ordure, and not wishing to offend the nostrils
of decent persons, we do not propose to analyse 'The Picture of Dorian Gray.'" The
experience of physical revulsion, the body's own felt self-evidence, stands surrogate for the critical analysis it thus renders superfluous. And if the novel, with its
comparatively limited arsenal of sensuous resources, can register its ideological
agenda somatically, how much more so can film? Steven Shaviro argues that "the
materiality of [filmic] sensation" is "irreducible to, and irrecuperable by, the ideality of signification":

The experience of watching a film remains stubbornly concrete, immanent, and prere-
flective. . . . Sitting in the dark, watching the play of images across a screen, any detach-
ment from "raw phenomena," from the immediacy of sensation or from the speeds and
delays of temporal duration, is radically impossible. Cinema invites me, or forces me, to
stay within the orbit of the senses.[53]

But this is to promote precisely the mystification that *Dorian Gray* labors to expose: there can be no simple opposition between "the materiality of sensation"
and the alleged "ideality of signification." The body itself is made to register, as if
from within, the meanings implanted in it, including the bodies sitting in the
dark watching the bodies on the screen. It is sometimes argued that Wilde wrote
for both an initiated and an uninitiated audience. It takes one to know one, and
only those already in the know knew what Wilde was about. A similar discretion
(or panic) informs the film, which, made under the auspices of the Hollywood
Production Code, is equally tight-lipped on the subject of homosexuality. But not
all forms of knowledge (or knowingness) are "reflective," reducible to the "ideality of signification." Sedgwick notes that both *The Picture of Dorian Gray* and *Dr.*
Jekyll and Mr. Hyde "begin by looking like stories of erotic tensions between men,
and end up as cautionary tales of solitary substance abusers."[54] To figure sexual deviance as addiction is to invoke the evidence of the body as a guard against both:
addiction, the "unnatural" expansion of the body's orbit of senses, presupposes
that the "natural" orbit knows better. ("Listen to your body," my doctor routinely
advises me, as if it were my body, not his ventriloquization of it, that wanted me
to quit smoking.)[55] Cocksucking, like cigarette smoking, may or may not be a
moral atrocity. There can be no argument, however, with the body's own felt judgment, and what better way to guard against even the thought of a perverse oral-
ity than to induce a gag reflex? Frank Harris once sought to convince Wilde that
the "prejudice" against homosexuality was simply reason incarnate:

"And what is such a prejudice?" I asked. "It is the reason of a thousand generations of
men, a reason so sanctioned by secular experience that it has passed into flesh and blood
and become an emotion and is no longer merely an argument. I would rather have one
such prejudice held by men of a dozen different races than a myriad reasons. Such a prej-
udice is incarnate reason approved by immemorial experience."[56]

But again, Wilde would have none of this. "Aversion therapy," the disciplining of
the body's responses to erotic stimuli, is no longer the preferred "cure" for homosexuality. It remains, however, at the vanguard of preventative measures.

49

Film would make flesh mean conscience, but the film version of *Dorian Gray* does not finally have the courage of its somatic convictions. The body itself (or that "human something" up there on the screen) should seem to speak, but what we hear is an anonymous, disembodied voice-over, the filmic equivalent of a nineteenth-century omniscient narrator. Hollywood cinema is not much given to extra-diegetic voice-overs—documentaries and film noir tend to be exceptions—and its use here suggests a certain uneasiness with the evidence (or self-evidence) of the visible. As Kaja Silverman notes,

The theological status of the disembodied voice-over is the effect of maintaining its source in a place apart from the camera, inaccessible to the gaze of either the cinematic apparatus or the viewing subject—of violating the rule of synchronization so absolutely that the voice is left without an identifiable locus. In other words, the voice-over is privileged to the degree that it transcends the body.[57]

To make a diegetically unanchored voice-over the ultimate arbiter of meaning is necessarily to betray a certain uneasiness with the principle of somatic intelligibility itself. Cinematography literally means "writing in motion," and the motion picture *The Picture of Dorian Gray* literally begins and ends with writing, a passage from the *Rubaiyat* of Omar Khayyam:

I sent my soul through the invisible,
Some letter of that after-life to spell:
And by and by my soul returned to me
And answered, "I myself am Heaven and Hell."

If this too heralds the presence of Art—a "film" rather than a "motion picture"— it is an art dominated by the "letter," by the arbitrary order of the signifier. The film is better equipped than the novel to register the "monstrous soul-life" (167) visually, but visual evidence is "always already" contaminated by the rhetorical. Appropriately, the film reverses the conventional hierarchy of image over voice. The cinematic body, no less than the body "itself," is a typology of signs.

There are two motion pictures in the motion picture *The Picture of Dorian Gray* —the motion picture proper and the motion picture that is the portrait—and twice over the movie thematizes the relationship between the two. When Dorian murders Basil, a light is disturbed; when Dorian stabs the painting, which has already registered the murder of Basil, the same light is disturbed. And in both cases, we see the motion picture that is the easel portrait in the context of a flickering light that figures the medium of film.

In the first instance, physical violence from without, the penetration of the body by a knife, is translated into hermeneutic violence from within, the saturation of the surface of a painting by meanings putatively lodged within. In the second instance, physical violence from without, the penetration of the surface of a painting by a knife, is translated into hermeneutic violence from within, the saturation of the surface of the body by meanings putatively lodged within. The two motion pictures—the surface of the painting and the surface of the screen—are clearly and crucially distinguished. Unlike, say, the famous shower scene in Hitchcock's *Psycho*—which aspires to the effect of "a knife slashing, as if tearing, at the very screen, ripping the film"[58]—there is no suggestion that the fragmentation represented on the level of content has its counterpart on the level of form. The motion picture proper answers cut with continuity: in the process of returning to its pristine state, the portrait sutures over the wound Dorian inflicts on it, and Dorian's own body seamlessly dissolves into the loathsome state of his portrait. Narrative energies are displaced, not destroyed, and the narrative energies that were initially transferred from Dorian's living body to his painted image are returned to it.

It is a process that exposes narrative technologies as such, the resistance of classic narrative cinema to such demystification notwithstanding:

The American Cinema's formal paradigm . . . developed precisely as a means for con-
cealing . . . choices. Its ability to do so turned on this style's most basic procedure: the sys-
tematic subordination of every cinematic element to the interests of a movie's narrative.
Thus, lighting remained unobtrusive, camera angles predominantly at eye-level, framing
centered on the principal business of a scene. Similarly, cuts occurred at logical points in
the action and dialogue.[59]

Small wonder that the novel about a motion picture has no desire to become one:
the systematic subordination of style to story is anathema to all things Wildean.
Bakhtin contends that genres that resist the imperialism of the novel appear
"more or less stylized," and Wilde's novel is certainly that: story is gloriously subordinated to style. "All the people speak equally strained Oscar," Henry James
complained of *Lady Windemere's Fan,* and the epigrams that are the essence of
Oscar transform linear unfolding, the syntagmatic axis of narrative, into a series
of quasi-sculptural, discontinuous moments.[60] (Again, the queering of Lessing.)
Dorian complains that Lord Henry "cuts life to pieces" with his epigrams (82), but
Dorian himself would arrest narrative, and when obliged to become a character in
a motion picture, he construes the "cut," the violence he directs against his portrait, as the promise of redemption. Theoretical takes on film tend to emphasize
its capacity for dismemberment and fragmentation. As the magician is to the
painter, Benjamin argues, so the surgeon is to the cameraman, and film and surgical pathology share between them a vocabulary of "cuts," "sutures," and the
like.[61] But the violence of physical dismemberment is easily matched by that of
narrative totalization, narrative continuity, and it is a violence that the motion
picture *The Picture of Dorian Gray* renders explicit. As the portrait sutures over the
wound Dorian inflicts on it, we witness the static image that is the easel portrait
become the kinetic process that is a motion picture, which is to say, we witness,
for the first and only time, the power of film to grant the appearance of motion to
bodies frozen within a frame. The procedure exactly reverses the "formal paradigm" of U.S. cinema: rather than the systematic subordination of every cinematic
element to the interest of the movie's narrative, we have the conspicuous mar-
shaling of cinematic gimmicks to produce the illusion of narrative, which is necessarily acknowledged as such. Neither Wilde's novel nor the film rationalizes its
supernatural phenomenon, but if an easel portrait that is made to sweat meaning
strikes us as a fantastic conceit, well and good. What *Dorian Gray* refuses to natu-
ralize is the weird technology of narrative itself.

But to demystify a technology of meaning production is not necessarily to escape its logic. In "The Decay of Lying," Vivian tells the story of a woman who "felt an absolutely irresistible impulse to follow the heroine [of a novel] in her strange and fatal progress," which leads to her final ruin. It was, she goes on to say, "a most clear example of this imitative instinct of which I was speaking, and an extremely tragic one" (985). But there are other examples, no less clear, no less tragic. Here is Wilde's description of the death of Dorian Gray: he was "withered, wrinkled, and loathsome of visage" (167). And here is Richard Ellmann's description of the death of Oscar Wilde:

Foam and blood came from his mouth during the morning, and at ten minutes to two in the afternoon [of November 30, 1900] Wilde died. He had scarcely breathed his last breath when the body exploded with fluids from the ear, nose, mouth, and other orifices. The debris was appalling.[62]

Reginald Turner, who was present at Wilde's deathbed, later denied this account, which Ellmann attributes to self-censorship.[63] But whatever the truth of the matter, the logic of Ellmann's own narrative clearly requires the scenario: it is Wilde's own body, not the judges at the Old Bailey, that must finally sit in judgment on the state of his soul. "The good ended happily, and the bad unhappily," and the narrative fulfillment of the ethical distinction, Miss Prism might have added, is ultimately written on the flesh. That is what Fiction makes Life mean.

Life magazine, September 1985: "AIDS was given a face everyone could recognize when it was announced that Rock Hudson, 59, was suffering from the disease." Some twelve thousand of the already sick (by the official 1985 count) had to find representation in that face; for the six thousand already dead (and still counting), it was too late. And today, that face denotes only AIDS:

The faceless disease now has a face. But it is not the ruggedly handsome face of Giant *or* Magnificent Obsession *or even* Pillow Talk *that will be Rock Hudson's greatest legacy. Instead, that legacy will be the gaunt, haggard face of those poignant [for whom?] last days.*[1]

This might seem homophobic enough, but it does scant justice to a "legacy" that denies even the "instead," the caesura between the "ruggedly handsome" and the "haggard" face. The contemporary response to the spectacle of Rock Hudson's once normative masculinity—the love scenes are now met with knowing laughter and smirks—argues a haggard face that retroactively structures the handsome one, a culture that alleges to see the gay death skull beneath the youthful skin. AIDS is not, then, simply the cause of Hudson's death, but the belatedly revealed truth of his life: the role Hudson can no longer play, if only because he once played it with such dexterity, is that of a heterosexual. The laughter is the purely defensive response of a homophobic culture to the knowledge that here (as elsewhere) its normative spectacle of heterosexual masculinity was (and frequently is) a gay man.

The "legacy" of Rock Hudson is still with us, a decade and a half later, and it presupposes a cultural context in which AIDS continues to be received—its changing demographics be damned—as what D. A. Miller calls "*the* narrative of gayness," subjective and objective genitive.[2] More precisely, AIDS is received as the revenge *of* narrative *on* gayness, the assimilation of the "homosexual" to the fully satisfying teleology that, in a Freudian technology of self-fashioning and self-knowledge, he is said to resist. It was once conventional to speak of AIDS as "an epidemic of signification"; Thomas Yingling, for instance, characterized it as "profoundly unimaginable, as beyond the bounds of sense . . . an epidemic almost literally unthinkable in its mathematical defeat of cognitive desire."[3] And, in one sense, so it is, so it remains. But this is to assume—and it is an assumption in which gays and lesbians participate at their own peril—that our culture finds genocide unthinkable, little less unpracticable, and that it construes the lives of perverts as nonexpendable. AIDS is related to a phenomenon "almost literally unthinkable in its mathematical defeat of cognitive desire," but in the mode of resolution or reconstitution. The pandemic has resolved, rather than occasioned, a crisis in signification, the crisis that has always been gay sexuality itself.

Consider the discrepancy between the medical formulation and the cultural phantasmagoric: AIDS is defined clinically as the appearance of specific opportunistic infections "in a previously healthy individual," but to contract AIDS, as Cindy Patton notes, is to relinquish any claim to a prior state of psychosexual health.[4] Susan Sontag distinguishes between the poetics of cancer, which "is first of all a disease of the body's geography," and AIDS, which "depends upon constructing a temporal sequence of events."[5] Yet if the latter evinces a "natural" or "proper" affinity, as Lessing might say, with the temporal art of narrative, it is for reasons that are fully ideological, not simply prognostic or epidemiological. The cultural function of AIDS has been to stabilize, through a specifically narrative or novelistic logic, the "truth" of gay identity as death or death wish. Every gay man living with AIDS is Dorian Gray come again, and the pandemic realizes the promise of Wilde's novel, of the novelistic itself. "The good ended happily, and the bad unhappily," and the final fulfillment of the ethical distinction is written on the face. AIDS is somatic outing, the final, fully legible spectacle of a hitherto occluded depravity.

Or if not somatic outing, then ersatz heterosexuality, virtual normality: every gay man is threatened with the face he deserves, but for that reason alone the pandemic provides the occasion for reflecting on the errors of their ways, the lethal wages of their sins. Better, it turns out, a belated complicity with the poetics of bourgeois spiritualization than a commitment to the pleasures that bring death. A medical condition in which the immune system effectively turns against itself may suggest, in the best postmodern fashion, a destabilization of identity, an effacement of the distinction between self and other, but the cultural logic that structures the pandemic tends toward the opposite. We are less various than we care to acknowledge and homosexuality elicits from our culture a response in which even the most diverse of its elements finds common cause. It is, therefore, without apology that I advance an argument quite this unnuanced: AIDS has served either (a) to confirm the truth of gay identity as death or death wish, the better to return to those whose capacity for love is itself proof against illness an image of their own innate health, or (b) to refigure the gay male subject as a heterosexual manqué, the better to vitiate the scandal that is gay sexuality.

It is without apology, moreover, that I advocate a sexual politics now associated—especially among a few media darlings—with the "mantras of decades gone by":

There are plenty of people—especially among a few activist elites—who prefer to chant mantras of decades gone by and pretend that somehow this is 1957 and straight America is initiating a Kulturkampf against sex in parks and that somehow this is the defining issue of our times. But this is nostalgia masquerading as politics. It is not "sex panic," as they call it. It is victim panic, a terror that with the abatement of AIDS we might have to face the future and that the future may contain opportunities that gay men and women have never previously envisioned, let alone grasped. It is a panic that the easy identity of victimhood might be slipping from our grasp and that maturity might be calling us to more difficult and challenging terrain. It is not hard to see what that terrain is. It is marriage.[6]

The hitherto unenvisioned future that "the abatement of AIDS" opens before us is distressingly familiar: "maturity" calls us to reproduce the social order that produced us. (But precisely who is this "us"? who is experiencing "abatement"? Ninety-five percent of people living with HIV are in developing countries, and the rate of infection is on the rise.) This is nostalgia masquerading as a *Bildungsroman*, sex panic recast as a narrative of maturation and development. There is always the danger, of course, that promising new therapies will promote the illusion that gay sex is not inherently death producing. Eliminate sex panic, Gabriel Rotello worries, and our new found maturity will devolve back into the old promiscuity:

As the new drugs become the therapy of choice, many individuals may not be able to maintain the strict regime and will develop multiple-drug-resistant HIV. At the same time, governments throughout the world may relax prevention efforts, while many people, rejoicing that the AIDS epidemic seems to be contained, drift back to a life style of unprotected sex with multiple partners. The drug-resistant strains could enter these newly reconstituted viral highways, and we might end up with a super-epidemic that stymies even the strongest drugs.[7]

The newer therapies are not in fact cause for undue optimism—a generalized "abatement of AIDS" would require a generalized reduction in their cost—but neither do they justify what Sontag terms "imaginative complicity with disaster" (175). St. Paul thought it better to marry than to burn. Rotello thinks it better to be monogamous than to pursue the pleasures that, even today, mean death. ("Imaginative complicity with disaster" is here indistinguishable from pragmatic commitment to normalization.) Sullivan associates the brave new world of same-sex unions (new to him) with "the abatement of AIDS." Rotello associates "the new monogamy" with the so-called second-wave resurgence of HIV illness. But whether waxing or waning, AIDS/HIV is made to mean (or motivate) only one thing: erotic impoverishment.

Michael Warner reminds us that there is no necessary connection between the two:

AIDS activism in its most powerful (and truly ethical) mode was formed by the need to confront the pseudo-ethics that consisted in a willingness to stigmatize those who had sex, to blame them for the virus that was killing them, to use their sex to let them die, to prevent at all costs any further talk of sex even if it could be shown—as it was—that safer sex was the best and healthiest and most ethical solution to the crisis of prevention.

The mantras of decades gone by refused the thematization of homosexuality as death or death wish; "the normalized movement" of recent times, however, can imagine no higher ideal than the attainment of the legal right to have and to hold, which virtually literalizes the promise of heterosexuality manqué.[8] The current orthodoxy is mystified St. Paul. (Marriage may indeed be better than hellfire, but does the lesser of two evils therefore become a positive good?) Today, little escapes the teleology of the marriage plot, including—to add narrative insult to injury—the history of gay activism that once seemed, among other things, a critique of it:

Whatever gravity life may have lacked in the disco seventies it acquired in the health crisis of the eighties. What it lost in youth and innocence it gained in dignity. Gay cruising and experimentation. . . . gave way to a more lesbian-like interest in commitment. Since 1981 and probably earlier, gays were civilizing themselves. Part of our self-civilization has been an insistence on the right to marry. . . . The AIDS epidemic that ripped through the eighties not only cast a pall over the sexual freedom of the seventies, but, more important, illustrated the value of interpersonal commitment for gay people generally.[9]

This is from William Eskridge's *The Case for Same-Sex Marriage: From Sexual Liberty to Civilized Commitment*, the subtitle of which makes clear the narrative promise of AIDS. The dignified or mature sexuality that the epidemic promotes is strategically identified as "lesbian-like" (why do gay men always feel free to impute monogamy to dykes? why hasn't GLAAD, the Gay and Lesbian Alliance Against Defamation, taken up the issue?), but it is actually heterosexuality-as-usual. Our disco adolescence was fun, but all things are appropriate to their time, and what we have lost in youth and innocence (not to mention friends and lovers) we have more than gained in maturity and dignity. Every gay man need not be Dorian Gray come again, but to escape the fate of that perpetual adolescent is to embrace the conventions (now freely scattered across a broad range of cultural practices and assumptions) of the genre in which he figures: AIDS is a nineteenth-century, a novelistic phenomenon.

i. The Wicked Queen's Anxieties

Our most prestigious technology of self-fashioning and self-knowledge, which remains even today the Freudian narrative of psychosexual development, construes homosexuality as a simple failure of teleology, as sexual impulses that have yet to find resolution and stabilization in heterosexual genitality, in proper object choices and organ specificity. Homosexuality, fetishism, scopophilia, exhibitionism, sadism, masochism: the sundry perversions catalogued in *Three Essays on the Theory of Sexuality* are but the "abortive beginnings and preliminary stages of a firm organization of the component instincts" of a law-abiding sexuality.[10] Perversion is distinguished from heterosexual genitality primarily in terms of its relation, or nonrelation, to "discharge," which Freud terms "end-pleasure":

This last pleasure [the pleasure of genital orgasm] is the highest in intensity, and its mechanism differs from that of the earlier pleasure. It is brought about entirely by dis-

charge: it is wholly a pleasure of satisfaction and with it the tension of the libido is for the time being extinguished. (TE 210)

Like the well-made narrative, normative sexual activity issues in climax, from which comes, as it were, quiescence. Like the well-made narrative, moreover, normative sexuality is end-haunted, all for its end. In "Dora," Freud holds that hysterical "patients' inability to give an ordered history of their life in so far as it coincides with the history of their illness is not merely characteristic of the neurosis. It also possesses great theoretical significance."[11] And so it does:

It is only towards the end of the treatment that we have before us an intelligible, consistent, and unbroken case history. Whereas the practical aim of the treatment is to remove all possible symptoms and to replace them by conscious thoughts, we may regard it as a second and theoretical aim to repair all the damages to the patient's memory. These two aims are coincident. When one is reached, so is the other; and the same path leads to them both. (D 18)

The ability to tell an "intelligible, consistent, and unbroken" history of the self— in effect, to construe oneself as a character in a *Bildungsroman*—is coincident with, not simply the royal road to, psychosexual health. The normative is the narrative:

Another physician once sent his sister to me for psychotherapeutic treatment, telling me that she had for years been treated without success for hysteria. . . . The short account which he gave me seemed quite consistent with the diagnosis. In my first hour with the patient I got her to tell me her history herself. When the story came out perfectly clearly and connectedly in spite of the remarkable events it dealt with, I told myself that the case could not be one of hysteria. (D 16–17 n. 2)

And if the normative is the narrative, the perversions of adults, as Leo Bersani notes, are intelligible only as "the sickness of *uncompleted narratives*."[12]

Narrative teleology is, therefore, a good or goal in itself. Attain to it and all else is forgiven:

In the majority of instances the pathological character in a perversion is found to lie not in the content of the new sexual aim but in its relation to the normal. If a perversion, instead of appearing merely alongside the normal sexual aim and object, and only when circumstances are unfavorable to them and favorable to it—if, instead of this, it ousts them completely and takes their place in all circumstances—if, in short, a perversion has the characteristics of exclusiveness and fixation—then we shall usually be justified in regarding it as a pathological symptom. (TE 161)

Perversions can be characterized as such only when they displace, rather than supplement, normative sexual development:

In ordinary speech, the connotation of sadism oscillates between, on the one hand, cases merely characterized by an active or violent attitude to the sexual object, and, on the other hand, cases in which satisfaction is entirely conditional on the humiliation and maltreatment of the object. Strictly speaking, it is only this last extreme instance that deserves to be described as a perversion. (TE 158)

Strictly speaking, the "merely" violent relation to the sexual object that routinely emerges alongside male heterosexual genitality must be considered normative. Sadism "deserves" to be considered pathological or perverse only when it is directed toward (as opposed to against) a masochist, a fully consenting individual. Consider, however, the theoretical incoherence of the argument. Freud insists that a "sadist is always at the same time a masochist" (*TE* 159); unlike the "single aim" (*TE* 232) that is normative end pleasure, sadism is neither fixated nor exclusive, an indeterminacy that, as Freud also notes, is characteristic of "inversion" in general: "The important fact to bear in mind is that no one single aim can be laid down as applying in cases of inversion. Among men, intercourse *per anum* by no means coincides with inversion" (*TE* 145). Anal intercourse is not coincident with perversion, yet perversion is positioned as an early and fixated form of a trajectory that, its commitment to a "single aim" notwithstanding, is celebrated as freedom from fixity. Heterosexual genitality knows only one way, but it would have it, as it were, both ways.

Perhaps the most radical suggestion of *Three Essays on the Theory of Sexuality* is buried in a 1915 footnote: "From the point of view of psycho-analysis, the exclusive sexual interest felt by men for women is also a problem that needs elucidating and is not a self-evident fact based upon an attraction that is ultimately of a chemical nature" (*TE* 146 n. 1). But the radicalism is finally gestural: *Three Essays* is structured in order to think heterosexuality, or to allow heterosexuality to emerge as a problem for thought, only as the chronologically "after" and the qualitatively "later." Because the various stages of psychosexual development are "normally passed through smoothly, without giving more than a hint of their existence," the full or complete form of the trajectory is subject "to superficial observation" (*TE* 198)—or, more precisely, hypothetical reconstruction—only in the lives of those who fail to attain to the norm. Freud thus feels free to begin *Three Essays* with the sexual aberrations even though when he began he had no clinical experience of the sexually aberrant whatsoever. The entire project is pre-posterous, ass-backwards: "The clinical 'verification' of the stages of infantile sexuality . . . [is] guided by a theory which already assumes [and requires] their existence."[13] Heterosexuality is spared the embarrassment of explanation—it resolves the "problem" of the sexual aberrations; it is not itself a problem in need of elucidation—but with results that are, at best, ambiguous.

On the up side: the exclusive sexual interest felt by men for women or women for men, like the unseen but all-seeing heart of Foucault's panopticon, is never implicated in the field it commands. (Note the paucity of departments of heterosexual studies in even our more liberal institutions. The aberrant are the objects of a coercive and normalizing logic; heterosexuality is the unmarked condition of knowing.)[14] But on the down side: the exclusive sexual interest felt by men for women or women for men is necessarily defined by what it is not. (A source of heterosexual comfort: "Whatever else you might say about it, at least it's not that." A source of heterosexual anxiety: "There is nothing else to say about it but that.") The celebration of the "highest satisfaction" is not, then, without its ambivalence: like the wicked queen in the fairy tale, who fears that someone, somewhere, may be more beautiful than she, the highest satisfaction is haunted by the possibility that it isn't. A pleasure that is coincident with the extinction of libidinal energy necessarily suggests that "the end of sex, the goal of sex" is also "its end, its disappearance,"[15] all of which plays havoc with the wicked queen's anxieties. A heterosexuality that is construed as what homosexuality fails to become can as easily be dismissed as what homosexuality refuses to be: erotic pessimism, sensual impoverishment. The Freudian construction of homosexuality, the pathos inherent in a failure of narrative teleology, is haunted by the Wildean, the pleasures attendant upon its refusal.

Dorian Gray recasts "the sickness of uncompleted narratives" as the pleasure of multiple narratives, endless narratives, nonnarratives, everything that our culture denigrates as "promiscuity," which is simply a sexuality that does not pursue, lemming-like, its own end or disappearance:

The attainment of the normal sexual aim can clearly be endangered by the mechanism in which fore-pleasure is involved. This danger arises if at any point in the preparatory sexual processes the fore-pleasure turns out to be too great and the element of tension too small. The motive for proceeding further with the sexual process then disappears, the whole path is cut short, and the preparatory act in question takes the place of the normal sexual aim. . . . Such is in fact the mechanism of many perversions, which consist in lingering over the preparatory acts of the sexual process. (TE 211)

The normative teleology is endangered not only by the mechanism in which fore-pleasure is involved, but by any teleology that is simply for pleasure, any sexual economy in which pleasure does not work toward its own effacement. Bersani notes that the now ubiquitous public discourse on gay sexual practices—the heated fantasies of gay men having sex twenty to thirty times a night—presupposes a thoroughly preternatural standard of sexual heroics, a phenomenon "almost literally unthinkable in its mathematical defeat of [straight] cognitive desire."[16] Simon Watney argues that the discourse resembles nineteenth-century speculation (no less heated) on the prostitute's capacity for multiple orgasms.[17] Both are forms of pleasure strictly superfluous to the (re)productive deployment of the body; both presuppose a capacity for end pleasure or discharge that does not herald an end to pleasure. But if the fantasy titillates, it also comforts: the whore's capacity for pleasure is analogized to disease and the homosexual's to death. The perverse coupling of Eros and Thanatos betrays a generalized cultural sadomasochism—even the most extravagant of Mapplethorpe's excursions into S/M seem positively candy-assed in comparison—but it relieves the wicked queen's anxieties. Gays, like girls, might think they just want to have fun, but we now know better. AIDS recasts "the sickness of uncompleted narratives" as "intelligible, consistent, and unbroken" narratives of sickness. The perverse, the promiscuous, just want to die.

Perverse sex aspires to the atemporal condition of lyric, but in the plague years, Sontag cautions, it necessarily compromises with narrative: "The fear of AIDS imposes on an act whose ideal is an experience of pure presentness (and a creation of the future) a relation to the past that is to be ignored at one's peril" (160). Sontag's formulation is itself, however, incapable of imagining the ideal it imagines AIDS to threaten: by definition, the experience of "pure presentness" can have no investment in the creation of a future, even so modest a future as breakfast the next morning. (Edna St. Vincent Millay to a trick: "Let me make it plain / I find this frenzy insufficient reason / For conversation when we meet again.") Pure presentness can be maintained as sexual ideal, moreover, only if all sexual activity aspires to the condition of perversion, which Freud construes as lingering in, dilating upon, the sexual present. But our culture is unwilling to entertain such a possibility, even if its most prestigious theoretician of sexuality unwittingly invites it. And today, the invitation can be declined with impunity. "So remember when a person has sex, they're having it with everybody that partner had it with for the past ten years." The grammar of this 1987 pronouncement from the secretary of health and human services is no less atrocious than its politics: fantasizing about all the others might up the erotic ante, but it hardly makes for safer sex. The point, however, is clear enough. Pleasure is not, as Dorian Gray would have it, the experience of pure presentness, but a narrative in which every moment is potentially contaminated by its past, and hence threatening to its future. "Strandentwining cable of all flesh," as Joyce says in a different context (and with a different referential thrust).

ii. Their Vehement Sexual Customs

In other words, it's back: the marriage plot and its attendant ideology, the erotics of scarcity, the poetics of monogamy, the prudent administration and distribution of desire. Indeed, it never left us. The hitherto unenvisioned future posited by Andrew Sullivan, for example, is already in sight in Sontag's *AIDS and Its Metaphors*:

The catastrophe of AIDS suggests the immediate necessity of limitation, of constraint for the body and for consciousness. But the response to AIDS is more than reactive, more than a fearful and therefore appropriate response to a very real danger. It also expresses a positive desire, the desire for stricter limits in the conduct of personal life. There is a broad tendency in our culture, an end-of-an-era feeling, that AIDS is reinforcing; an exhaustion, for many, of purely secular ideals—ideals that seemed to encourage libertinism or at least not provide any coherent inhibition against it—in which the response to AIDS finds its place. The behavior AIDS is stimulating is part of a larger grateful return to what is perceived as "conventions," like the return to figure and landscape, tonality and melody, plot and character, and other much vaunted repudiations of difficult modernism in the arts. The reduction in the imperative of promiscuity in the middle class, a growth of the ideal of monogamy, of a prudent sexual life. (166)

But which is it? Is "the reduction in the imperative of promiscuity" a reactive (not to say reactionary) pressure that has gained momentum because of the pandemic? Or is it the great good that will emerge, phoenix-like, from it? Is Sontag one of the "many" for whom the "positive" desire to "constrain" the non–HIV-positive body is in fact a welcome development? Or is she merely functioning as an amanuensis to a culture that now believes it has forged a "coherent inhibition against libertinism," a narrative of perversion and promiscuity that need no longer begrudge the deviant their fun?

The journalistic *style indirect libre* to which *AIDS and Its Metaphors* is given suggests the latter, and it is difficult to imagine so distinguished an apologist for the avant-garde recommending a repudiation of "difficult modernism" *tout court*. Not surprisingly, then, both *Illness as Metaphor* and *AIDS and Its Metaphors* fortify themselves against the seductions of narrative:

I decided to write about the mystifications surrounding cancer. I didn't think it would be useful—and I wanted to be useful—to tell yet one more story in the first person about how someone learned that she or he had cancer, wept, struggled, was comforted, suffered, took courage . . . though mine was also that story. A narrative, it seemed to me, would be less useful than an idea. For narrative pleasure I would appeal to other writers. (101)

These reflections on *Illness as Metaphor* stand as preface to *AIDS and Its Metaphors*, which suggest that they are no less proleptic than retrospective. Certainly the project of the latter, the attempt to "retire" metaphor from the discourse of AIDS, would logically involve a rejection of narrative. As Paul de Man notes, "From the recognition of language as trope, one is led to the telling of a tale, to the narrative sequence. . . . The temporal deployment of an initial complication, of a structural knot, indicates the close, though not necessarily complementary, relation between trope and narrative, between knot and plot."[18] Or Peter Brooks: narrative "operates as metaphor in its affirmation of resemblance"; it brings into relation different actions, combines them through perceived similarities, and appropriates them to a "common plot," which requires "the rejection of all merely contingent (or unassimilatable) incident or action."[19] The identity of these surd elements is never specified, but in a culture in which a single "common plot" dominates the field—every Jack shall have his Jill—it is easily surmised.

Yet Sontag does not just say no to narrative. The gesture of refusal is conspicuous, but "narrative pleasure" reasserts itself in a fully motivated, fully coherent narrative of gay sexual pleasure as death or death wish:

An infectious disease whose principal means of transmission is sexual necessarily puts at greater risk those who are sexually more active—and is easy to view as a punishment for that activity. True of syphilis, this is even truer of AIDS, since not just promiscuity but a specific sexual "practice" regarded as unnatural is named as more endangering. . . . Addicts who get the illness by sharing contaminated needles are seen as committing (or completing) a kind of inadvertent suicide. Promiscuous homosexual men practicing their vehement sexual customs under the illusory conviction, fostered by medical ideology with its cure-all antibiotics, of the relative innocuousness of all sexually transmitted diseases, could be viewed as dedicated hedonists—though it's now clear that their behavior was no less suicidal. (114)

The phrase "their vehement sexual customs" is an embarrassment. Sontag is fluent in the vocabulary of moral condemnation, but she is apparently less comfortable with what she proceeds to call, euphemistically and thus nonspecifically, "a specific sexual 'practice.'" (She means, of course, perverse end pleasure, pleasure taken the wrong end round, fucking or getting fucked in the ass, which she regards as regarded as unnatural and "more endangering." But what is actually "more endangering"—and it apparently bears repeating—is unprotected anal intercourse, or how "the specific sexual 'practice'" is practiced. "An infectious disease whose principal means of transmission is sexual" does not "necessarily" put at risk those "who are sexually more active," although statements like Sontag's, which associate "promiscuity" qua "promiscuity" with unsafe sexual practices, do.) Granted, Sontag seems only to be rehearsing various homophobic constructions of the epidemic—"it is easy to view," "regarded as," and the like—against which she will come to define her own position. But as the two ultimately coalesce, she is spared the trouble. It is not homophobia, but gay sex itself, that is predicated on culturally determined illusions: AIDS is not a catastrophe that the powers-that-be have allowed to happen, but the result of gay men's "illusory conviction . . . of the relative innocuousness of all sexually transmitted diseases." (Why illusory? Why "the imaginative complicity with disaster"? HIV may yet prove, at least in the first world, a relatively innocuous, if not ultimately curable, condition.) It's now "clear": their behavior always was "suicidal," full stop. Like all good stories of a certain kind, the narrative of AIDS is both fully motivated (the active agent is not a retrovirus, which would hardly do, but a gay community intent on collective suicide) and in possession of a final twist (the suicidal intent is not just received opinion, as it might first appear, but the belatedly revealed truth of things). No matter that many gay men initially knew nothing of the existence of AIDS or the means of transmitting HIV infection while engaging in their "vehement sexual customs": narrative retroactively brings to light causalities that always were operable, even if they passed temporarily unrecognized or unacknowledged as such. (What else to make of an otherwise unintelligible oxymoron: "inadvertent suicide"?) No need, moreover, to specify the specific sexual practice. Behavior is but the incidental manifestation of a deep psychological truth.

Hence, the broad cultural tendency to construe "risk," the medical evidence notwithstanding, under the novelistic category of "character," as if E. M. Forster's *Aspects of the Novel* were not only still, but everywhere, with us:

"Character," says Aristotle, "gives us qualities, but it is in actions—what we do—that we are happy or the reverse." We have already decided that Aristotle is wrong and now we must face the consequences of disagreeing with him. "All human happiness and misery," says Aristotle, "take the form of action." We know better. We believe that happiness and misery exist in the secret life, which each of us lives privately, and to which (in his characters) the novelist has access. And by the secret life we mean the life for which there is no external evidence.[20]

To translate all this into the idiom of AIDS: it is not by what we do that we are healthy or the reverse, for homosexuality, unlike sodomy, is not a category of behavior. Foucault's sense of the historical divide that separates the sodomite, the perpetrator of a category of "forbidden acts," from the modern homosexual, "a certain quality of sexual sensibility," is much disputed, but it has found unwelcome confirmation in the poetics of AIDS. Health and illness, no less than happiness and misery, exist in the secret life, which each of us lives privately, but to which AIDS, like Dorian's portrait, provides privileged access. (Forster's celebration of "the discourse of the secret singularity" is itself implicitly or unwittingly Foucauldian. A secret life for which there is no external evidence is necessarily betrayed by its novelization, which, in registering it, provides external verification of it.) The behavior AIDS is stimulating is not, therefore, simply part of a "larger grateful return to what is perceived of as 'conventions,'" for as Sontag's own narrative of gay sexual pleasure evinces, they never really left us. To make "their vehement sexual customs" but the incidental manifestation of an innately suicidal impulse is to perpetuate the novelistic subordination of plot to character, behavior to identity, that has subtended the category of the homosexual from its inception.

And it is still too much with us, perhaps more so now than ever. Gabriel Rotello, for instance, dismisses the "condom code" as a "technological fix," as a "minimally transformative" intervention into gay sexual practices, but what the pandemic requires is a transformation of consciousness, a new homosexual "ecology," a new homosexual person.[21] It is not in actions—what we do—that we are healthy or the reverse, but in who we are, and AIDS is nature's way of telling us that we are untenable, unsustainable. The Vatican and the quasi-official spokespersons of "the normalized movement" are in substantial agreement. Love the sinner, hate the sin. Affirm the dignity of the homosexual "person"; condemn the perverse or promiscuous deployment of the body. Warner argues that the failure of contemporary gay politics is precisely its fixation on the category of identity:

The concept of perversion, as distinct from perverse acts, led to the concept of sexual identity (or its close kin, sexual orientation). Each distinguishes between identity and sex, between the person and the act, status and conduct. The doctors had inadvertently made it possible for their former patients to claim that being gay is not necessarily about sex. Homosexuals could argue that any judgment about their person, irrespective of their actions, was irrational prejudice. In so doing, they could challenge the stigma of identity, without in the least challenging the shame of sexual acts. To this day, a similar logic governs much of gay politics. That is why lawyers who challenge military antigay policy or discrimination by the Boy Scouts usually take pains to find test cases in which the victim is a model victim because he or she has never done anything wrong—that is, had sex.[22]

The mantras of decades gone by taught us "how to have promiscuity in an epidemic." Today, we are schooled in the poetics of bourgeois spiritualization, in what Warner, following Hannah Arendt, terms "the world-canceling" force of the ideology of love.[23] The normalized movement exactly reverses the priorities of an earlier activism: it privileges ethos rather than praxis, being rather than behavior. Its failure is thus the triumph of all things novelistic. Freud maintains that people fall in love "in order not to fall ill."[24] People, not unreconstructed perverts: they continue to have sex in order to die.

Or so our culture insists and Sontag unwittingly reiterates, which renders her larger project little more than gestural:

My aim was to alleviate unnecessary suffering—exactly as Nietzsche formulated it. . . . Thinking about illness!—To calm the imagination of the invalid, so that at least he should not, as hitherto, have to suffer more from thinking about his illness than from the illness itself—that, I think, would be something! It would be a great deal! (101–2)

Perhaps this would be a great deal, but it is difficult to know how the belatedly revealed knowledge that your sex life or drug habit always was "suicidal" serves to release the sick from the suffering of self-incriminating thinking about their illness. Nor is it clear, given the current obsession with same-sex unions, that the collective imagination requires calming. (T. S. Eliot once remarked that religion will probably continue to modify itself, as in the past, into something that can be believed. Marriage, an institution closely allied with it, will no doubt do the same. Here the lunatic Right is wrong: the eventual—I am tempted to say "inevitable"— recognition of same-sex partnerships will be the true "Defense of Marriage Act," evidence of an inclusiveness that will allow all right-thinking people, in every sense of the phrase, to participate in it.) The project of calming the imagination needs, moreover, to consider the risks (if such is not already its implicit agenda) of quietism. Liberal readings of the pandemic tend to follow Sontag in rejecting the metaphor of "plague," but only to recover the equanimity of, say, a Pat Robertson. For it makes no practical difference whether AIDS is construed as a punishment from above ("God's way of weeding his garden") or within ("inadvertent suicide"): Sontag's New Age psychology is as much an apology for homophobia as that old-time religion. Responsibility for the pandemic resides not with a generalized and genocidal homophobia ("on the whole," Sontag blithely notes, the medical es-tablishment has been "a bulwark of sanity and rationality" [169]); rather, it is of the essence of homosexuality itself.

Sontag is not unique, of course, in forgoing the pleasures of narrative, in name if not deed, for a muse more rigorous. The Freud of "Dora," for example, might be claimed as a significant precursor:

I must now turn to consider a further complication to which I should certainly give no space if I were a man of letters engaged upon the creation of a mental state like this for a short story, instead of being a medical man engaged upon its dissection. The element to which I must now allude can only serve to obscure and efface the outlines of the fine poetic conflict which we have been able to ascribe to Dora. This element would rightly fall a sacrifice to the censorship of a writer. . . . For behind Dora's supervalent train of thought which was concerned with her father's relations to Frau K. there lay concealed a feeling of jealousy which had that lady as its object—a feeling, that is, which could only be based upon an affection on Dora's part for one of her own sex. (D 59–60)

Were Freud embarked on a short story or a "*roman à clef*" (D 9), Dora's lesbianism would fall victim to the censorship of the writer, who, "after all, simplifies and ab-stracts when he appears in the character of a psychologist" (D 60). Yet if there is a censorship that is imposed from without, there is also one that inheres within, in the symmetries of the well-made narrative itself: to register same-sex desire is nec-essarily "to efface and obscure the outlines of a fine poetic conflict." For Freud as for Brooks, narrative brings into relation different actions, combines them through perceived similarities, and appropriates them to a "common plot," which requires "the rejection of all merely contingent (or unassimilable) incident or ac-tion." Freud, however, gives those surd elements a name: the man of science calls "un chat un chat" (D 48)—albeit only in French—and a dyke a dyke. Even for Freud, however, same-sex desire remains the most inert of facts, curiously devoid of narrative life, and at no point is Dora's lesbianism allowed to impinge on the fine poetic symmetries of the case study. "The girl has married," Freud triumphantly announces in the concluding paragraph,

and indeed—unless all the signs mislead me [they did]—she has married the young man who came into her associations at the beginning of the analysis of the second dream. Just as the first dream represented her turning away from the man she loved to her father—that is to say, her flight from life into disease—so the second dream announced she was about to tear herself free from her father and had been reclaimed once more by the realities of life. (D 122)

Reality is the plot of normative psychosexual development; heterosexual genitality is health, and both are governed by the symmetries ("just as the first dream . . . so the second") that any man of letters might envy. In *Three Essays*, Freud argues that there are "good reasons why a child sucking at his mother's breast has become the prototype of every relation of love. The finding of an object is in fact a refinding of it" (*TE* 222). The heroics of heterosexual genitality are recuperative, not progressive, and regression apparently exhausts the meaning of love.

A child sucking at his mother's breast can be construed as "the prototype of every relation of love," however, only if every relation of love is construed as autoerotic. (Wilde: "To love oneself is the beginning of a lifelong romance.") In the second of the three essays, Freud observes that the "most striking feature" of infantile sexuality "is that the instinct is not directed towards other people, but obtains satisfaction from the subject's own body. It is 'auto-erotic,' to call it by a happily chosen term introduced by Havelock Ellis" (*TE* 181). If, then, the heterosexual finding of an object is always a refinding, the recovery of the experience at (not of) the mother's breast, heterosexuality can only be construed as the perpetual elision or re-elision of the object. "The Transformations of Puberty," the final of the three essays, seeks to rehabilitate this autoeroticism as selflessness. With the emergence of heterosexual genitality, "the sexual instinct is . . . subordinated to the reproductive function: it becomes, so to say, altruistic" (*TE* 207). (Prior to 1965, when the U.S. Supreme Court struck down the last law prohibiting the sale of birth control to married couples, contraception was routinely charged with fostering sexual "egotism.")[25] But if anything is subordinated here, it is the integrity of the broader argument itself. Nothing in *Three Essays* issues logically in this sexual pastoral.

To approach the issue obliquely: the conventional academic critique of Foucault—and hell hath no fury like a specious radicalism exposed—might be better directed against Freud:

At the same time as these plainly incestuous fantasies are overcome and repudiated [the son's desire for the mother, the daughter's for the father], one of the most significant, but also one of the most painful, psychical achievements of the pubertal period is completed: detachment from parental authority, a process that alone makes possible the opposition, which is so important for the progress of civilization, between the new generation and the old. At every stage in the course of development through which all human beings ought by rights to pass, a certain number are held back: so there are some who never get over their parents' authority and have withdrawn their affection from them either very incompletely or not at all. (TE 227)

Foucault is routinely dismissed as a fetishist of power, but nothing in his work rivals the ease with which Freud recuperates opposition for the status quo. The "reward for filial disobedience," to mar Jane Austen, is the recovery of parental, heterosexual privilege, and only those of us unable to detach ourselves from parental authority fail to attain to it. (For example, boys who don't turn out to be the marrying kind or girls who do but who thereafter refuse "to give their husbands . . . what is due them" [*TE* 227].) Opposition to compulsory heterosexuality is evacuated of all efficacy even as the heterosexual cloning of Oedipal desire, the urge inherent in all social life to recuperate a prior state of affairs, is preserved as "hetero." Lacan is perfectly explicit:

Freud reveals to us that it is thanks to [grâce au] the Name-of-the-Father that man does not remain in the sexual service of the mother, that aggression towards the father is at the principle of the Law, and that the Law is at the service of desire, which it institutes through the prohibition of incest.

It is, therefore, the assumption of castration which creates the lack through which desire is instituted. . . . Desire reproduces the subject's relation to a lost object.[26]

The psychoanalytic production of desire reproduces the subject's relation to the lost object that is itself produced by Oedipal familialism. It is not, therefore, simply the negative prohibition against incest, the *non* latent in the paternal *nom*, that is "at the principle of the Law," for the Oedipal family is itself a structural incitement to, a perpetual solicitation of, "those plainly incestuous fantasies" it allegedly guards against. Freud maintains that respect for the prohibition "is essentially a cultural demand made by society. Society must guard against the danger that the interests which it needs for the establishment of higher social units may be swallowed up by the family" (*TE* 225). But the bourgeois family recognizes no social unit or value higher than itself, and it is only by systematically producing what it nevertheless prohibits that the bourgeois family reproduces itself. Oedipal familialism places desire "at the principle of the Law" the better to reproduce Oedipal familialism.

Or so Foucault, in open opposition to the Freudian settlement, insists:

The [psychoanalytic] guarantee that one would always find the parents-children relation at the root of everyone's sexuality made it possible—even when everything seemed to point to the reverse process—to keep the deployment of sexuality coupled to the system of alliance. There was no risk that sexuality would appear to be, by nature, alien to the law: it was constituted only through the law. Parents, do not be afraid to bring your children to analysis: it will teach them that in any case it is you whom they love. Children, you really shouldn't complain that you are not orphans, that you always discover in your innermost selves your Object-Mother or the sovereign sign of your Father: it is through them that you gain access to desire.[27]

In a premodern, predisciplinary "system of alliance," children are distributed in marriage as so many prizes or possessions. In the kinder, gentler world of bourgeois familialism, however, children give themselves, for better or worse, in love. The contractual and the consensual govern the modern marriage market, yet neither the family nor the social order it subtends is thereby threatened with heterogeneity. True, parents are denied sovereign authority over their children's bodies, but only to be granted a compensatory, if less immediately discernible, privilege: the overt coercion of an older familialism is simply translated into an ideology of desire. Thus it was possible, even when everything seemed to point to the reverse process, to keep the deployment of sexuality coupled to the system of alliance. Freud's rather lurid study of the sexual dynamics that sustain the conjugal family might seem to threaten naively idealizing celebrations of it, but the hand that delivers the blow, as Jacques Donzelot suggests, is also the hand that heals:

[The discourse of psychoanalysis] is a fortunate one, since it credits the family with being both the only model for socialization and the source of all dissatisfactions. An excess or deficiency is always imputed to the family in order to explain the oppressions and frustrations of individuals within it. In the suffering or pride of those who flee, there is always something that points back to a singular, baleful experience of the family, which invalidates or excuses the action taken but refers the subject of it back to the family. . . . [The "psy" disciplines] make possible a situation in which the family disappears as a social protagonist but continues to exist as a means of individual attainment, as a place where ambitions are inscribed, a real origin of failures and a virtual horizon of successes.[28]

71

Sad to say, Dorothy is wrong. In a psychosexual economy that always points back to the singular, baleful experience of the family, all places are like home.

An economy so utterly domestic and domesticating is, of course, perfectly at home in what Henry James calls "the house of fiction." Freud openly acknowledged that the poets were there before him, and poets have long occupied a privileged position in humanist education. Yet if psychoanalysis revives a prior state of literary affairs, or at least literary wisdom, its affinities are not necessarily with the poets Freud himself chooses to name. The bourgeois novel, not the classical Greek stage, is the significant precursor. Freud has good reasons for mystifying the genealogy: to construe the conjugal family in the image of ancient Greek tragedy is to eternalize its tawdry sexual intrigues as oracular destiny. It is the nineteenth-century novel of psychological depth, however, that is most fully complicit with the cultural work of psychoanalysis. "Some things . . . were not to be done," the eponymous hero of John Weir's *The Irreversible Decline of Eddie Socket* insists, "like voting Republican and drinking Coors." But some things are, and Eddie, who is HIV-positive, comes to regret his "failure to imagine a world in which there were any options other than the ones his parents presented."[29] The novel expresses the failure in psychological terms, but Eddie's predicament, like Dorian Gray's, may well reside with his generic dispensation. The novel is in fact a genre, Bakhtin notwithstanding, and its refusal to speak its name, to acknowledge its structural determinates and limitations, betrays its complicity with both the class and the sexuality that-would-not-be-named. (I mean, of course, heterosexuality, which both goes without saying and is the privilege of never having to say; indeed, the privilege rarely emerges unscathed from the saying.) To risk a formulation that, in an earlier manifestation of these paragraphs, exposed me to the charge, which I initially mistook for a compliment, of throwing out the baby with the bathwater: traditional narrative is at once heterosexual and heterosexualizing. The novel is less accommodating to perverse elements than its P.R. would suggest, and its heterosexual and heterosexualizing conventions are all the more insidious for defining themselves against the "merely" literary.

iii. Radical Heterosexuality, Heterosexuality Manqué

Consider what Weir's novel might have been in the good-old-bad-days, in the time before the plague: not the "irreversible decline" but the "coming out" of Eddie Socket. Ethan Mordden celebrates the *"Bildungsroman* of gathering self-awareness and coming out" as the gay writer's unique contribution to literature, which is true enough: narratives of "gathering [heterosexual] self-awareness and coming out" are few and far between.[30] Homosexuality has an etiology; otherwise, it would not be preventable or curable. Heterosexuality, like death and taxes, just is. Proto-homosexuality, the story of gathering gay self-awareness, is amenable to narrative elaboration; heterosexuality, the completed or closed form of the normative trajectory, isn't. (Proto-heterosexuality is homosexuality, the "sickness of uncompleted narratives.") Freud is right: the exclusive sexual interest felt by men for women or women for men "is a problem in need of elucidation and not a self-evident fact that is ultimately of a chemical nature," yet neither the man of science nor the man of letters is willing to submit the normative to the indignity of explanation. The straight writer's unique contribution to literature is thus not the coming out narrative, but the marriage plot, which assumes an infinitely renewable reserve of cross-gender desire.

Yet for all its ubiquity, the marriage plot isn't quite: betrothal, not the eternity of having and holding, is the conventional fulfillment. The narrative dynamics of heterosexual desire characteristically suspend their operations on the threshold of a future that strategically remains future, the better to mystify their relation to the past. In Fielding's *Tom Jones*, for example, the belated revelation of parental identity resolves multiplicity back into a primal unity, the aptly named family "cell," and the knowledge gleaned from the past as the secret of Tom's birth is re-created on the threshold of the future as the promise of his marriage.[31] The finding of an object, here as in Freud, is effectively a refinding, and the family remains, despite its temporary eclipse, the real origin of failure and the virtual horizon of success. ("Until recently," Lady Bracknell concedes, "I had never heard of a family that had its origin in a terminus." In one sense, the great lady's bewilderment is understandable: train stations and the like are not, after all, conventional sites for heterosexual coupling. In another sense, however, it is entirely beside the point. The true scandal would be a family that did not have its origins in its terminus and its terminus in its origins, a family that did not endlessly clone itself.) If, then, the homosexual is without a narrative future, it is because the alleged love of the same is irreducible to the narrative return of the same. In *Beyond the Pleasure Principle*, Freud defines the instinctual as the "*urge inherent in organic life to restore an earlier state of things.*" Far from "impelling us toward change and development," as common sense or convention would have it, "the instincts are the expression of the *conservative* nature of living substance."[32] But what may or may not be true of all organic life is certainly true of all traditional narrative life. It is thus structurally incapable of imagining a world in which there are options not predetermined by origins.

Rotello argues that the restorative or recuperative is the logic of sexual "ecology" itself:

The task of bringing HIV prevalence down to lower levels is equivalent to what environmentalists call restoration ecology, the goal of which is to return damaged eco-systems to something approximating their "predisturbance state." Restoration ecology is particularly applicable to gay men because levels of HIV prevalence are so high that strategies that might otherwise work in low-prevalence populations—simply reducing the number of partners or using condoms most of the time—cannot work for gay men. High prevalence means high risk, and high risk will continue to face us until we go beyond mere prevention and achieve some measure of restoration to a lower level of prevalence. (206–7)

Biology may be powerless to realize the dream of a world without the homosexual—even if AIDS were to claim every gay man tomorrow, heterosexuals unlucky at reproduction would continue to restock the supply—but it is capable of recovering homosexuality for heterosexual norms. Nature apparently abhors promiscuity as much as a vacuum, and it is nature, not ideology, that demands a prudent regulation and administration of desire. Gays are thus obliged to translate the "implacable" (300) logic of nature into its natural psychosexual analogue: "The question facing us . . . is not only whether we can learn these ecological lessons [from heterosexuals] . . . but also whether we are psychologically and politically willing to implement such lessons if they tend to fly in the face of cherished ideals about sexual liberation" (183). Rotello's ambition is the creation of a "sustainable" future for homosexuality, which, here as in Freud, means the recuperation of an earlier, "predisturbance" state of affairs, and hence a future functionally indistinguishable from the past. God made Adam and Eve, not Adam and Steve, as the religious right witlessly reminds us, and as Adam and Steve represent the irruption of difference into the heterosexual reproduction of the same, a predisturbance state can only be that happy, mythological time before the homosexual. There is no getting back to the Garden, our original home, but even perverts can aspire to something approximating a "predisturbance state."[33] Ecology literally means "home wisdom" (*oikos logia*), and if homosexuals are powerless literally to reproduce the domestic economy that produced them, close counts in more than horseshoes. Rotello's vision succeeds where mere biology fails: the future belongs to heterosexuals, actual or ersatz.

The heterosexual reproduction of the same might seem curiously at odds with its P.R., but a little etymological speculation apparently sets things straight. From Jane Gallop's *The Daughter's Seduction: Feminism and Psychoanalysis*: "I wish to speak of a radical heterosexuality, a true openness and love for the *heteros*, the other, an intercourse between two modalities. . . . And any relation between members of the same sex which allowed their difference, did not assimilate both to one fantasy, would be heterosexual."[34] But surely a fantasy that reduces the other to an honorary version of itself defines the meaning of assimilationist—Gallop's "radical heterosexuality" is Sullivan's "virtually normal"—and no amount of etymological play (routine at that) can translate a category of social privilege into an ontology of difference. Michael Warner notes that a "sexuality organized by its self-understanding as *hetero*sexuality" also "includes the category of homo- and autoerotics against which it defines itself," which is to say, the claims made for radical heterosexuality are already implicit in the garden variety version of the same.[35] "Homosexuality," Gallop's term of choice, is itself a homophobic category, but then so too is "radical heterosexuality," and better the devil one knows. (What have perverts to gain from Gallop's oxymoronic designation? "Oh, they count as Tories," Lady Bracknell says of Liberal Unionists. "We dine with them.") Gallop does have the good sense, or the good rhetorical instincts, to cop to a certain ambivalence. "We cannot be certain," she concedes, "that this radical notion of 'heterosexuality' is not just an alibi for the comforting norm" (127–28). But on the contrary: we can be and it is. And never is the comforting norm more comfortable than when taking up residence in and as the novel.

None of this is meant to deny the obvious: there are novels written by homosexuals and novels in which homosexuals figure. Yet if there is a homophobia of exclusion, so too is there a homophobia of inclusion. A once notorious case in point:

> *Back in the bathhouse, when the moaning stopped, the young man rolled over on his back for a cigarette. Gaetan Dugas reached up for the lights, turning up the rheostat slowly so that his partner's eyes would have time to adjust. He then made a point of eyeing the purple lesions on his chest. "Gay cancer," he said, almost as if he were talking to himself. "Maybe you'll get it too."*[36]

"Their vehement sexual customs" is here reduced to "his," and "inadvertent suicide" is refigured as willful murder: this is Gaetan Dugas, the "Patient Zero" of Randy Shilts's *And the Band Played On*. Dugas answers, of course, to the most conventional of narrative exigencies. The novel traditionally figures structural injustice as individual villainy, and "Patient Zero" is very much the villain of a nineteenth-century multi-plot novel.[37] Part 2 of *And the Band Played On* takes as its epigraph a passage from Emerson's "Self-Reliance": "All history resolves itself quite easily into the biography of a few stout and earnest persons" (9). Altogether too easily, as it happens. The "history of AIDS," like "the history of sexuality," may be its discursive construction, but this is hardly a compelling argument for re-solving a history of criminal silence and institutional homophobia into the biog-raphy of a few stout and earnest persons, Randy Shilts and friends, and one par-ticularly "dedicated hedonist." *And the Band Played On* is finally the story of the bad faggot too many people slept with and the good faggot too few people listened to: Gaetan Dugas and Randy Shilts. "THE MAN WHO GAVE US AIDS"—I am quoting from the *New York Post*, which obligingly gave Shilts the headline his book so ob-viously solicits—is also the story of "THE MAN WHO GAVE US THE MAN WHO GAVE US AIDS." "Patient Zero" makes Randy Shilts's name.

There are, then, good faggots: they have—the term is from the Auden poem "September 1, 1939," although the Larry Kramer play gave it new currency—"nor-mal hearts":

What mad Nijinsky wrote
About Diaghilev
Is true of the normal heart;
For the error bred in the bone
Of each woman and each man
Craves what it cannot have,
Not universal love
But to be loved alone

. . .

There is no such thing as the State
And no one exists alone;
Hunger allows no choice
To the citizen or the police;
We must love one another or die.[38]

I cannot pretend to speak for or from the normal (or virtually normal) heart, but this seems to me exactly wrong. "What mad Nijinsky wrote / About Diaghilev" is not the norm, although the assertion that it is can only serve the cause of the regime of the norm. Even if one were to concede the biologism—and it is a gen-erous concession: hunger is meaningless in isolation from its social distribution and regulation—the physiology of hunger cannot be conflated with the poetics of love. (People do get hungry without first reading about it in books; they do not fall in love without prior literary or cultural experience.) Freud, no enemy to biologism, worries the relation between the two:

The fact of the existence of sexual needs in human beings and animals is expressed in biology by the assumption of a "sexual instinct," on the analogy of the instinct of nutrition, that is of hunger. Everyday language possesses no counterpart to the word "hunger," but science makes use of the word "libido" for the purpose. (TE 135)

The sexual drive (*Trieb*) is not an instinct (*Instinkt*); it cannot be understood as a "response to a natural need whose paradigm is hunger." Were the analogy compelling, sexual maturation would be "a behavioral sequence narrowly determined by its 'source,' with a fixed and quite precise 'object,' since sexuality would focus uniquely and in a manner predetermined for all eternity on the other sex."[39] In effect, the sexual aberrations would be unthinkable or thinkable only as incidental variations on the norm, which is precisely the burden of Kramer's normalizing deployment of Auden's poem. The state is internalized, not eluded: to conflate the physiology of hunger with the poetics of love is to invite the psychoanalytic cop into the heart of the gay citizen, the better to render those other cops—I mean those whose uniforms bear the official sanction of the state—superfluous to the regulation of the bedroom or T-room. "We must love one another or die": the virtual reiteration of Freud's epigram ("People fall in love in order not to fall ill") might better read, "we must become heterosexuals manqué or die."

And nothing is now easier to become: in a world in which twelve steps will take you virtually anywhere you want to go, virtual normality is open to us all. Gay literature itself provides any number of how-to narratives. Paul Monette's *Afterlife*, for instance, a story of a trio of self-proclaimed AIDS "widows," is a crash course in the pursuit of the normal heart. One such "widow," Sonny Cevathas, returns from a memorial service for his lover only to find "the locks changed at the Bel-Air house," which is not the normal experience of the heterosexual-heart-in-mourning.[40] But if a certain local irony is directed against the categories of heterosexual privilege, it is belied by a deeper complicity in narrative forms of the same. In *Afterlife*, only the sexualities have been changed and only to protect the ideological innocence of the normative plot. "Do you love him?" Mr. Inman senior asks his son Mark, an AIDS "widow" who has returned home to tell his father that he is both gay and HIV-positive. "I guess," Mark concedes, "but not like *you* mean," a response that is met with paternal puzzlement: "At this the father finally turned and looked at his son. Not judgmental, not even ironic, just curious to know how many meanings love could have" (177). Just one meaning, as it turns out, which means in practice heterosexuality, ersatz or actual: Mark learns to love Steven as his father learned to love Roz, his second wife. Like the hunger that allows no choice to the citizen or the police, love allows no choice to the gay son or the straight father, for love means the privatized, bourgeois couple; love is the heterosexual policing of desire. Freud characterizes perverse sexual practices as "ethically objectionable, for they degrade the relationships of love between two human beings [he never entertains the possibility of "among"] from a serious matter to a convenient game, attended by no risk and no spiritual participation."[41] This is clearly not the liberal apologist for sexual diversity and tolerance, but so much the better: perversion must struggle against Freud (and the Mr. Inmans of this world) to reclaim its "ethically objectionable" character. And never more so than today. Even in the plague years, perverse sexual activity can be attended by minimal risk; even now, perversion can avoid participation in the poetics of bourgeois spiritualization.

Afterlife notwithstanding. It is finally unimportant, for example, that gay "widows" do not enjoy the same legal and economic privileges as their straight counterparts, for they too can find a place, be put in their place, in that most impoverished of all arrangements: the marriage plot. The Freudian injunction is modified—we must learn to love each other because we are dying—but it is otherwise heterosexuality as usual:

"That's all there is, son. Someone to love. You ask anybody here." And he [Mr. Inman] gestured grandly over the Pitch 'n' Putt, but also included the mid-rise condos banked on every side, full of seniors in lonely efficiencies. "They've either been married for forty years, and they're holding on to what little time they got left, or they're widowed and only half alive. The lucky ones are like Roz and me, we get another chance. We know it's not for long. Two years, three years—just like you say. But it's all there is, so you take even a little." (178)

To which the gay subject might be expected to respond, "This is not my beautiful wife, this is not my beautiful home." But *Afterlife* recognizes no differences between the politics of the father's triglyceride and the son's T-cell counts. Death is acknowledged only as the most universal of dispensations. And, in one sense, so it is. We are all, as Pater (following Hugo) famously remarks, *condamnés*. A universal dispensation does not, however, a neutral biological fact make, and if nothing else, AIDS is a reminder that the death sentence, like hunger, is meaningless in isolation from its cultural distribution and regulation. Even the most lyrical evocation of the dominion of death, moreover, need not issue in a counsel of despair (or heterosexuality). *The Renaissance* refuses the conventional wisdom that maintains that enough is as good as a feast: "Our one chance lies in expanding the interval, in getting as many pulsations as possible into the moment." (Wilde: "Enough is as bad as a meal. More than enough is as good as a feast.") Pater's celebration of "our one chance" anticipates Freud's definition of perversion, which is perhaps why *The Renaissance*, particularly its concluding moments, proved something of a scandal. Sex and death, as Yeats maintained, may be the only subjects worthy of a serious mind, but the inevitability of the latter need not serve as an argument for the productive (or reproductive) deployment of the former. Pater refuses to advance that most normalizing of all social imperatives under the guise of a metaphysical heroism: the reproductive egoism of the conjugal family is not a sublime lie against time. Rather, the inevitability of death is an argument for cramming "as many pulsations as possible into the moment," for dilating upon, for lingering in, the sexual present.

The Renaissance does not labor to reconcile us to what it terms our "listlessness," which seems to me the true source of its scandal. Boredom, as Bataille reminds us, has long since replaced religion as the opium of the masses, or at least the professional classes, and it may be that the primary spiritual discipline of the novel is to reconcile us to it. Mark Inman, after having been schooled in the logic of heterosexual love, learns that he has desired too much, too many, which he thus comes to acknowledge as too little—he leaves his father only to meet with and reject the advances of "a young god":

How many times had he . . . walked this dock in a horny swoon of desire, too late to drive to the bars in Miami? He'd always been up for another encounter like this, the chance to plunder beauty. That was the point: you could never have enough. But now he could feel himself recoiling, because if he'd lost the pleasure of this, then what was left? (180)

This is the entire point of *Afterlife*. Pre-AIDS gay sexuality could never suffice, could never satisfy, for in pursuing too many bodies it was content with too little spiritual entanglement. So Mark must learn to abandon the docks, to recoil from pleasure, to accept the end of pleasure, the very little that is left him, as the great good that emerges from the devastation of the plague years. The gay body becomes for Mark what it has always been for the novel: a window unto the soul. Good pecs, for instance, betray a pathological taste for promiscuity; Sonny Cevathas is a hunk, which means that he will end badly. Steve Shaw is the man for

Mark, if only because Steve has developed a pot belly, which the novel construes as the outward sign of an inward grace: a capacity for monogamy. Mark thus turns from the young god's good pecs to Steve's big belly, and the two learn to ape, if only in an empty formalism, the "radical heterosexuality" of Mr. and Mrs. Inman.

If AIDS thus provides an alibi for reclaiming the gay subject for the comforting norm, it can only be construed retroactively as a perverse resistance to that plot. Here, for example, is Ned, the Larry Kramer figure in *The Normal Heart*: "Having so much sex makes finding love impossible." And again: "I said the gay leaders who created this sexual-liberation philosophy in the first place have been the death of us. Mickey, why didn't you guys fight for the right to get married instead of the right to legitimize promiscuity?"[42] Both *The Normal Heart* and *Reports from the Holocaust* position AIDS as but an episode in an ongoing family romance, and both conclude with the Larry Kramer figure embracing his brother and sister-in-law. ("Those poignant last days"—but again, poignant for whom? How many more made-for-TV movies will ask us to applaud the moral heroism of families that reconstitute themselves over the corpse of a gay son?) Paul Monette's *Halfway Home* might seem an exception, if only because it entertains the possibility that not all families have their origin in their terminus and their terminus in their origin. "Home is the place you get to," we are assured in the final moments of the novel, "not the place you start from."[43] But Tom, a PWA, can "get home," can learn to love another man before he dies, only after he has reconciled with his brother Brian, a homophobic high school jock who repeatedly raped him as a child. The family disappears as a social protagonist—no Christian Coalition idealizations here—but only to take up residence in and as the psychosexual. Tom claims that he "put that all behind him" when he came out, "Brian and Dad and their conspiracy of silence" (2), and the novel is fully sympathetic to the suffering and pride of those who flee. The family is never more disabling, however, than in the futility of one's resistance to it, and Tom must learn to rid himself of a prejudice that, finally, can deform only him. To find love is thus to reconcile oneself to the family that, in the very act of withholding it, provides the only viable paradigm for its attainment. ("It's not my mother, it's not my mother," to which the good doctor can only respond: "But Paul, it is your mother." Miranda rights, as they are rather curiously termed, need never be articulated, but here too they are fully in place: everything you say can and will be used against you. So parents, don't be alarmed if your sons and daughters are in analysis: their words can never be turned against you. And sons and daughters, those of you who persist in looking for sex in all the wrong places: you will learn soon enough that it is really only love that you are after, and that you have only to look in your own backyard.) This Tom, unlike his namesake in Fielding's novel, "gets home" without the promise of producing another Tom to sustain the line. (He in fact gets home to the family beach home of his lover who, through Tom, comes to experience it once again as a home.) But even ersatz heterosexuality can participate in the consolations of the real thing. Thus Tom comes to discover in his nephew the promise of that "small immortality" (191), the lie against time, that fuels the reproductive egoism of the bourgeois family. Tom and his lover want in fact for nothing, except the legal, social, and economic privileges that attend actual, if not ersatz, heterosexuality.

But then our culture allows Tom and his kind to want only in accordance with a rigid binarism: choose between a sexuality that works toward its own effacement, the erotic pessimism that calls itself love, or the erotic excess that is called perversion. Refuse the terms of the opposition and you are committed, willingly or not, to forcing what all the deaths have not yet occasioned: a crisis in signification.

4 Coffee Table Sex

If nothing else, the furor occasioned by *The Perfect Moment*, the still notorious Robert Mapplethorpe retrospective, has served to delimit the scope of the conservative mania for deregulation. Good government may now mean virtually no government at all, but the museum, the ultimate arbiter of value in the modern art market, remains fully the object of anxious scrutiny and control. It is not surprising, then, that museum existence, albeit in the form of a traveling exhibit, should have been the focus of the Mapplethorpe controversy.

Or not-quite museum existence. To date, U.S. courts have been reluctant to judge a museum or exhibit show obscene, so absolute is the museum in conferring aesthetic worth. (The law defines obscenity as lacking in "serious artistic content or redeeming social value," but museum existence is itself proof positive of that value.) The Cincinnati Arts Center, which exhibited *The Perfect Moment* without NEA funding, came perilously close to being an exception, due in part to the unprecedented decision by the courts to distinguish between "gallery" and "museum" existence. (The center was legally demoted to the status of a gallery, the better to foster the illusion that the museum, unlike the gallery, is innocent of market forces.) Both the center and its director were, happily, vindicated in the courts, but the efficacy of the anti-obscenity laws brought against them is in no way dependent on their legal enforceability. The legal challenge itself, moreover, testifies to the difficulty of recuperating Mapplethorpe—even the Mapplethorpe granted entry into the aestheticizing space of the museum—for the category of the aesthetic.

There are other Mapplethorpes. The work that so troubled the walls of the Cincinnati Arts Center also graced the pages of gay porn magazines, also without NEA funding, but also without legal challenge. Context is determining. Porn magazines are not conventional venues for the disinterested contemplation of beauty, but the museum is, and if Mapplethorpe troubles, it is because he refuses to confirm the highbrow art consumer in the experience of freedom that the aesthetic is conventionally said to afford. The specious (and therefore much insisted upon) distinction between the pornographic and the erotic is a matter of context, not content, and Mapplethorpe plays knowingly on the relation between the two. The force of the sexuality depicted in the work—in what follows, I focus primarily on *Bill, New York, 1976–77, The Slave* (1974), and *Brian Ridley and Lyle Heeter* (1979)— is inseparable from the conditions under which it is displayed, disseminated, and consumed.

D. A. Miller speaks of "the identity of the liberal subject who seems to recognize himself most fully only when he forgets or disavows his functional implication in a system of carceral restraints."[1] It seems unlikely, however, that the literally carceral subjects depicted in many of Mapplethorpe's photographs—say, the cuffed and manacled Ridley of *Brian Ridley and Lyle Heeter*—could ever forget their somewhat different implication in a system of restraints. In *The German Ideology,* Marx observes that "in all ideology, men and their relations appear upside down, as in a camera obscura."[2] The men who appear in Mapplethorpe's camera, however, particularly those who appear in manacles and chains, reverse this idealist inversion: at the very least, they render problematic the opposition between the apparent freedom of the museum-going art consumer, he or she who views the photographs, and the apparent unfreedom of (what once would have been called) Mapplethorpe's "inverts." Miller's understanding of the "liberal subject" is clearly Foucauldian, and Foucault is frequently dismissed as a fetishist of power, the theorist (or fabulous artificer) of a panopticism from which there is no exit, against which there can be no resistance. But the carceral subjects who populate Mapplethorpe's work suggest otherwise. Disciplinary power cannot survive its theatricalization: when openly embraced as bondage and discipline, the disciplinary is no longer itself.

This is not to advocate kinky sex as a form of new age political activism, although the suggestion is no more bizarre than what frequently passes for polit-ical engagement in the academy. But neither is it to evacuate Mapplethorpe's work (and this is perhaps more to the point) of its perversity. Everyone knows that only the good bourgeois is ever shocked, and to register disgust or fascination before (yet another) photograph of (say) a man ramming a whip up his ass—see Map-plethorpe's *Self-Portrait, 1978*—is to abandon all claims to sophistication. A re-sponse "pathologically conditioned," as Kant terms it, does not qualify as free, and the aesthetic is meant to confirm the liberal subject's transcendence of the world of necessity and compulsion. The highbrow art consumer thus learns with the force of a learning-turned-intuition never to engage the body in the Olympian contemplation and appropriation of form. True, the flesh has been experiencing something of an academic resurrection of late, and where the body is, Kantian "disinterestedness" or Arnoldian "free play" cannot be. Edmund White, for ex-ample, would seem to demand more flesh, less formalism. He dismisses the "pu-rity" of Mapplethorpe's work as "the least functional, least personally expressive, least psychological" dimension of it, and he criticizes the reduction of the male body, particularly the black male body, to so many isolated symmetries. The for-malism is said to "tranquilize [Mapplethorpe's] anxieties," but if there is indeed a sedating formalism at work here, it is in the eye of the beholder.[3] Today, the hip highbrow art consumer learns with the force of a learning-turned-intuition to pre-tend to engage the body, but the Olympian contemplation of form, the old Kan-tianism, proceeds apace. And what better way to evacuate the work of its troubling or enticing content—without, that is, appearing positively bourgeois—than to ac-cuse the artist of not providing it? White is obviously more sophisticated than Helms—the know-nothing senator would repress content; the all-too-knowing connoisseur renders it incidental—but it amounts to much the same thing.

The anxieties are, however, ours, not Mapplethorpe's, and if we refuse to see what is actually there, it is the better to hallucinate what is not. The audacity of *The Perfect Moment* is precisely its insistence that there are perfect moments, that there always have been, the devastations of the plague years notwithstanding. Like Dorian Gray, Mapplethorpe rejects the narrative logic that would reduce his life and career to a gay rake's progress, but like Dorian, he too is reclaimed by it. All the perfect moments, all the individual photographs, are made to line up—as in a police lineup, although here everyone and everything is guilty—in the spec-tacle of gay sexual crime and punishment. No matter that Mapplethorpe's notori-ety predated *The Perfect Moment* and the attentions of Jesse Helms, for today every-thing about the artist, everything about the controversy that has come to envelop him, is structured by a fact that is presented simply, openly, as one among many, but that surreptitiously determines all: Robert Mapplethorpe died of complications arising from AIDS. His name has appeared in print in forms as various as "Mapplewood," "Mappleton" and "Mapplesex"; it is frequently misspelt as "Maplethorpe." But whatever the violence directed against the name—and apparently Jesse Helms has never pronounced it the same way twice, a rhetorical ploy he no doubt learned from Archie Bunker—the acronym is invariably noted and noted accurately. All artists or authors, the very category of the author or artist, died some time ago. Or at least the academy issued a generalized death notice. But when it is death-by-AIDS, the death of the artist is again news. The compulsion to make of AIDS the deep truth of the homosexual brooks no opposition, least of all from gay self-representations themselves. Any given photograph may prove recalcitrant—photography is itself, of course, an aggressively nonnarrative art—but one has only to look around or through it to discern the narrative logic in which they all cohere. It's now clear: their behavior always was suicidal.

i. Photography Is Like Perversion

Any number of modern art objects take as their title the exact moment of their composition, "the perfect moment." Where a medieval fresco is properly a fragment of "the general tableau of the universe," in which continuity and reversibility are operable, the modern art work, even the modern representational or photographic work, refers back to the temporality of its subject-creator, to the signature or subjectivity of the artist in the act of self-indexing.[4] The various "moments" in the Picasso oeuvre do not combine by virtue of their contiguity and likeness to reproduce an image of the world and its order; rather, they refer back, by virtue of their difference and likeness (a "blue" Picasso, a "cubist" Picasso, and the like), to the authority of their subject-creator, to the temporality of moments within an individual oeuvre. Artists may choose to copy or reproduce themselves, as Rauschenberg's *Factum II* (the example is Baudrillard's) reproduces his *Factum I* almost down to the last daub of paint. But the very category of the copy presupposes a logic of content, and the modern art object is predicated on the value, in all senses of the word, of the signature or proper name. (The academy may have decreed the author or artist dead, but the modern art market paid it no heed.) Were *Factum II* not signed by Rauschenberg, it would be a forgery, subject to legal action, and not, oxymoronically, an authentic or unique copy, and hence a critique of an economy that can only construe the copy, the generally disseminated or the readily available, as a forgery. Broadly speaking, what was once representation, "the redoubling of the world in space," is now repetition, "the redoubling of the [creative] act in time."[5] Derrida argues that no name can ever be truly proper, no signature ever truly unique: both are already structured by their iterability, by their capacity for repetition. But whatever this may mean for Occidental metaphysics—and for Derrida, it is profoundly subversive—it is business as usual in the modern art market.[6]

The economy in which the modern art object functions (as opposed to the world it represents) is, then, narrative, at least to the extent that narrative can be defined as the relation of moments one to the other in their temporal likeness and unlikeness. Any given photograph, as Susan Sontag argues, may be incapable of narrative, and for Sontag, narrative is the precondition of all understanding:

Photography implies that we know about the world if we accept it as the camera records it. But this is the opposite of understanding, which starts from not accepting the world as it looks. All possibility of understanding is rooted in the ability to say no. Strictly speaking, one never understands anything from a photograph. . . . The camera's rendering of reality must always hide more than it discloses. As Brecht points out, a photograph of the Krupp works reveals virtually nothing about that organization. In contrast to the amorous relation, which is based on how something looks, understanding is based on how it functions. And functioning takes place in time, and must be explained in time. Only that which narrates can make us understand.[7]

Photography is like perversion: both aspire to the condition of "pure presentness" that is inimical to the demands of narrative. Like all modern art objects, however, the very category of "the photograph" presupposes a narrative context, if not content. Where "the snapshot" remains bound to its mimetic capacity to reproduce the world in space, "the photograph," at least to the extent that it has attained the status of a "fine art," is referred back to the temporality of moments within an individual oeuvre. "Art" photography has tended to ape the fortunes of easel painting, the prototypical fine art object, and modern easel painting has, on the whole, tended to eschew representational content (or it is no longer valued in terms of that content). Mapplethorpe's *White X with Silver Cross* (1983) and *Star with Frosted Glass* (1983), for example, are largely formal explorations of geometrical design, no less painterly in the modern sense than Julia Margaret Cameron's photographic portraits are in the old. The distinctive genius of photography—or its distinct technological advantage, which may be the same thing—is its ability to reproduce the world in space. But as Mapple-thorpe's *White X with Silver Cross* or *Star with Frosted Glass* suggests, photography has been more than willing to forgo this advantage, to evacuate the photographic image itself, if it thereby gains access to the space of the museum, the traditional home of easel painting.

All modern art is, then, what Philip Fisher terms "a probationary candidate for the museum," and all knowing modern art, like all knowing graduate students and assistant professors, structures itself in relation to what it labors to make its final destination.[8] The signature, real or virtual, remains the index of value and authenticity for the modern art object, and that signature, like all signatures, is meaningful only in terms of its continuity with and difference from the same signature penned at different temporal moments. (Unlike painting, photography is not generally signed, although for a snapshot to attain to the status of a photograph, the metaphorical equivalent of the signature, the "personal style" of its subject-creator, must be discernible.) But if the value of the art object is thus construed in relation to a series, the series is recognizable as such, valuable as such, only if one of its "moments" or works finds its way into a relation of juxtaposition with other objects of established aesthetic value, which is the space of the museum. The fundamental organizational principle of the modern art object thus tends to be the collection itself, the juxtaposition of discrete objects, events, or styles, a miniature version of the heterogeneity that is the museum.[9] The collection as organizational principle is most readily apparent in the early Mapplethorpe, particularly in the work that appropriates printed matter and commercially produced images, but it is also operable in the larger context of the individual show or exhibit. The organizational principle of *The Perfect Moment,* to return to Lessing, is not the *Nacheinander,* the narrative order of one-after-the-other, but the *Nebeneinander,* relations of spatial contiguity, the juxtaposition of discrete "portfolios" (the "X" or S/M portfolio, the "Y" or portrait portfolio, and the "Z" or flower portfolio). *The Perfect Moment* is both an individual exhibit within the larger space of the museum and a replication of the relations of juxtaposition and contiguity—here a highly formal study of an orchid, there the most explicit exploration of sadomasochism—that are the museum. Mapplethorpe, the most "knowing" of modern artists, knowingly plays with the space of the museum.

But Mapplethorpe is not simply one artist among others: he is the artist-who-died-of-AIDS, a hip or highbrow analogue to Rock Hudson or Liberace, and AIDS apparently exhausts the meaning of all he was and did. Not that Mapplethorpe constructs a closet for AIDS: to refuse any thematization of the pandemic as the belatedly revealed truth of the pervert's life is not to deny its devastating impact, and *The Perfect Moment* seeks to reclaim some measure of control over the representation, in sickness and in health, of the gay body. The show includes, for example, the highly theatrical and frequently reproduced *Self-Portrait* of 1988.

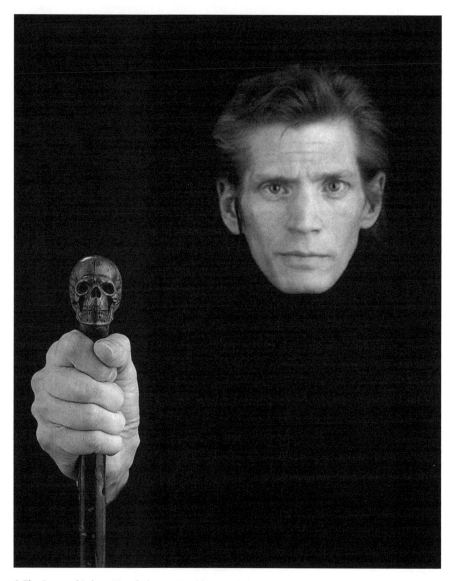

© The Estate of Robert Mapplethorpe. Used by permission.

The death skull is not, as it were, hidden beneath the skin, but theatrically fore-grounded, as if to insist that no hidden psychology or pathology structures AIDS. The image registers the somatic repercussions of AIDS, but unlike the portrait of Dorian, there is no pretense that the "corruption" emerges from within. The self-portrait is, moreover, but one moment among many, and the whole is not rendered retroactively (or posthumously) less perfect for its inclusion. Yet if *The Perfect Moment* refuses to make the death skull the belatedly revealed truth of the pervert's life, critics have evinced no such reluctance. Dominick Dunne, *Vanity Fair,* February 1998: Mapplethorpe's work is a documentation "of the homoerotic life in the 1970s at its most excessive, resulting, possibly, in the very plague that was killing its recorder." Susan Weiley, *Artnews,* December 1998: Mapplethorpe's erotic images "provoke a shudder similar to the one we feel looking at smiling faces in photographs of the Warsaw ghetto."[10] It's now clear: homosexuality = death.

The journalistic shuddering would reduce *The Perfect Moment* to a cautionary tale, but Mapplethorpe's work does not permit the comforting illusion that the corruption emerges from within. For that reason alone, however, it apparently threatens everything without. "This pornography is sick," Jesse Helms informed his colleagues in the Senate on July 26, 1989,

But Mapplethorpe's sick art does not seem to be an isolated incident. Yet another artist exhibited some of this sickening obscenity in my own state. . . . I could go on and on, Mr. President, about the sick art that has been displayed around the country.[11]

In a bizarre literalization of the aesthetic affect that Plato terms "contagion"— "Few persons ever reflect, as I should imagine, that the contagion must pass from others [poets] to themselves"—HIV passes from the artist's body to his work, from the work to the body politic.[12] Mapplethorpe is thus made to bear a burden of responsibility for a pandemic that is properly Helms' own: the disastrous Helms amendment of 1987, which prohibited public funding to projects that "promote homosexuality" (read: that specify safer sexual practices), betrays a homophobia literally genocidal in its intensity. But if the senator is opposed to the promotion of safer sexual practices, he is clearly an advocate of safer aesthetic experiences, and here the know-nothing senator knows better than Mapplethorpe's liberal apologists and critics. Mapplethorpe's work consciously vies for position within the aestheticizing space of the museum; it knowingly plays with that space; but it is not thereby assimilated to the category of the aesthetic.

There is a sense in which the academy owes a debt of gratitude to Jesse Helms. The Big Easy, for example, is not so easy when it comes to gay sex—heterosexuality is the only legal game in town—yet I recently traveled to New Orleans to deliver a paper in defense of our right of access to, among other things, Mapplethorpe's representations of gay sex. Without Helms's attack on the public funding of the Mapplethorpe and Serrano shows, I could not have represented myself in New Orleans—at some profit to the city, at some profit to my own institution (or so it must have thought: it paid the bills), and at some profit to my own career (or so I hoped)—as a champion of artistic freedom. Yet if we are to continue to exercise our right to consume in representation the perversions of others, logic, if nothing more, dictates that someone, somewhere, must first have the right to engage in perverse sexual acts. The point is obvious, yet it bears emphasizing, if only because the defense of Mapplethorpe has, to my knowledge, remained exclusively on the level of our right of access to representation. For Kant, this is as it should be:

Interest is what we call the liking we connect with the presentation of an object's existence. Hence such a liking always refers at once to our power of desire, either as the basis that determines it, or at any rate as necessarily connected with that determining basis. But if the question is whether something is beautiful, what we want to know is not whether we or anyone cares, or so much as might care, in any way, about the thing's existence, but rather how we judge it in our mere contemplation of it (intuition or reflection).[13]

But in Mapplethorpe, so much depends (to mar William Carlos Williams) upon the actual existence of something called "gay sex," and if this is to refer aesthetic contemplation back to the faculty of desire, so much the better. True, Helms's attack on the NEA funding of the Mapplethorpe and Serrano shows had as little to do with money as the defense of Mapplethorpe has to do with the right to engage in perverse sexual acts. The entire 1986 NEA budget, some $172 million, was largely a symbolic expenditure, meager beside Great Britain's budget, $720 million, and pathetic beside France's $1.6 billion and West Germany's $4.5 billion.[14] It in no way follows, however, that a purely symbolic defense or counterattack is to be mounted. A politics that defends our right to consume in representation a sexuality that is routinely condemned in practice—a politics that actively colludes, through its conference dollars, with the legal harassment and persecution of gay and lesbian people—is functionally indistinguishable from political opportunism.

The conservative attack on all that "sick art" now serves as one of the con-
texts—Kobena Mercer suggests that it is *the* determining context—in which Mapplethorpe's work is necessarily positioned:

It is impossible to ignore the crucial changes in context that frame the readings . . . ne-
gotiated around Mapplethorpe and his work. Mapplethorpe's death in 1989 from AIDS,
a major retrospective of his work at the Whitney Museum in New York, the political "con-
troversy" over federal arts policy initiated by the fundamentalist Right in response to a
second Mapplethorpe exhibition organized by the Institute of Contemporary Art in
Philadelphia—these events have irrevocably altered the context in which we perceive,
argue about, and evaluate Mapplethorpe's most explicitly homoerotic work.[15]

The "crucial changes in context" changed Mercer's own mind about Mapplethorpe. His 1987 essay "Imagining the Black Man's Sex" accuses the photographer
of fetishizing and objectifying the black male body; his 1991 essay "Skin Head Sex
Thing: Racial Difference and the Homoerotic Imaginary" emphasizes the "subversive dimension" of the "homoerotic specificity" in Mapplethorpe's representations of the racially other.[16] The earlier essay imports its theoretical premises more
or less wholesale from Laura Mulvey's influential analysis of the gender politics of
the gaze; the later essay explores the complex imbrication of racialized and sexu-
alized subject positions, both Mapplethorpe's and Mercer's own. Between the two
intervenes Jesse Helms, art critic: "I [Mercer] want to emphasize that I've reversed
my reading of racial signification in Mapplethorpe not for the fun of it, but because I do not want a black gay critique to be appropriated to the purposes of the
Right's antidemocratic cultural offensive" (192).

My own concern is with the white, liberal (sexually unmarked, and so presumably straight) critique of racial signification in Mapplethorpe, which often
seems functionally indistinguishable from (and not simply open to appropriation by) the Right's antidemocratic cultural offensive. "Why art thou / Solici-
tous?" Christ asks Satan in *Paradise Regained* (III. 199–200), and the same might
be asked of Mapplethorpe's liberal critics: why the intense interest in the racial
politics? Two possibilities suggest themselves: (1) ours is a culture that receives
exploitive images of black men with immediate and well-nigh universal condemnation, or (2) the charges of racism serve to mystify a somewhat different
agenda. I suspect the latter.

Jesse Helms, to give the devil his due, has the courage of his prejudices. He
doesn't like images of men pissing on men—or, for that matter, the actuality to

which they refer—and he says so. Mapplethorpe's liberal critics, however, possess greater cultural capital than the senator, and cultural capital precludes experiencing (or at least registering) shock at the sexually explicit: water sports hardly trouble them. But racism apparently does, although the outing of Mapplethorpe's colonial fantasies, real or imputed, is characterized less by shock than triumphalism. (To reiterate an earlier point: to be entirely pleasurable, sexual knowledge must be extricated from, not freely given by, the subject, and Mapplethorpe makes a spectacle of his perversions. The triumphalism denied the critic on the level of the sexual is, however, recuperated on the level of the racial.) We everywhere read, for example, of his relentless drive toward "idealization" ("it is a subtle tactic of those in power to praise the excluded"), "objectification" (he "looked at males in the same way that centuries of male artists have looked at females"),[17] and "classicism" ("the least interesting, the least psychologically complex" dimension of his work). But surely this is not to tell the photographs anything they don't already know. To charge an image of, say, a beautiful black man draped over a pedestal with "idealization"—see *Bob Love* (1979) or *Tom on a Pedestal* (1986)—is to confuse criticism with content. Paraphrase is generally considered to be the most debased form of critical activity, but the white, liberal critique of Mapplethorpe's racial politics rarely rises above it. Much of the suspicion of Mapplethorpe seems predicated on the conviction that no notice can be taken of the body of the racially other without confirming the terms of an abusive mythology, which is reasonable enough.[18] Certainly physiology figures prominently in the racist imaginary. As Fanon notes, "I am the slave not of the 'idea' that others have of me but of my own appearance. . . . I am being dissected under white eyes. . . . I am fixed"—"Look, a Negro!"[19] To which the good liberal responds, "Don't look, it's an African American," which is no less a fetishization of physiology. But Mapplethorpe does look, intensely, perversely. His notorious *Man in Polyester Suit* (1980), for example, stages a cultural fantasy that no white liberal would touch with a ten-foot pole: black men have big dicks. A fantasy is no less powerful, however, for being relegated to silence, and it is the cultural fantasy, not simply the black man's dick, that the photograph exposes. To modify Fanon: what we see is what we would rather not see, which is how we see (even when we refuse to look) "a Negro."

But precisely who is this universal and universalizing "we"? Mercer's "return to Mapplethorpe" involves a reconsideration of the complex determinants of his own subject position(s); the liberal response to Mapplethorpe merely confirms the critic in the comforting knowledge of his or her own (apparently disembodied) liberalism. Like the portrait of Dorian Gray, which Basil fears reveals more about its creator than its subject matter, Mapplethorpe's work allegedly has everything to do with the photographer's fetishization of the black body, very little to do with the unique subjectivity of any given black man. (For people who feel that no proper notice can be taken of the body of the racially other, Mapplethorpe's liberal critics have considerable faith in the ability of physiology to reveal psychology.) But on the contrary, it would seem that the work is insufficiently revelatory of the photographer, for it is precisely "the homoerotic specificity" of Mapplethorpe's gaze that his liberal critics fail or refuse to see. Mercer is virtually alone in acknowledging the wit and irony of Mapplethorpe's representations of the racially other:

The binarisms of classical racial discourse are emphasized in Mapplethorpe's photograph [Man in Polyester Suit] *by the jokey irony of the contrast between the black man's private parts and the public respectability signified by the business suit. The oppositions exposed/hidden and denuded/clothed play upon the binary oppositions nature/culture and savage/civilized to bring about a condensation of libidinal investment, fear, and wish-fulfilment in the fantasmatic presence of the other. (177)*

To which I would add: the jokey irony of the contrast between dick and phallus, which is very much part of the "homoerotic specificity" of Mapplethorpe's gaze. On the one hand: the flaccid (but still impressive) private parts. On the other: the perpendicular uniform of normative masculinity, the abstract, sublimated form of the penis—the phallus, the polyester suit.[20] Charles Bernheimer suggests that male subjectivity emerges allegorically in the struggle for authority between the penis and phallus, which is precisely the agon that *Man in Polyester Suit* stages.[21] Normative masculinity is of the party of the phallus; if the straight white racist is obsessed with the black man's big dick, it is because he fears black ascendancy to phallic mastery. Mapplethorpe, however, fetishizes a dick that he may wish to master or be mastered by, but which in its very specificity and materiality precludes elevation to the phallic. The specificity bears emphasizing. The charge of objectification presupposes that only the face, which is nowhere present in *Man in Polyester Suit,* is individualizing, but for those who bother to look, the gonads are at least equally so. "Look, a Negro" is a generic, categorizing gesture; Mapplethorpe's gaze, by contrast, registers the precise contours and textures of a very specific organ. It is individualizing, not psychologizing. Hence, the jokey irony of the title: what is least individualizing about *Man in Polyester* Suit is what is specified by it, the polyester suit. Indeed, it is because Mapplethorpe does not hold that physiology reveals psychology that he can take "proper" notice of the body of the racially other. (Mapplethorpe is highly conventional in terms of his "sculptural codes," in the posing and positioning of bodies. He frequently departs, however, from the exclusive focus on the face that is a staple of portraiture.) All of which issues in the panicked cry of his liberal critics: "Look, a white homosexual is looking at a Negro!" Mapplethorpe is clearly the least repressed of homosexuals, and the homophobic contention that the negrophobic man is a repressed homosexual hardly applies. But it requires only slight modification in order to preserve the political innocence of white heterosexuality, which, as usual, is nowhere implicated in the field it surveys: the negrophilic homosexual is really negrophobic.

ii. The Sadomasochism of Everyday Life

In one sense, the elision of the political burden of Mapplethorpe's work (or its strategic displacement) merely rehearses the founding gesture of aesthetics in its modern form, which the academy, in various guises, is in the business of perpetuating. The assimilation of photography to the standards of aesthetic autonomy has been a relatively recent phenomenon, and it everywhere betrays the anxieties of the arriviste. It is no longer necessary, for example, to speak of the "art film," so thoroughly has the movie been colonized by and for the academy. Today, the "art" of the motion picture literally goes without saying, or is said in the word "film" itself, which is virtually the symmetrical opposite of "movie." But the "art" in "art photography" still needs to be said, and the academy has yet to develop a nomenclature that would distinguish it—without, that is, anxious recourse to the word "art" itself—from photography of the "merely" instrumental or pragmatic kind. (The opposition photograph/snapshot does not have the force of the film/movie binarism). The academy has not, of course, been derelict in its duty: its defense of Mapplethorpe is clearly continuous with its general aestheticization of photography. Pierre Bourdieu argues that the propensity to appreciate a work of art in isolation from its content presupposes "the distance from the world," specifically the world of necessity, that is "the basis of the bourgeois experience of the world."[22] In Mapplethorpe, however, the bourgeois experience of the world becomes entangled in the pervert's, in discipline and bondage, leather and chains. For if there is much in Mapplethorpe that encourages a purely formal response, there is also much that defeats it.

Take, for example, the triptych *Bill, New York, 1976–77:*

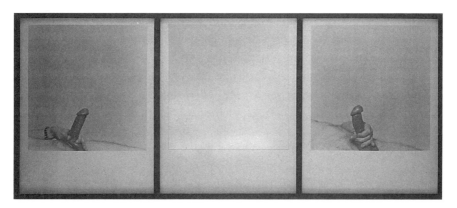

Two side panels, two views of a man pursuing, as we say, his own happiness, divided by a central panel, a mirror. (Or, better, two views of only those portions of a man strictly necessary to the pursuit: the meeting of hand and dick. No head, no face, and thus no "personal expression" or "psychology" to intervene between the two.) Yet if the formal symmetries of the work are obvious, so too is the challenge to any purely formal contemplation of them. The central mirror, which reflects the head of the spectator, transforms the disinterested or literally distanced contemplation of the autoerotic into something resembling a participatory act of oral sex: the spectator literally gives (his or her) head. Those who would deny Mapplethorpe access to the museum characteristically argue that museum existence does not a work of art make. Mapplethorpe, however, not only knows better, he insists that the museum-going art consumer knows as well. His *Julius of California* (1971) and untitled kissing boys (1972), for example, are both spray painted pages torn from what are clearly porn magazines, in which the areas that would have received the censor's black rectangle, the crotch and the kissing mouths respectively, are highlighted. In their original context, their porn magazine manifestation, the images referred only to the faculty of desire. But duly framed and hung on a museum wall—and *Bill, New York, 1976–77* needs to be hung, so to speak, at head level—pages torn from a porn magazine do occasion aesthetic reflection, are acknowledged and valued as "fine art." Or so Mapple-thorpe's assault on the piety that would distinguish the erotic from the pornographic, the better to disavow its interest in the sexually explicit or perverse, would suggest.[23] The very category of the "erotic" presupposes access to content that can then be disavowed as such, but both *Julius of California* and kissing boys openly acknowledge—spray paint, frames, and museum walls notwithstanding—their origins in, the museum-going art consumer's interest in, the pornographic.

If Mapplethorpe's work thus challenges the commonsensical argument that the museum does not a work of art make, it also suggests the necessary repercussions, which extend well beyond Mapplethorpe himself, of any attempt to deny his work the space of the museum. Consider a 1974 self-portrait, *The Slave,* which is a photograph of two photographs in an open book of two views of Michelangelo's *Dying Slave* (see illustration opposite). Mapplethorpe reverses the conventional process by which art objects are disseminated—from the museum or gallery, the site of the original, to the art catalogue or book, the site of its reproduction—even as he knowingly defines his self-portrait in relation to that process. *The Slave* demands entrance into the aestheticizing space of the museum by reproducing the process by which *Dying Slave* is disseminated beyond it, yet in returning a reproduction of a reproduction to the museum (which becomes, then, an original, a unique object; hence, the conspicuous presence of the proper name "Mapplethorpe"), *The Slave* also insists on the sadomasochistic content of the art already in the museum, of which Michelangelo's *Dying Slave* is a distinguished example. Any attempt to deny Mapplethorpe the space of the museum would need, therefore, to deny Michelangelo as well. *Dying Slave* and its companion piece, *Rebellious Slave,* were originally commissioned for the tomb of Julius II; although both are now housed in the Louvre, they were never intended for it. And translated into the dehistoricizing, aestheticizing space of the museum, both stand as enigmas. There is a general consensus that *Dying Slave* does not represent a dying figure, but there is little agreement as to what the youth is actually about, although sleeping—either falling into or awakening from—is a frequent suggestion. Mapplethorpe advances a somewhat different possibility: his return of a reproduction of a reproduction of the statue to the museum retroactively positions *Dying Slave* as a precursor of any number of Mapplethorpe's own sexual slaves. The pervert Michelangelo is about as canonical as they come, and the canonical, in the conservative imagination, is the redeemed counterpart to the sorry spectacle of contemporary art. (Cultural conservatives who recommend a return to the classics as an antidote to all that "sick art" are clearly unfamiliar with them.) The pervert Mapplethorpe, however, knows that all that separates the canonical from the perverse is the difference in cultural capital between the proper name "Michelangelo" and the not-quite proper name "Robert Mappleton" or "Mapplesex" or "Mapplethorpe." At the very least, *The Slave* now suggests that had the system of patronage under which

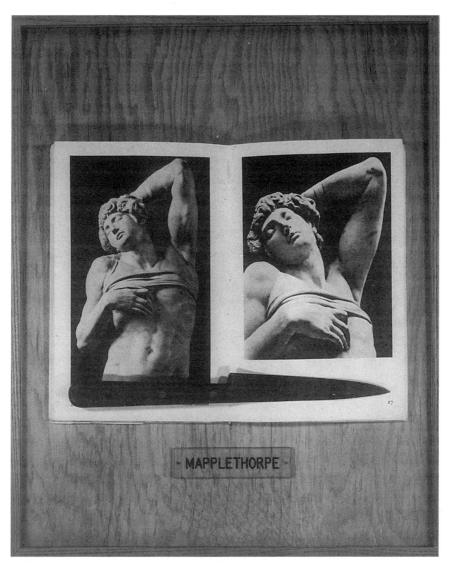

Michelangelo labored included the stipulations that Helms would have govern NEA grants, which are part of the patronage system in its modern form, *Dying Slave* would never have been commissioned.

In reversing the process by which Michelangelo's *Dying Slave* is disseminated beyond the museum, Mapplethorpe's *The Slave* also reminds us that modern art is

97

in no way restricted to the museum. (Although it does not thereby elude the scrutiny and control that are routinely focused on the museum. The art video and the performance piece, for example, may bear a relation to the art market and hence the museum different in kind from the traditional commodity forms of easel painting and sculpture. These same genres, however, are virtually the creation of the public funding of the arts.) The museum confers value not only on the objects it houses, but also on the individuals who visit it, which is the right thereafter to be known as someone who has been to the museum, the proof of which is in the catalogue, the glossy coffee table art book, conspicuous consumption in its cultural form. (Or one proof among many, all of which are class-specific. In the age of the museum "blockbuster," which is the result of the unprecedented influx of corporate dollars into the museum, paraphernalia once identified with a visit to an amusement park—T-shirts and the like—are now evidence of a certain cultural investment and ambition. The courts may consider museums to be innocent of market forces, but museums themselves now house elaborate commercial emporia and "museum shops" flourish in isolation from any actual museum.) Consider the curious status of the copy or reproduction in the aesthetics of the bourgeois interior. The framed print, the reproduction, is an aesthetic gaffe of the first magnitude, for the print is without the value-bearing presence of the artist's signature. The print in book form, however, the textual reproduction of the art object, confers value on its owner, precisely to the extent that it is proof positive that its owner values culture.

Thus Mapplethorpe's work may well find its final destination on the coffee tables of the culturally privileged, your coffee table or mine. Where once there was, say, a large glossy book of photographs of ancient Japanese fabrics, there is now a large glossy book of photographs of, among other things, sadomasochistic sexual practices (see illustration opposite). Mapplethorpe is fully at home on the cover of *Metropolitan Home* (March 1991); indeed, the coffee table Mapplethorpe, unlike the book of ancient Japanese fabrics it displaces, pays a double dividend. It is simultaneously inscribed with the message "I value culture" and "I'm hip." I have the right of access to representations of the perverse, and I exercise that inalienable right by owning a coffee table miscellany of perversions. The third dividend—I need never acknowledge my interest in the perverse—goes without saying.

Yet if the coffee table Mapplethorpe thus comes to displace the coffee table book of ancient Japanese fabrics, there is a sense in which the former, unlike the latter, always was intended for the coffee table. (Ancient Japanese fabrics cannot

be accused of a knowing relation to the modern art market.) For the use value of the coffee table Mapplethorpe—or at least of the image of *Brian Ridley and Lyle Heeter* that is contained therein—is its existence as a coffee table book of photographs of perverse sexual practices. The portrait conspicuously features a side table on which rest a number of books, any one of which might be a catalogue from the Whitney or the Wadsworth Athenaeum, a coffee table Mapplethorpe.

© The Estate of Robert Mapplethorpe. Used by permission.

The photograph contains within itself a representation of one of the conditions of its own consumption, an anticipation of its destiny as a photograph in a coffee table art book. Unlike *The Slave*, which moves knowingly from the pages of an art book back to the museum wall, *Brian Ridley and Lyle Heeter* moves knowingly from the museum wall to the art book. The photograph, by virtue of the extravagance of its subject matter, might easily have provided the hip highbrow art consumer with little more than a holiday in other people's perversions. (What's a holiday without photos?) But like *Bill, New York, 1976–77, Brian Ridley and Lyle Heeter* resists any distanced or disinterested contemplation. Looking out from your coffee table book is a couple looking back at you who might well be—minus, of course, chaps and chains—the couple in your living room looking into your coffee table art book.

It would seem, then, that sadomasochism, like charity, begins at home. Certainly the portrait of Ridley and Heeter disturbs, as I think many of Mapplethorpe's S/M photographs do not, precisely in its combination of the extravagantly alien, the full leather drag, and the utterly domestic, the leather drag at home. Even in its museum existence, the portrait, which is not part of the "X" or S/M portfolio, threatens the various demarcations that organize *The Perfect Moment*. The "X" portfolio was sequestered in a cabinet: the generally smallish photographs were displayed in a manner that forced the spectator—in anticipation of the expected response?—literally to "look down," to understand by standing over or above. But like the conventional photographic portrait, *Brian Ridley and Lyle Heeter* holds the museum wall at eye level, one portrait among others. And in its post-museum existence, in its coffee table art book manifestation, *Brian Ridley and Lyle Heeter* is fully at home in your home.

The disconcerting combination of the alien and the domestic on the level of content also obtains on the level of form: the technical virtuosity of the photograph, which is thoroughly characteristic of Mapplethorpe, belies the utter banality of its composition, which is rare in Mapplethorpe. Indeed, *Brian Ridley and Lyle Heeter* resembles nothing so much—chaps and chains notwithstanding—as the twenty-fifth wedding anniversary or senior prom snapshot. One subject duly seated; one subject duly standing—the decorum is simultaneously sexual and aesthetic—and both resplendent in their Saturday night best. *Brian Ridley and Lyle Heeter* does not, then, only anticipate arriving in your living room; it insists that it might have been taken there, by you or of you.

It is perfectly obvious, of course, who wears the chaps in Ridley and Heeter's relationship: they both do. In other words, it is not perfectly obvious—despite the obvious evidence to the contrary—who is master and who is slave. Granted, Ridley is elaborately manacled and Heeter is fully in control of the manacled Ridley. Ridley, moreover, is fully visible, totally accessible to visual consumption and objectification, whereas the bearded Heeter, whose eyes are slightly obscured by his leather cap, sees without himself being fully seen. Nothing, however, is easier to deconstruct, at least under the current theoretical regime, than a binary opposition. It would require little ingenuity, for example, to show how Ridley recovers on the level of composition something of the dominance he is denied on the level of content. His partially obscured crotch, to which Heeter's crop directs our attention, is a point of visual focus, a compositional cynosure. But the portrait is concerned neither with the internal dynamics of Ridley and Heeter's relation—both men look outward toward the spectator, not laterally toward each other—nor with the sexual politics of a bondage and discipline that openly acknowledges itself as such. Rather, *Brian Ridley and Lyle Heeter* explores the relation that obtains, the relation that it insists does obtain, between a bondage and discipline that is theatrically construed and embraced as such and a bondage and discipline that dare not speak its name.

iii. There Is Too Much Sexual Relation

Unlike novel reading, museum going does not presuppose a private space that is free from surveillance, in which the viewing subject sees without himself or herself being seen. True, the closed-circuit cameras that regularly monitor the interior of museums, or even the uniformed men and women who stand in low-tech guard, tend to pass unnoticed, so thoroughly have we grown accustomed to our visual accessibility. (Or at least unnoticed by me. I had to phone the Wadsworth Athenaeum, where I first saw *The Perfect Moment,* to confirm that closed-circuit cameras had in fact monitored the exhibit. They had.) We have grown accustomed to our accessibility, however, in a manner different in kind from Ridley, who actively solicits—in the etymological as well as the familiar sense of the word: *sollus,* whole, and *ciere,* to move, stir, agitate—the visual surveillance to which we are routinely subjected, to which we routinely subject ourselves. Even fully manacled, Ridley stages the conditions of his own objectification, an objectification to which the museum-going spectator does not, indeed cannot, contribute. The very nature of the museum presupposes the relation of a thoroughly autonomous viewing subject to thoroughly accessible and exposed objects. In holding up a mirror to the viewing subject, however, *Bill, New York, 1976–77* effaces the distance between subject and object positions. The ontological privilege that the viewing subject enjoys vis-à-vis the aesthetic object, which is always the right to see without oneself being seen, to consume in representation without oneself being represented, is itself violated.[24] And in staging the conditions of his own objectification, in proleptically assuming the object position, Ridley beats the museum-going art consumer at his or her own game.

Liberal critiques of visual representation tend to rehearse some form of the opposition between the "naked" and the "nude," the better to preserve the body natural from the body cultural. I am naked when I experience my body in all its mammalian warmth and innocence; I am nude when my body is given over to (or appropriated by) the culturally determined space of representation. Nakedness is natural and thus heterosexual, although today the paraphernalia of safer sex apparently threaten to translate the condition of heterosexual nakedness into a perverse nudity:

Sex partners of uncertain [HIV antibody] testing status [could] . . . wear disposable plastic gloves during all intimate moments. These gloves, after all, aren't too different from condoms. Yet we [Masters and Johnson] are unwilling to seriously entertain such an outlandish notion—right now, it seems so unnatural and artificial as to violate the essential dignity of humanity.[25]

Gloves are among the least outlandish of props in Mapplethorpe's spectacularly "artificial" sexual scenarios, but if the opposition between the naked and the nude has little relevance to the likes of Ridley and Heeter, it is not simply because the two appear in skins other than their own. "Staginess" is perhaps the most common criticism directed against Mapplethorpe's erotic photographs: the camera-as-voyeur is said to violate or suspend the operations of an otherwise spontaneous sexuality, thereby transforming a condition of nakedness into nudity. But because the criticism presupposes both a myth of photographic transparence (the camera, in hands less theatrical or theatricalizing than Mapplethorpe's, records rather than constructs its world) and a myth of natural or spontaneous sexuality (sex, at least for individuals less kinky than Mapplethorpe's subjects, is all animal vitality, utterly innocent of cultural determination), it hardly proves devastating. Indeed, the criticism may evince little more than an attempt to deny perhaps the most disturbing implication of Mapplethorpe's work. Nakedness is not the condition of a body that eludes or resists cultural inscriptions, but the misrecognition of a cultural appropriation so thorough as to be experienced as the Adamic.

If this is to suggest that one is always and only nude, that the object position or objectification is the normal condition of subjectivity in the bourgeois West, it is also to suggest that the objectifying gaze that is structurally formative for the closed institution, be it the museum or the academy, is in no way limited to its four walls. "Seeing, but not seen myself," as Freud said of the physical relation of analyst to analysand, and the human scientist occupies a position that is structurally analogous to the all-seeing but unseen heart of Bentham's Panopticon, which is Foucault's most fully articulated figure for panoptic power.[26] What are termed, appropriately enough, the modern "disciplines" of knowledge—

psychology, pedagogy, sociology, political science, and cultural anthropology, among others—seamlessly mesh with a technology of power that acknowledges subjects only as the objects of a nonparticipatory observation and knowledge.[27] At its most efficient, disciplinary power is participatory, precisely to the extent that it passes over to what Foucault calls "the other side—to the side of its surface of application."[28] Like the museum-going subject, who characteristically overlooks the closed-circuit camera that nevertheless over-looks everything, including the museum-going subject, modern subjectivity is most fully itself only when it forgets or disavows its functional implication in a system of carceral restraints. Video surveillance of the culturally ambitious may seem the most trivial of examples, but an ostensible triviality is precisely the point: disciplinary power, which is diffused in the very minutiae of social existence, strategically labors not to speak its name, not to be known or acknowledged as such. But again, it is difficult to imagine that Ridley could ever forget or disavow his radically different implication in a system of carceral restraints, and his visibility advertises not the triumph of a normalizing regime, which exercises its gentle violence over the soul, but the spectacular perversity to which he gives his body.

The ideal of an all-seeing but unseen surveillance is intimately bound to the propagation of a regime of the norm, to the dissemination of normalizing prescriptions and sanctions throughout the social fabric, which also implicates the subject in the principle of its own subjection. The goal is normalization (as opposed to repression), and any recourse to the iron fist rather than velvet glove—say, the discipline and bondage that is theatrically exercised over Ridley's body—can only suggest a "soul" lost to the regime of the norm. And Ridley and Heeter are indeed lost. Unlike the binarism of same- or cross-sex object choice that determines sexual discourse and practice in the bourgeois West, sadomasochism does not define itself in relation to the sex of object choices; unlike "mature" sexuality, which is always ghettoized in the genitals, sadomasochism is not organ-specific. The hierarchical impulses to which it is so obviously given, to which Ridley and Heeter are so obviously given, are not anatomical, at least not in the manner prescribed by Freud. The perversity of *Brian Ridley and Lyle Heeter* would thus be its refusal of, its threat to, the very category of the sexual subject, a classification that includes both the "homosexual" and the "heterosexual," which are themselves unique to modern discursive technologies of self-fashioning and self-knowledge.

Leo Bersani argues that it is the "degeneration of the sexual into a relationship that condemns sexuality to becoming a struggle for power." Love cheapens sex and Bersani's paradoxical project is to redeem the latter from the various redemptive projects intended for it:

Gay men's "obsession" with sex, far from being denied, should be celebrated—not because of its communal virtues, not because of its subversive potential for parodies of machismo, not because it offers a model of genuine pluralism to a society that at once celebrates and punishes pluralism, but rather because it never stops re-presenting the internalized phallic male as an infinitely loved object of sacrifice. Male homosexuality advertises the risk of the sexual itself as the risk of self-dismissal, of losing sight of the self, and in so doing it proposes and dangerously represents jouissance as a mode of ascesis.[29]

Point well taken: gay men's obsession with sex cannot be reduced to the official pieties of liberal culture, the anodyne rhetoric of much contemporary gay (non)activism notwithstanding. Nor should AIDS provide the occasion for re-imagining perversion as heterosexuality manqué:

Far from apologizing for their promiscuity as a failure to maintain a loving relationship, far from welcoming the return to monogamy as a beneficent consequence of the horror of AIDS, gay men should ceaselessly lament the practical necessity, now, of such relationships, should resist being drawn into mimicking the unrelenting warfare between men and women, which nothing has ever challenged. (218)

Yet if Bersani recalls perverts to the full political implications of their practices, he does so by universalizing "the unrelenting warfare between men and women" as the logic of desire itself. (I find myself in the uncomfortable position of enthusiastically endorsing Bersani's conclusion while remaining wary of what I take to be the implications of the argument that issue in it.) Sex is to be cherished for its capacity to undo the categories of sexual subjectivity that inform it. The rectum is the grave (and good riddance to it) of internalized phallic mastery:

Women and gay men spread their legs with an unquenchable appetite for destruction. This is an image with extraordinary power; and if the good citizens of Arcadia, Florida, could chase from their midst an average, law-abiding family, it is, I would suggest, because in looking at three [HIV-positive] hemophiliac children they may have seen—that is, unconsciously represented—the infinitely more seductive and intolerable image of a grown man, legs high in the air, unable to resist the suicidal ecstasy of being a woman. (211–12)

Yet if the rectum is the grave of a particularly unappealing form of masculine subjectivity, nothing here challenges the logic that is constitutive of the category of sexual subjectivity itself. Sedgwick warns that a "damaging bias toward hetero-sexual or heterosexualist assumptions inheres unavoidably in the very concept of gender," which gives heteronormativity a "conceptual privilege of incalculable consequence."[30] Bersani provides a compelling argument against aping, in the emptiest of all possible formalisms, heterosexual norms. He does so, however, while simultaneously reaffirming the hegemony of the analytical axis of gender, and hence the conceptual privilege afforded heteronormativity, that the likes of Ridley and Heeter challenge.

The image that the good citizens of Arcadia see—and sight is here clearly the result of prior ideological naturalization—conforms to good Freudian principles. Compare, for example, the spectacle "of a grown man, legs high in the air, unable to resist the suicidal ecstasy of being a woman" with a 1920 footnote to *Three Essays on the Theory of Sexuality*:

Lou Andreas-Salomé . . . in a paper which has given us a very much deeper understanding of the significance of anal eroticism, has shown how the history of the first prohibition which a child comes across—the prohibition against getting pleasure from anal activity and its products—has a decisive effect on his whole development. This must be the first occasion on which the infant has a glimpse of an environment hostile to his instinctual impulses, on which he learns to separate his own entity from this alien one and on which he carries out the first "repression" of his possibilities for pleasure. From that time on, what is "anal" remains the symbol of everything that is to be repudiated and excluded from life. The clear-cut distinction between anal and genital processes which is later insisted upon is contradicted by the close anatomical and functional analogies and relations which hold between them. The genital apparatus remains the neighbour of the cloaca, and actually (to quote Lou Andreas-Salomé) "in the case of women is only taken from it on lease."[31]

In the very act of describing the "first repression," Freud "carries out" an inaugurating repression of his own: the anus, which is at once primal and gender-neutral, must be marked as feminine, at least if the logic of gender, understood as the visual self-evidence of the body, is to retain its definitional hold on sexual self-fashioning. What is at stake here is not simply "the clear-cut distinction between anal and genital processes," but the hegemony of the sexual regime that the "later" distinction between male and female genitalia underwrites. If, then, what the good citizens of Arcadia see is not three HIV-positive hemophiliacs, but the "infinitely more seductive and intolerable image of a grown man, legs high in the air, unable to resist the suicidal ecstasy of being a woman," it may be in order not to see something even more seductive and intolerable: the nonsuicidal ecstasy of a grown man pursuing a pleasure that is available, willy-nilly, to men and women.

A war that "nothing has ever changed" easily suggests a war that nothing ever could change, a recalcitrance that Bersani attributes to some basic "anatomical considerations":

Human bodies are constructed in such a way that it is, or at least has been, almost impossible not to associate mastery and subordination with the experience of our most intense pleasures. This is first of all a question of positioning. If the penetration necessary (until recently . . .) for the reproduction of the species has most generally been accomplished by the man's getting on top of the woman, it is also true that being on top can never be just a question of physical position—either for the person on top or for the one on the bottom. . . . In short, the social structures from which it is often said that the eroticization of mastery and subordination derive are perhaps themselves derivations (and sublimations) of the indissociable nature of sexual pleasure and the exercise or loss of power. (216)

Bersani insists that "this is not to propose an 'essentialist' view of sexuality" (216), but the "indissociable" imbrication of anatomy, sexual desire, and social power seems to me precisely that. And if essentialism it is, it does not always seem to serve him well: "the butch number swaggering into a bar in a leather get-up opens his mouth and sounds like a pansy, takes you home, where the first thing you notice is the complete works of Jane Austen, gets you into bed, and—well, you know the rest" (208). Indeed I do know, but then anyone for whom the category of the butch bottom is not a contradiction in terms would know. A misplaced faith in the erotic legibility of the body makes for the disappointment: neither anatomy nor costume resolves "the question of positioning" before the fact. Leather drag sometimes includes specific codes that indicate a preference for top or bottom, but a red handkerchief in a left seat pocket is hardly the evidence of "the body itself." The medico-juridical construct that is the modern homosexual, to return to Foucault, is ideology made flesh: "Nothing that went into his total composition was unaffected by his sexuality. It was everywhere present in him: at the root of all his actions because it was their insidious and infinitely active principle. . . . It was a secret that always gave itself away." The practicing pervert responds by carrying his sexual aims lightly in his pocket.

Freud's contention that "the sadist is always at the same time a masochist" is relevant here, although for reasons not intended by Freud. "At the same time" is crucial: tomorrow Ridley and Heeter may reverse positions (or not), but versatility or reciprocity, the values informing liberal apologies for sadomasochism, is hardly the point. Freud holds that sadism deserves to be characterized as such only when "satisfaction is entirely conditional on the humiliation and maltreatment of the object," but the old joke knows better: to the masochist's desire to be maltreated, the "true" sadist, like Nancy Reagan, would just say no. That is, a sadomasochistic relationship that deserves to be characterized as such is no relationship at all. Presumably, however, Heeter says yes, which necessarily prevents sex with Ridley from ever degenerating into a relationship of love. To the extent that Ridley takes pleasure in the maltreatment that Heeter is thus powerless to deliver, he is the top; to the extent that Heeter directs his sadism toward a consenting masochist who actively solicits it, he is the bottom. In *Three Essays,* Freud ultimately "solves" the problem of the exclusive sexual interest felt by men for women or women for men tautologically: "No doubt the strongest force working against a permanent inversion of the sexual object is the attraction which the opposing sexual characters exercise upon one another" (229). Because the diacritics of gender presuppose a myth of natural complementarity, heterosexuality is condemned to fetishizing relationship. (Or a myth of natural antagonism, which issues in much the same thing. If the female genitalia are taken "on lease" from the cloaca, and if the cloaca represents all that is to be "repudiated and excluded from life," male heterosexual desire is indistinguishable from revulsion. Swift's pathology is textbook Freudianism: "Nor wonder how I lost my Wits; / Oh! Caelia, Caelia, Caelia shits.") But because sadomasochism is radically asymmetrical, nonreciprocal, it is innocent of the poetics of bourgeois spiritualization. "Il n'ya pas de rapport sexuelle." There is no sexual relation. What Lacan mistakes for an accomplished fact—there is altogether too much sexual relation—Bersani advances as a sexual ideal. Ridley and Heeter suggest that it is not an impossible one.

But what, then, of the bondage and discipline that is exercised without recourse to manacles? The bondage and discipline that is exercised over (or within) the couple in your living room looking into your coffee table art book at the couple looking back at them? *Brian Ridley and Lyle Heeter,* which anticipates and incorporates within itself a representation of its existence as a coffee table art book, cannot be reduced to the merely exotic. But neither can it be assimilated to the merely domestic, to a consensual relation not different in kind from heterosexual coupling. Any appeal to the standard of the contractual or the consensual, which tends to dominate the discourse of S/M, both pro and con, can only rebound to the credit of Ridley and Heeter. The two may think they are exercising free choice, or so the argument usually goes; they may even think (more fool they) that they are deriving pleasure from their choice. But what Ridley and Heeter do not know—and here knowledge functions as a less palpable but more fully carceral form of the chains that bind one to the other—is that they are merely replicating the phenomenon of oppression that they mistake for the exercise of free choice. (Sadomasochism and bondage and discipline, which tend not to be named in the numerous statutes that regulate sexual activity, are sometimes prosecuted as felonies. It is legally impossible to consent to a felony.) This is not to defend anything, least of all kinky sex, on the basis of the liberal myth of the free subject, who is in practice, to the extent that he exists in practice, always a straight white male of a certain class. Neither is it to evacuate the consensual of all meaning, which would have obvious repercussions for the already limited efficacy of our laws governing rape and domestic violence. It is to insist, however, that arguments that assume that consent cannot be an operable category for the likes of Ridley and Heeter—arguments that tend to replicate the logic that informs the legal prosecution of sadomasochism—are blind to their own carceral determinants. Ridley's relation to Heeter might be characterized as a theatricalization, in photographic negative, of the myth of consent that structures a law-abiding sexuality, a legally determined sexuality: if S/M or bondage and discipline is a consensual relationship, often undertaken in defiance of criminal law, which is thereafter theatricalized as the non-consensual, heterosexual genitality is first and foremost a social, religious, and legal obligation, which is nevertheless experienced as the consensual. Heterosexual genitality tends to be the least regulated of sexual practices, but only because what is so thoroughly of the law need not be massively subject to it. In a city like New Orleans—and, in this respect, the Big Easy is anything but unique—the only possible sexual contract between or among adults, at least to the extent that contract implies consent and choice, is necessarily nonheterosexual. To make the obvious point yet again: if we are to continue to enjoy our right to consume in representation the perversions of others, someone, somewhere, must first contract himself or herself, often in defiance of criminal law, to engage in perverse sexual acts. Alternatively, we might labor to change criminal law, or at least not actively abet the legal harassment and prosecution of gays and lesbians with our conference dollars.

Conservatives tend to know better than most that a legal right without the economic means to exercise it is effectively no right at all, and the conservative attack on Mapplethorpe strategically limited itself to the public funding, as opposed to the private consumption, of the arts. Not a stern master in (what one takes to be) the manner of Lyle Heeter, the House voted down the punishment it initially proposed to inflict on the NEA: no more money for five years was apparently too overt an exercise of the iron fist. The compromise legislation that did pass, however, was all the more effective for being less overtly punitive. Under the new dispensation, sexually explicit material, specifically the homoerotic, was pulled from the funding lineup to undergo further obscenity tests. Given the relatively liberal Supreme Court obscenity guidelines incorporated into the legislation, the tests proved, on the whole, negative, but they were no less efficacious for that. For their purpose was not, or not only, to prevent the funding of another Mapplethorpe or Serrano, but to render testing itself superfluous, to discipline the artistic community proleptically. Even the retroactive withdrawal of the relatively modest sum of $45,000 from the NEA budget, the amount spent on the Mapplethorpe and Serrano shows, was less a retroactive punishment than a proleptic warning. Not a full censorship—in the opinion of certain conservatives, not a censorship at all, as it involved only the public funding, not the private consumption, of the homoerotic and the sexually explicit—it is perhaps best characterized as a disciplinary censorship.

Censorship is not now, as it was in the premodern world, an overt intervention by the state before the fact of publication, exhibition, or public dissemination. Rather, modern censorship, while holding in reserve the possibility of a preemptive strike, characteristically functions as a deterrent, as an invitation to, or inoculation of, self-discipline. Its earliest and most eloquent formulation remains Milton's *Areopagitica,* which, as Francis Barker notes, marks both a decisive caesura in the history of censorship (from what came after it as well as before, as its recommendations were not immediately implemented) and a new formulation of the relation of the state to social life.[32] In what is generally taken to be an impassioned polemic against censorship, but what is in fact an argument for its reconceptualization and reintroduction in less overt forms, censorship is for the first time guaranteed by an "apparent withdrawal," however limited, of state control from the production and consumption of discourse.[33] Milton holds out the eventuality of punishment for offending books should they be published, yet he nevertheless maintains, in a paradox that is still central to liberal culture, the "right" or "freedom" of individuals to write and publish such books. In the prepublication licensing of Tudor, Stuart, and early parliamentary England, the state openly acknowledges its power as such. It assumes the possibility of undisciplined discourse, and hence the need for overt, preemptive, and externally imposed controls. With Milton, however, "the overt violence of the older settlement," as Barker terms it, is transformed into a "more indirectly ideological control," to an ideology of the subject or the citizen itself.[34] "How great a virtue is temperance," Milton writes in *Areopagitica*, "how much of moment through the whole life of man! Yet God commits the managing of so great a trust, without particular law or prescription, wholly to the demeanor of every grown man."[35] As with food, so too with books: the decisive moment of control is not the imposition of a "particular law or prescription" from without, but the internalized self-discipline that already preconstitutes the subject as temperate. Power passes over "to the other side—to the side of its surface of application," to the citizen who is no longer subject to the law only because he or she is now so thoroughly of it.

Like Milton—to compare small things to great—Helms did not propose a preemptive censorship. The government should not be in the business of subsidizing the sexually explicit and the homoerotic, although it need not, or perhaps cannot, actively prohibit their production and consumption. In *Areopagitica*, the state limits itself to threatening a punishment that ideally needs never to be inflicted; with Helms, the state limits itself to devising obscenity tests, for the purpose of withholding money, that in practice cannot work. But the Helms amendment, like censorship in Milton, needs to be understood not simply in terms of what it prohibits or prevents, the few who might henceforth be denied funding, but in relation to what it actively produces, the artists who will henceforth receive it. It is not, perhaps, necessary to remind an academic audience of the structuring force of grant money: if all knowing modern art defines itself in relation to the institution that it seeks to make its home, all knowing grant applications structure themselves in relation to their funding agency. If, then, the obscenity tests cannot work, ideally they need never work, need never be put to the test. *The Perfect Moment* encountered much-publicized legal challenges in Cincinnati, which involved the rather droll spectacle of men in uniform confiscating photographs of men in uniform. Disciplinary power is, however, rarely so overt, and its resources are not, in any case, limited to the courts.

Even given the now defunct Helms amendment, the NEA did not threaten the First Amendment rights that govern artistic production and consumption in the United States, rights that were regularly invoked in defense of Cincinnati's Contemporary Arts Center. The center and its director won the legal battle, however, only to concede the economic war. Given the controversy in which *The Perfect Moment* was already embroiled, the Contemporary Arts Center "voluntarily" withdrew, as the *New York Times* saw fit to put it, from the Cincinnati Institute of Fine Arts, an umbrella organization that raises money for the arts, lest its decision to exhibit Mapplethorpe should prove damaging to fund-raising efforts in general.

But surely such voluntarism is anything but voluntary, or is voluntary only to the extent that institutions, like individuals, "voluntarily" participate in the principle of their own subjection. Museums cannot routinely afford to withdraw, however "voluntarily," from major funding sources; neither can they routinely afford to be involved in litigation. The laws under which the center and its director were indicted are still very much on the books, and even if they are never again invoked against a Mapplethorpe, which seems unlikely, their disciplinary power is all the more effective for never having to be deployed. Even the reauthorization of the NEA under terms that did not include the Helms anti-obscenity pledge represents less the defeat of censorship than its "Miltonic" reconceptualization and reintroduction in less overt forms. Under the new provisos, the chair of the NEA is enjoined to "take into consideration general standards of decency and respect for the diverse beliefs and values of the American public." Censorship now enjoys a properly liberal alibi—"respect" for "diversity" in such a context almost always means its opposite—and a strategically unspecified agenda, which amounts to little more than a censorship that is no longer obliged to speak its name. Like the freedom granted the writing subject in *Areopagitica*, which is meaningful only to the extent that it internalizes the state control it thus renders superfluous, the freedom granted the modern artist may be meaningful only to the extent that it solicits (in many senses of the word, but not the etymological) the institutional approbation, be it public funding or museum existence, that has, in any case, already preconstituted it. (The reader is free to substitute academic for artistic freedom, the institutional approbation that is tenure for the approbation that is museum existence.) The freedom granted the museum, moreover, may be meaningful only to the extent that it solicits, explicitly or implicitly, the funding that sustains it, and in sustaining determines it. The legal guarantee of a freedom, the subjective experience of freedom, is not, it would seem, incompatible with its functional implication in a system of carceral restraints to which it remains effectively or strategically blind. Or, to return to the photograph that occasioned many of these reflections: the most conspicuous theatricalization of bondage, the most overt imposition of discipline, is not incompatible with a certain freedom from disciplinary restraints.

5 Muscles

Beauty pageants betray women into subjectivity. Bodybuilding contests afford their participants—of either gender, of any amalgamation thereof—the respect due beautiful objects. A case in point: there is no Mr. Congeniality in the Mr. Olympia contest, no recourse to the alibi of talent (say, a deft rendition of a light classic on a baby grand) or personal opinion (an earnest hope for world peace; a deep admiration for the novels of J. D. Salinger) to mystify the guilty pleasures of exhibitionism and spectatorship. The bodybuilding contest stages the body wholly as body, in all its perverse unnaturalness; the beauty pageant cannot imagine flesh unencumbered by spirit. John Berger argues that the visual economy of the West is structured by a rigid and gender-specific binary: women appear; men do.[1] In the beauty pageant, however, women do; in the bodybuilding contest, men appear.

There are exceptions. Arnold Schwarzenegger, to cite but the most obvious example, routinely betrays his body: he speaks. (I am referring to the politics, not the accent or the acting.) But then Schwarzenegger always was something of an exception in physical culture: he is, or has taken to staging himself as, straight.[2] A string of action pictures followed hard on the heels of the bodybuilding career, as if so much frenetic doing could retroactively compensate for—ontologically as well as financially—so much sublime and useless appearing. As Conan the Barbarian, Arnold does not threaten the straight male gaze. The exigencies of narrative "motivate" the loincloth, and the loincloth provides an alibi that the posing pouch does not. Laura Mulvey argues that an "active/passive heterosexual division of labor," a gender-specific split between spectacle and narrative, structures the visual economy of film:

Man is reluctant to gaze at his exhibitionist like. Hence the split between spectacle and narrative supports the man's role as the active one of forwarding the story, making things happen. The man controls the film phantasy and also emerges as the representation of power in a further sense: as the bearer of the look of the spectator, transferring it behind the screen to neutralize the extra-diegetic tendencies represented by woman as spectacle. This is made possible through the processes set in motion by structuring the film around a main controlling figure with whom the [male] spectator can identify.[3]

Again, men do; women appear, and again, the muscled male body disrupts the opposition. Conan the Barbarian does a great deal, but the "masculine" thrust of narrative is clearly subservient to the "feminine" stasis of spectacle. Plot provides the occasion for Arnold the Bodybuilder to strike poses.

A process that is set in motion "by structuring the film around a main controlling figure with whom the [male] spectator can identify" obviously runs the risk of confusing identification, the wish to be like the other, with desire, the wish to have the other. And the risk might seem considerable. Freud, for one, labors mightily to distinguish between the two. Nothing less than the conceptual coherence of heterosexuality—and the incoherence of its demonized obverse—depends on the stability of the opposition. (It is, of course, identification with one's sex that underwrites desire for its alleged opposite.) Yet if conceptual coherence requires the binarism, strategic considerations work toward its effacement. Consider, yet again, the famous 1915 footnote to *Three Essays on the Theory of Sexuality*, which implicitly concedes the impossibility of ever separating identification from desire:

Psycho-analytic research is most decidedly opposed to any attempt at separating off homosexuals from the rest of mankind as a group of a special character. By studying sexual excitations other than those that are manifestly displayed, it has found that all humans are capable of making a homosexual object-choice and have in fact made one in their unconscious.[4]

114

The shift in tenses is crucial. Homosexuality moves from a present, abiding possibility ("all human beings are capable") to an already superseded stage ("have in fact made one") in normative psychosexual development. Been there, done that, if only in my unconscious: a homosexuality that is construed as both integral to and superseded by the developmental logic of heterosexuality threatens nothing. The perversions that might otherwise be considered alternatives to heteronormativity are little more than defective forms of it. Narrative dissipates, even as it contains, the threat of perversion. To dwell on Arnold's physique as spectacle, as lyrical presence, is deviant in the extreme. To consume Conan's body in narrative— and the evidence suggests that the consumer of Conan's body will be male—is normative. The plot that motivates Conan's poses is as flimsy as the costumes it thus allows Arnold to wear, yet plot there must be, at least if the straight male gaze is to retain its composure. So long as the spectacle of male beauty can be construed as the incidental by-product of a narrative that directs its energies elsewhere or otherwise, man is comfortable gazing at his exhibitionist like. For a man simply to appear, however, or for a man to look at a man who simply appears, is itself proof that he is no man at all.

The bodybuilder is routinely demonized as the hyper-butch, the more-than-masculine, which means, in effect, the hardly-butch. Bodybuilding contests were initially dismissed as "male beauty pageants," and the analytical axis of gender, which underwrites the hetero/homo binary, continues to structure the cultural intelligibility of the muscled body.[5] But if I begin with what seems a variation on the familiar opposition—here it is the woman, the beauty queen, who occupies the "subject" position—it is not to confirm the explanatory privilege conventionally afforded gender. On the contrary. A body that openly declares itself "built," not born, necessarily challenges the inevitability of the operations by which gender, understood as the body's naturally given imperatives, come to organize the erotic field. Tertullian condemned the muscled body as an attempt "to surpass the plastic art of God" (*De Spectaculis*, 18). My own project refigures Tertullian's censure as celebration. The plastic art of God is precisely that—plastic, malleable—and if nothing else, the musclehead reminds us that the ideological order in which we have come to be naturalized is neither natural nor inevitable. Foucault invites us to construct alternative orders: "We have to invent with our bodies—with their elements, their surfaces, their masses, their volumes—a non-disciplinary eroticism: an eroticism of the body in its volatile and diffuse potentialities."[6] The normative subject is committed to the head-doctor's couch; the musclehead, to the weight lifter's bench. The normative subject is given to a poetics of the face; the muscle-head pursues new technologies of the flesh. The normative subject is the object of a disciplinary *scientia sexualis*; the musclehead invents a perverse *ars erotica*. The poets were there before Freud; the muscleheads were there before Foucault.[7]

i. Matter and Ghost

"It is only the superficial," Oscar Wilde once remarked, "who refuse to judge by appearances," and by Wilde's lights, it is the beauty pageant, not the bodybuild-ing contest, that is profoundly superficial. True, the man who also quipped he would do anything to stay young—except take exercise, get up early, or be re-spectable—might not seem the presiding genius of physical culture. But the ide-ology of exercise, with its normalizing celebration of self-development, self-real-ization, and the like, is at an extreme remove from the voluptuous uselessness of the muscled body. Consider the following exchange from Samuel Wilson Fussell's *Muscle: Confessions of an Unlikely Bodybuilder*:

"Is this a gay gym?" I asked.

"Look, honey," he replied, "All gyms are gay."

I examined the men by the machines. There Austin seemed right. "But what about them?" I asked, pointing to the free-weight lifters.

Austin laughed out loud. "Especially them," he said. "They just don't know it yet!"[8]

Fussell's interlocutor does not say all "health clubs," all "fitness centers." Wilde is here, as always, exactly right. Gay men do not in fact exercise; they work out. In their modern forms, both bodybuilding and weight lifting trace their origins to the career of Eugen Sandow, whose vaudeville act deftly combined posing, the body as spectacle, and highly theatrical feats of strength, the body in action. What Sandow amalgamated, however, bodybuilding and weight lifting now divide be-tween them. In a weight lifting competition, men do. The object is to demonstrate strength, not to command the visual field. In a bodybuilding contest, however, men appear only after having done (there is no lifting on stage). The object is to enthrall. Legitimate sports provide alibis. When men do, we need never cop to the guilty pleasures of spectatorship. It is but a happy accident, for instance, that com-petitive swimmers are obliged to don the skimpiest of trunks. The immodesty of the bodybuilder, however, is without apology or alibi; the (non)activity in which he engages is thus denigrated as spectacle, not celebrated as sport. And as sport is always the promise of a normative gender identity—for men if not women: young girls take tennis or golf lessons at their own peril—the nonsport that is body-building can only be an invitation to deviance.

That Fussell speculates on the sexual orientation of the space of the gym more than justifies the adjective of his title: we are indeed in the presence of an "unlikely" bodybuilder, although for reasons that are class as well as sexually specific. Fussell is the Oxford-educated son of university professors, and the Oxford-educated do not prefer the fraternity of the weight room to, say, the prattle of an MLA cash bar. The fate of wrestling is instructive. Once the most aristocratic of sports, it is now relegated to the cultural wasteland—or, in an alternative social register, to the postmodern chic—of pay-per-view TV. Like any number of activities predicated on conspicuous male embodiment, it has suffered a massive cultural devaluation (or at least a significant transformation in its class affinities). Yet if Fussell's memoir worries the class determinants of its titular activity, it is considerably more sanguine about the sexual orientation that the muscled body may betray. "Is this a gay gym?" he asks, as if the ability to recognize a "gay body" were not itself compromising. Fussell evidently thinks himself immune to the logic of "it takes one to know one," which, at least in this case, he may in fact be: his pursuit of the muscled body comes to us already structured as a confession, as a pathology recollected and represented in discursive tranquility. Writing both redeems the Oxford education and reestablishes the proper subordination of body to spirit.[9] To pose, to make a visible spectacle of the body, is a sign of pathology. To confess, to make a discursive spectacle of the soul, is an index of maturity. Or so, in any case, the normalizing logic of Fussell's memoir would have us believe. The Reverend Sydney Smith once complained that a certain man "had not body enough to cover his mind decently with, [so that] his intellect is improperly exposed."[10] Much the same might be said of Fussell.

Yet if Fussell is guilty of indecent intellectual exposure, so are we all, for there is a sense in which our culture renders it impossible to gain sufficient bulk—and Fussell's body was, at one time, massive—to cover the mind or soul decently with. The muscled body is received as a pathology, not as an aesthetics or an erotics, and the more intense the pursuit of bulk and definition, the more obvious the pathology it betrays. Freud teaches us to regret the separation of body from spirit that is our Cartesian inheritance, but for the musclehead, the imbrication of matter and ghost is, if anything, too intricate; as in the beauty pageant, our culture acknowledges no flesh unencumbered by spirit. (The organizers of the Miss America pageant recently considered renegotiating the relation of flesh to spirit by abolishing the swimsuit portion of the competition. The gesture, which was intended to

117

establish feminist credentials, was overwhelmingly rejected by the public. It seems to me, however, that the legitimately feminist gesture would be to nix the tiny talent time. Miss Idaho has considerably more to fear from subjectification than objectification.) The ideological uses to which Freud subjects the body, for example, require both its specific materialities, its burden of bulk and weight, and the limited resistance of those materialities to the meanings they will nevertheless be made to bear:

We must recall the question which has so often been raised, whether the symptoms of hysteria are of psychical or of somatic origin, or whether, if the former is granted, they are necessarily psychically determined. Like so many other questions to which we find investigators returning again and again without success, the question is not adequately framed. The alternatives stated in it do not cover the real essence of the matter. As far as I can see, every hysterical symptom involves the participation of both sides. It cannot occur without the presence of a certain degree of somatic compliance offered by some normal or pathological process in or connection with one of the bodily organs. And it cannot occur more than once—and the capacity for repeating itself is one of the characteristics of a hysterical symptom—unless it has a psychical significance, a meaning.[11]

Freud is discussing the hysterical symptoms exhibited by Dora, but the somatization of psychological states or moral judgments is in no way restricted to female hysteria. (Witness the cultural construction and reception of AIDS.) To be cured, Dora, like Fussell, has only to confess. The body itself speaks; the "talking cure" consists in translating the eloquent, if opaque, discourse of the body— Lacan terms hysterical symptoms "letters of suffering in the subject's flesh"— into discourse proper.[12] (A strategy that finds its loony, if logical, culmination in the nothing new of New Age psychology. Marianne Williamson's hateful *A Return to Love,* for example, recommends that the HIV-ill write love letters to AIDS and AIDS will lovingly write back.)[13] Dora, however, refuses to offer her body up in evidence, as evidence. Like Fussell, she withdraws from visibility (she famously walks out on Freud before the "talking cure" is completed); unlike Fussell, however, she does so in order to prevent making, or allowing Freud to make, a discursive spectacle of her soul. Anatomy is alibi rather than destiny: Freud can translate the opaque discourse of the flesh into discourse proper only because his own discourse has already been insinuated, however imperfectly, within the body's "naturally given" imperatives. Were it not for the limited resistance of the body to the meanings it will nevertheless be forced to bear, the translation into discourse proper would be redundant. The doctor would not be necessary. Were the resistance not limited, the translation would be impossible. The doctor would not prevail. The body always knows better than the subject who occupies it; the doctor, in turn, knows best.

Žižek views hysteria as "a kind of 'existential dramatization,'" the rendering somatic of "a theoretical position whereby a certain *surplus* is produced":

We can see . . . how the logic of this dramatization subverts the classical idealist relationship of a theoretical Notion and its exemplification: far from reducing exemplification to an imperfect illustration of the Idea, the staging produces "examples" which, paradoxically, subvert the very Idea they exemplify—*or, as Hegel would say, the imperfection of the example with regard to the Idea is an index of the imperfection proper to the Idea itself.*[14]

The rendering somatic of a "theoretical position" must never *seem* the mere exemplification of an Idea, but only because therein lies its ideological efficacy: the sermons already hidden in the body must be experienced as its naturally given imperatives. Thus, the excess such "staging" produces subverts only the subject's self-knowledge, not the cultural order that would put the subject in its place, teach the subject to know its place.[15] In the early decades of this century, fetishists of the male physique satisfied their perversion in the pages of Bernarr Macfadden's *Physical Culture*, the title of which precisely defines the space the muscled body occupies: not on either side of the nature/culture binary, which would only reinforce the logic of the divide, but in the space opened up by the lifting of the bar. Granted, Schwarzenegger, who should know better, insists that bodybuilding is the rendering somatic of a theoretical position, that the imagination produces muscles. But practice belies the inanities of theory, and in practice all serious muscleheads know that the body is not the word made flesh. By the same token, however, any musclehead who began his career as a proverbial ninety-pound weakling knows that physiology is ideology. Hence, the threat posed by the oxymoron that is "physical culture" to the operations of our modern bio-power: how to insinuate the workings of ideology in the "naturally given imperatives" of a body that openly declares itself built, not born, that knows itself to be always nude, never naked?

ii. Face Value

The Freudian logic of somatic compliance threatens us all with the face we deserve. Charles Atlas promises us the body we want,

CHARLES ATLAS, World's No. 1 Body Builder, says:

Don't Be Half A Man!

THE INSUL THAT MADE A MA OUT OF 'MA

Let ME SHOW How I Can Make You a Real HE-MAN From Head to Toe — in Just 15 Minutes a Day! Take a good honest look at yourself! Are you proud of your body — or are you satisfied to go through life being just "half the man" you could be? No matter how ashamed you are of your present physical condition — or how old or young you are — the "sleeping" muscles already present in your body can turn you into a real HE-MAN! Believe me, I know — because I was once a skinny, scrawny 97-pound half-alive weakling! People used to laugh at my build and make fun of me. I was ashamed to strip for sports or the beach . . . shy of girls . . . afraid of healthy competition.

HOW I CHANGED FROM A "MOUSE" TO A MAN!
One day, I discovered a secret that changed me from a timid, frightened scarecrow into "The World's Most Perfectly Developed Man" — a "magic formula" that can help turn you, too, into a marvellous physical specimen . . . a real HE-MAN from head to toe . . . a man who STANDS OUT in any crowd! What's my secret? "DYNAMIC-TENSION" — the natural method! No theory. No gadgets or contraptions. You just do as I did. Simply take the "sleeping" muscles already present inside your own body — build them up — use them every day in walking, bending over, reaching, even sitting! Almost before you know it, you're covered with a brand-new suit of beautiful, rock-hard SOLID MUSCLE!

MY SECRET BUILDS MUSCLES FAST!
Just 15 minutes each day in the privacy of your room is all it takes to make your chest and shoulder muscles swell so big they almost split your coat seams . . . turn your fists into sledge-hammers . . . build mighty legs that never tire! Mail coupon today for my famous book showing how "Dynamic-Tension" can give you a Body by Atlas. Charles Atlas, Dept. C60 115 E. 23 St., New York, N. Y. 10010.

WIN THIS VALUABLE TROPHY

5 FREE GIFTS
If you act now, in addition to my complete course, you will also get these five valuable outline courses.

DO YOU WANT...

A DEEP CHEST?	BIG ARM MUSCLES?	TIRELESS LEGS?	MAGNETIC PERSONALITY?

...THEN MAIL THIS NOW!

	CHARLES ATLAS
HERE'S THE KIND OF BODY I WANT	Dept. C60 115 E. 23 St., N.Y. N.Y. 10010
☐ MORE MUSCLE —BIGGER CHEST	I enclose 10¢. Show me how "Dynamic-Tension" can make me a new man. Send your famous 32-page book, full of pictures, valuable advice. No obligation.
☐ BIG ARM MUSCLES	
☐ BROAD BACK & SHOULDERS	Print Name .... Age ....
☐ TIRELESS LEGS	Address ....
☐ MORE WEIGHT	City &
☐ MAGNETIC PERSONALITY	State .... Zip Code ......
	In England send to Charles Atlas, 21 Poland St., London W 1

BROAD SHOULDERS?
"Dynamic-Tension" will broaden your shoulders. You'll see and feel BIG differences in 7 DAYS!

MORE WEIGHT?
You'll put on pounds in the right places. "Dynamic-Tension" rebuilds you in size and out.

CHARLES ATLAS ON TV

MY 32-page illustrated book, Charles Atlas, 115 East 23 St., N. Y. 10010.

Our culture is given to a patently moralized fixation with the face; Charles Atlas celebrates a frankly utopian relationship to the body. Face is to body, moreover, as beauty queen is to musclehead, as Miss Idaho is to Mr. Olympia. The beauty pageant purports to judge the whole person, and the face, as Susan Sontag notes, is always a privileged synecdoche for subjectivity:

All the debunking of the Cartesian separation of mind *and body by modern philosophy and modern science has not reduced by one iota this culture's conviction of the separation of* face *and body, which influences every aspect of manners, fashion, sexual appreciation, esthetic sensibility—virtually all our notions of appropriateness. . . . Our very notion of the person, of dignity, depends on the separation of face from body, on the possibility that the face may be exempt, or exempt itself, from what is happening to the body.*[16]

The face *is* the self, and the ontological decapitation renders "our very notion of the person, of dignity" an effect of consciousness rather than sentience. The beauty pageant participates in this familiar idealization, and so finds itself caught in a curious (and disingenuous) paradox: to judge the face is not to take the individual at face value. The bodybuilding contest, however, fetishizes only those body parts that are responsive to the baroque discipline of the gym. Small wonder, then, that the term "musclehead" is not considered pejorative among serious bodybuilders.[17] The face is fully implicated in "what is happening to the [muscled] body," and where individuality and subjectivity conventionally are, there bulk and definition will be. Recall the passage from Hegel quoted earlier:

The external element [of the work of art] has no value for us simply as it stands; we assume something further behind it, something inward, a significance by which the external semblance has a soul breathed in it. . . . Just so the human eye, a man's face, flesh, skin, his whole figure, are a revelation of mind and spirit. . . .

The art of bodybuilding has as its distinctly non-Hegelian task the creation of an irreducible opacity, an exteriority resistant to the imperialism of the spirit. The face itself is subsumed into the phenomenal, and a wild proliferation of bulk and sinew threatens to sever the body's constitutive relation to the soul.

In *Three Essays on the Theory of Sexuality*, Freud holds that the face both is and is not implicated in the economy of normative sexual desire:

The use of the mouth as a sexual organ is regarded as a perversion if the lips (or tongue) of one person are brought into contact with the genitals of another, but not if the mucous

121

membranes of the lips of both of them come together. This exception is the point of contact with what is normal. Those who condemn the other practices (which have no doubt been common among mankind from primaeval times) as being perversions, are giving way to an unmistakable feeling of disgust, *which protects them from accepting sexual aims of the kind. The limits of such disgust are, however, often purely conventional: a man who will kiss a pretty girl's lips passionately, may perhaps be disgusted at the idea of using her tooth-brush, though there are no grounds for supposing that his own oral cavity, for which he feels no disgust, is any cleaner than the girl's. (151–52)*

The use of the mouth as a sexual organ is indeed regarded as a perversion if the lips or tongue of one person are brought into contact with the genitals of another. But why? The limits of disgust are conventional, not unmotivated, and how is one to explain the aversion to a sexual practice that our culture, and not simply our forty-second president, might reasonably be expected to promote? Conventional wisdom holds that sex is meaningful only to the extent that it respects the unique individuality of both partners; conventional wisdom posits the face as the privileged synecdoche for that individuality. This same wisdom does not, however, promote the use of the mouth or face as a sexual organ. "You don't fuck the face." "Put a bag over their heads and they're all alike." These, the misogynist mantras of my own misspent adolescence, were meant to induce an aura of worldly wisdom, a reputation for rather jaded sexual knowledge. In practice, however, their ritual reiteration merely served to establish thoroughly conventional sexual aims: "you don't fuck the face" turned out to mean precisely that. The face or mouth participates in a normative sexual economy only as forepleasure. The mucous membranes of both partners come together as a prelude to sex, as a guarantee that sex is a relationship between two faces, two subjects. Prelude is not, however, to be confused with the act "itself," and to give or to get head is apparently to violate the separation of face from body that is constitutive of subjectivity itself. (The transgression may be ontological, but its repercussions are practical: oral sex can get you arrested in some seventeen of these United States.) The face, the self, underwrites the value of sex and sexuality. "Making love," we are regularly assured, is nothing but the deepest, most intimate, expression of the self. It can be idealized as such, however, only if the face is effectively exempt from sexual use. (The one exception is the mind or brain, the "translucent" form of the face, which TV talk sexologists routinely promote as *the* erogenous zone. "Sex in the head" is a cultural ideal; sex in the mouth is a perversion.) The feeling of disgust does not, then, simply protect the normative from an unsavory sexual practice. Rather, it guards against an unwanted, unsettling knowledge. Sex is potentially incompatible with the various idealizations—the poetics of the face, the ideology of love, the metaphysics of the subject—that allegedly subtend it. This the musclehead knows: to sever the body's constitutive relation to the soul is to refuse any category of personhood that would allow sex to degenerate into love.

Freud argues that visual eroticism is properly "intermediate," a "preparatory" step either in the high road that leads to "artistic aims" or in the low (but not therefore to be despised) road that leads to full, genital, cross-gendered intercourse:

It is usual for most normal people to linger to some extent over the intermediate sexual aim of a looking that has a sexual tinge to it; indeed, this offers them a possibility of directing some proportion of their libido on to higher artistic aims. On the other hand, this pleasure in looking [scopophilia] becomes a perversion (a) if it is restricted exclusively to the genitals, or (b) if it is connected with the overriding of disgust (as in the case of voyeurs or people who look on at excretory functions), or (c) if, instead of being preparatory to the normal sexual aim, it supplants it. This last is markedly true of exhibitionists. . . . The force which opposes scopophilia, but which may be overridden by it . . . is shame. (156–57)

So much for "most normal people," although for the rest of us, it is damned if we do and damned if we don't. That is, the intermediate stage of looking shades over into perversion (a) if "it is restricted exclusively to the genitals" and (b) if "instead of being *preparatory* to the normal sexual aim"—and normative sexuality is always fixated on the genitals—it multiplies the sites and occasions for pleasure. To linger indefinitely on the genitals or to refuse the teleology that makes a beeline toward them: both qualify you as a pervert. Freud, the apologist for the face we deserve, argues that the force that opposes scopophilia is "shame." Charles Atlas, the purveyor of the body we want, holds that shame inheres in the failure to incite scopophilia. (Physical culture is always the promise, as the comic books of my youth put it, that your body might bring you "FAME instead of SHAME.") "I am ashamed of myself *as I appear* to the other": for Sartre, shame is the condition of being-looked-at, the experience of being seen.[18] The subject, understood as an effect of consciousness, imagines himself (the politics of the gaze are gender-specific) as what Lacan terms a "non-empirical punctum of observation."[19] What he is loathe to imagine, however, is that he is also subject, as object, to the gaze of the other. (The gaze is easily reversible, and there is more than one non-empirical punctum of observation in town.) Lacan reads Sartre through Freud: openness to the gaze of the other is tantamount to the threat of castration, annihilation. (Or, in what amounts to the same thing, the charge of homosexuality. For a man to give himself over to visual consumption and fetishization, to repeat an earlier formulation, is itself proof that he is no man at all.) But if Sartre and Lacan are in substantial agreement, Charles Atlas is the odd man out. His advice to Sartre would be to bulk up, butch up: even for an existentialist, "as I appear to the other" is not a grim ontological inevitability, but a specific performative possibility, and Atlas offers a crash course in the erotics of appearance. Shame inheres, moreover, less in the experience of being seen than in the inability to solicit the gaze, in the failure to command the visual field. A looking that extracts from the subject meanings already implanted in it is a *scientia sexualis*. A looking or a demand to be looked at that has an unembarrassed "sexual tinge" to it is an *ars erotica*. You decide: the face you will learn to think you deserve, physiology as poetic justice, or the body you want, flesh as erotic opportunity.

Poetic wisdom has it that only God can make a tree. Charles Atlas insists that it takes only the privacy of your room, fifteen minutes a day, and an official Charles Atlas chest expander to make a real man.

But can Atlas be trusted? The risk might seem small, but as anyone who ever gambled a stamp in order to get his "FREE book" knows, "real" masculinity can never be actively or willfully pursued. A word, then, to the wise: you will graduate from Atlas's crash course in "DYNAMIC TENSION" not metamorphosed into a butch butterfly, but marked by a desire for a "real" masculinity that, in the very pathos and futility of your attempt to construct it, argues its utter naturalness, and hence its unavailability to you. Listen to the whinings of one would-be Mr. America: "We're everything the U.S. is supposed to stand for: strength, determination, everything to be admired. But it's not the girls that like us, it's the fags."[20] The title to which the musclehead aspires figures the body politic as the body natural, but therein lies the problem: our "Mr. America" protests too much, tries too hard. In laboring to render the body allegorical—to make it "stand for" normative, heterosexual, U.S. masculinity—he succeeds only in exposing the fissure between signifier and signified that is constitutive of allegory as such. Lee Edelman notes that "a relation wherein the body is indulged and disavowed at once, emphatically 'worn' or inhabited, but inhabited with a distance that renders such embodiment ironic," is inevitably construed as "decadent." And decadence, in turn, is culturally intelligible only as a euphemism for gay. Edelman is speaking of an "auntyish littérateur," the character of Waldo in Otto Preminger's *Laura,* but what is true of the less-than-masculine male body is also true of its more-than-masculine counterpart.[21] He Man and Sissy Boy. The former has greater bulk to inhabit than the latter, yet he too "wears" his flesh with an emphasis and lightness that render such embodiment ironic. Trollope insists that clothes do not make the man, that "manliness" cannot be "worn":

Before the man can be manly, the gifts which make him so must be there, collected by him slowly, unconsciously, as are his bones, his flesh, and his blood. They cannot be put on like a garment for the nonce,—as may a little learning.[22]

For a real man, the body, the signifying medium, always "partakes of," as opposed to "stands for," the nature of the reality it renders intelligible; normative masculinity is symbolic in Coleridge's sense of the term. (As is perversion, if only because the distance that renders gay male embodiment ironic or allegorical easily comes to serve as its symbolic "truth" or "essence.") The excess in which the pursuit of masculinity issues always betrays the lack in which it originates. It is available only to those for whom the issue of its availability never arises as such.

That it is not girls who fetishize the muscled male body is not the newest news in town; indeed, nothing is more routinely or triumphantly outed than the muscle magazine. Here again class and sexual anxieties effectively coalesce. Were it not for the perceived class identity of its readership, for example, the obscenity charges brought against Macfadden's *Physical Culture* would never have stuck.[23] In *Pumping Iron*, Schwarzenegger advises neophyte muscleheads to visualize themselves "as a piece of sculpture"; in the same movie, Lou Ferrigno's father rhapsodizes, "What symmetry, Louie. You look like something Michelangelo cut on." A (frequently high-camp) deployment of the conventions of Greco-Roman art virtually defines the open secret that is homoerotic visual representation, and the soft-core porn to be had in the pages of *Physical Culture* was nothing if not classicizing. (Unlike contemporary muscleheads, who tend to favor store-bought tans, bodybuilders in Sandow's time coated their already pale bodies with white powder, the better to transform flesh into marble.) But neither the glory that was Greece nor the grandeur that was Rome saved Macfadden. In a 1907 court of appeals judgment, the image of the *Discus Thrower* that appeared on the cover of *Physical Culture* was deemed obscene. The high art credentials of the image would seem impeccable, yet the judge ruled that to translate a highbrow icon into a lowbrow context was necessarily to awaken its obscene content. (A reverse form of the same logic, a similar imbrication of class and sexual anxieties, guaranteed that the obscenity charges brought against *Ulysses* would not stick. The cultural capital required to read the book, the judge more or less ruled, effectively prevented the wrong sort of people from skimming it for the naughty bits. Sex is theoretically available to everyone, but as the proverbial lady puts it, it's much too good for most people.) To his credit, the judge in the Macfadden case implicitly acknowledged that the disinterested contemplation of beauty is a class-specific acquisition. What never quite gets acknowledged, although its logic everywhere informs the case, is that the perverse have no interest in the disinterested, no investment in the erotic impoverishment of art. The culturally privileged see, or learn to pretend to see, only the play of light and shadow, the formal perfection of the composition. The culturally disenfranchised see a naked man. The sexually perverse see a hot naked man.

Soft-core porn may be too good for some people, but it is only what is due others, and the devaluation of gay goods, here as elsewhere, is but prelude to a straight appropriation. Add "fitness" to the title and a woman to the cover: you have just transformed the muscle magazine, that sorry spectacle of failed masculinity, into *Muscle and Fitness* or *Men's Health*, the gospels of a new and revivified heterosexuality. (Chances are, however, that the woman on the cover will be a swimsuit model or an aerobics instructor. Female bodybuilders are dubious assets for a magazine seeking to establish heterosexual credentials.) Thus, the straight boy, the Johnny-come-lately to the gym, need never cop to his pursuit of the perverse body. Heterosexuals are free to clone the body that has already been dismissed as a clone, and a homophobic culture is spared the knowledge that, here as elsewhere, its normative spectacle of masculinity tends to be a gay man.

The gym—or, in its heterosexual and heterosexualizing manifestation, the "fitness center" or "health club"—is not, therefore, a restricted access club. It can be appropriated by any sexuality or class, provided that the pursuit of bulk and definition remains, like Dorian's portrait, a manifestation of soul:

Human beings are more than bodies, and a preoccupation with the world of physicality or outward appearance to the exclusion of deeper and ultimately more meaningful concerns can turn the pursuit of the developed body from an engrossing imaginative exercise into a futile obsession with the shallow surface of existence or a narcissistic cult of the self. More dangerously still, the distortion of physical development from a subjective means of personal expression into an ideological program is to pervert its creativeness and reduce it to the crudest form of physical suprematicism and social intolerance.[24]

To the sexually deviant, sad victims of the shallow surface of things, working out merely confirms them in their narcissistic self-absorption. To the sexually normative, devotees of the deep truth of things, exercise means releasing the inner self. The perverse cult of the body easily degenerates into the most reactionary of political agendas. The straight pursuit of self-expression, the apparent antidote to all things "ideological," is liberalism as usual.

The only politically responsible, psychologically healthy relation to the muscled body is, then, heterosexual; as it turns out, the gym is, or at least should be, a restricted access club. But what of race? Bodybuilding was among the first "sports" to be integrated, and although black competitors were initially denied major titles (the legendary Sergio Olivia never won the coveted Mr. Olympia), they soon emerged as a dominant force. Lee Haney, for instance, is an eight-time Mr. Olympia. The participation of blacks in an activity once associated with criminals and social misfits may only confirm racist expectations, but the diversity of bodybuilding is not always so comforting. Post–World War II economic developments have obliged the West to acknowledge what it nevertheless experiences as a scandalous oxymoron—"the Japanese giant"—and bodybuilding literalizes the offense.[25] Yukio Mishima poses a double threat: writers, least of all Japanese writers, are not expected to make a spectacle of their buff bodies. Racial difference is conventionally thought to be secured by visual difference, yet both the anachronistic habit of powdering the body and the contemporary taste for store-bought tans would seem to challenge the conventional diacritics. Indeed, the challenge may be too conspicuous, too confident: the very willingness to play with the visual signs of racial difference bears paradoxical testimony to a retrograde faith in their stability. It is anxiety over the fluidity of gender/sexual categories, not racial, that motivates the advisory sent by the International Federation of Bodybuilding to the judges of the February 1992 Ms. International competition in Columbus, Ohio:

First and foremost, the judge must bear in mind that he/she is judging a woman's body-building competition and is looking for an ideal feminine physique. Therefore, the most important aspect is shape. . . . The other aspects are similar to those described for assessing men, but in regard to muscular development, it must not be carried to excess where it resembles the massive muscularity of the male physique.[26]

Read: heterosexual credentials are to be maintained at all costs. Thus, in the film *Pumping Iron II: The Women*, which chronicles the Ms. Olympia contest of 1983, the only black contestant, Carla Dunlop, beats out the more highly developed (but therefore more sexually suspect) Bev Francis. "If muscles make a man 'masculine,'" the video jacket asks, "what do they make a woman?" But it is a big "if": muscles rarely, if ever, make a man more masculine. They do, however, make a woman more mannish, and it is the specter of the mannish lesbian—the more-than-natural, more-than-masculine musculature of Bev Francis—that haunts *Pumping Iron II*. Until, that is, Carla Dunlop emerges triumphant. The conspicuous (re)assertion of racial difference, as Ann Pellegrini notes, compensates for the apparent effacement of sexual difference that the contest enacts.[27] Heterosexual credentials are maintained, albeit at considerable cost to the integrity of the contest. The triumph of Carla Dunlop, the racially other, is really the defeat of Bev Francis, the sexually ambiguous.

"The ideal feminine physique" is, then, the outward manifestation of an innate femininity: a liberal ideology of self-expression defines the proper limits of somatic architecture. But how liberal is this liberalism? Consider the gentle and not-so-gentle forms of violence that our culture routinely directs against the fat, straight female body, a category that potentially includes every woman and no woman. Every woman, because in a misogynist culture, to rehearse the Duchess of Windsor's murderous wisdom, no woman can ever be too thin; and no woman, because in a misogynist culture, there are no fat women, much less an erotics of the fat female body, but only thin women struggling to escape fat encasements. Here it is the natural body, precisely to the extent that it has gone "natural" or "let itself go," that is construed as artificial. To diet, to exercise, or to go under the knife is not to construct a "real" body in Charles Atlas's sense of the term, which could only serve to denaturalize the object of heterosexual desire. Rather, it is to release the real, inner, thin you. Jenny Craig knows better than to promise, at least in so many words, that your body will bring you fame instead of shame; she directs her normalizing energies toward the soul, the psyche, in the knowledge that the body will follow suit. A promotional brochure for Bally Total Fitness, which features a buff young woman on its cover, punningly reads "A great body starts with what's *inside*" (emphasis in original); Cybertrim, a diet supplement, invites its potential consumers (presumably biological females) to "reveal the woman you really are." For Charles Atlas, a "real" body is built; for Jenny Craig, a "real" body is revealed. Yet if the discourse of the "real" functions differently for straight women and gay men, there is a sense in which the twain meet, which makes for that most familiar of strange not-quite-bedfellows: the fat straight woman and the muscled gay man. The former refuses to become what she naturally is, thin, the proper object of male heterosexual desire. The latter endeavors to become what no course in "DYNAMIC TENSION" will ever allow him to be, a real man, a proper male subject.

Thus, the non-man who is a bodybuilder, like the non-man who is a woman, can only want what he is in want of—the phallus. The power of the phallus is, however, abstraction, its never quite complete transcendence of the penis it strategically veils, and bodybuilding is nothing if not embodiment. Membership has its privileges, but they involve trading up, as it were, in the symbolic register. Deleuze and Guattari argue that Freud's "greatness lies in having determined the essence or nature of desire, no longer in relation to objects, aims, or even sources (territories), but as an abstract subjective essence—libido or sexuality."[28] Like the capitalist wealth that is its logical corollary, Freudian sexuality has no weight, no specific density or materialities. Lacan's contention that the phallus "can only play its role veiled" is thus exactly right: to expose the penis is to put the phallic function at risk. Physical culture characteristically stops short of full frontal nudity, but it is given—to borrow a phrase from a 1958 federal indictment brought against Kris Studio, a leading supplier of physique photography—to "excessive genital delineation." (The head of the studio later admitted that he soaked the already flimsy

129

fabric of the pouches the better to ensure precise delineation.)[29] Granted, delineation, no matter how precise, cannot guard against a hermeneutic that refuses to look. "The general public doesn't know how to look," Schwarzenegger complains in *Pumping Iron*, and academics are hardly exempt from the general censure.[30] Melody D. Davis, for example, maintains that by "becoming 'hard' all over," bodybuilders seek to transform themselves into "a perpetually erect phallus,"[31] and most readings of the muscled body, even the explicitly celebratory, tend to see only what can never be seen: the phallus. ("What's a penis but another phallic symbol?" Jung is reputed to have asked.) But sad to say, not all muscles respond equally well to working out; factor in steroid use, moreover, and bodybuilding is positively counterproductive. The posing pouch gives the dick its proper due, but nothing more: precise delineation works against a general phallicization. (Contestants who do appear with hard-ons, we are told in *Pumping Iron*, sully the spectacle.)[32] To the extent that the phallic bears any relation to a specific psychosexual dispensation, it is constitutively heterosexual. Even in Freud, the "abstract, subjective essence" that is libido occasionally issues in sex, and *Three Essays* begins by distinguishing between the sexual "object" ("the person from whom sexual attraction proceeds") and the sexual "aim" ("the act towards which the instinct tends"). But what is "merely soldered together" (135–36, 148) in the opening essay is organically fused in the concluding: "mature" sexuality knows only a single object and act. If, then, the phallus is the "all," as Lacan contends, it is all only for the heterosexual subject, who narcissistically imagines the perverse body in the image of its own erotic fixation. (The "all" of deviant sexuality is imagined differently as homophobic convenience dictates. In the discourse of AIDS, for example, gay men tend to be equated with the "all" of their assholes.) Certainly no bodybuilding contest would be complete without getting it, as it were, ass-forward, without the flaunting of body parts and apertures that are wonderfully responsive to the discipline of the gym. (By which I mean, as the narrator of *American Studies* puts it, not only "backsides, whose virtues are . . . generally appreciated, but backs, whose owners never see them, and whose baroque, superabundant complexity is squandered, given away freely to those who look.")[33] The so-called armored body flaunts, and the posing pouch lovingly contours, the chinks in it (see illustration opposite).[34] Turned ass-forward, Mr. America may well be soliciting a dick. Or not. To bifurcate the body in terms of the symmetry of dick and asshole, "the shrine of masculinity" and its "mythic violation," is to reiterate the terms of a heterosexual and heterosexualizing economy, which the musclehead rejects.[35] He traffics in flesh, not the abstract currency of the phallus.[36]

iii. Phallic Subjectivity

The phallus, Lacan is at pains to emphasize, is a discursive construct, not a physiological dispensation. The confessions of a bodybuilder can attain to it; bodybuilding itself, however, is precluded from the start. The heated fantasy of "becoming 'hard' all over" is phallocentric; the bodies that occasion the fantasy are not. Hysterical phallicization is, however, only one charge among many; the meanings extracted from the muscled body (the sermons hidden in it) are legion. There is, for example, the familiar cry of "physical suprematicism" or "body terrorism," which implicitly seeks to localize violence against women and effeminate men, which is endemic to heterosexual patriarchy, in a body that, precisely to the extent that it is marked as gay, is itself an open invitation to violence. There is the closely related charge of "body fascism," which implicitly translates a crime of compulsory, state-sponsored heterosexuality into a specifically gay atrocity. Or, finally, there is the charge of commodification, which, in reducing gay sexuality to the squalor of getting and spending, seeks to raise heterosexuality above the marketplace.

Commodification, as description if not accusation, can be readily admitted: the muscled body constructs itself with an eye to a specific sexual market. (One of many, as the gym body is hardly the "all" of perverse sexuality.) But commodification presupposes mystification, and the musclehead knows full well what he is about. For Sontag, the sexual and economic booms of the 1970s were two sides of the same coin:

In the 1970s . . . urban homosexual life became a sexual delivery system of unprecedented speed, efficiency, and volume. Fear of AIDS enforces a much more moderate exercise of appetite, and not just among homosexual men. In the United States, sexual behavior pre-1981 now seems for the middle class part of a lost age of innocence—innocence in the guise of licentiousness, of course. After two decades of sexual spending, of sexual speculation, of sexual inflation, we are in the early stages of a sexual depression. Looking back on the sexual culture of the 1970s has been compared to looking back on the jazz age from the wrong side of the 1929 crash. (164)

For Baudrillard as well:

I don't know . . . whether a stock market crash such as that of 1987 should be understood as a terrorist process of economy or as a form of viral catharsis of the economic system. Possibly, though, it is like AIDS, if we understand AIDS as a remedy against total sexual liberation, which is sometimes more dangerous than an epidemic, because the latter always ends. Thus AIDS could be understood as a counterforce against the total elimination of structure and the total unfolding of sexuality.[37]

The analogy—boom or bust—is specious. However it looks "looking back," junk bonds did not equal junk sex, and irresponsible gay male "licentiousness," "total sexual liberation," was not the psychosexual analogue of irresponsible capitalist speculation. Baudrillard is simply offensive. Sontag is cagey. The passive voice of her concluding sentence—"Looking back on the sexual culture of the 1970s has been compared . . ."—seeks to evade responsibility for the comparison she nevertheless (or therefore) feels free to make:

The ideology of capitalism makes us all into connoisseurs of liberty. . . . In rich countries, freedom has come to be identified more and more with "personal fulfillment"—a freedom enjoyed or practiced alone (or as alone). Hence much of recent discourse about the body, reimagined as the instrument with which to enact, increasingly, various programs of self-improvement, of the heightening of powers. Given the imperatives about consumption and the virtually unquestioned value attached to the expression of self, how could sexuality not have come to be, for some, a consumer option: an exercise of liberty, of increased mobility, of the pushing back of limits. Hardly an invention of the male homosexual subculture, recreational, risk-free sexuality is an inevitable reinvention of the culture of capitalism, and was guaranteed by medicine as well. The advent of AIDS seemed to change all that, irrevocably. (165)

No. Capitalism guarantees only the pursuit of happiness—abstract nouns are notoriously difficult to catch—and Sontag is confusing a normative ideology of desire, which is always in excess of any possible fulfillment, with a perverse "subculture" of pleasure. It is the poetics of erotic spiritualization, the ideology of love, that is the "inevitable reinvention of the culture of capitalism." Sontag has a point: "much of recent discourse about the body, reimagined as the instrument with which to enact . . . various programs of self-improvement," is capitalist commodification. Much, but not all, and the heterosexual appropriation of gym culture cannot be conflated with the practice it travesties. The injunction to exercise is dependent on a discourse of self-development and the like; bodybuilding is not. The behavior Sontag is pleased to attribute to the perverse "some"—a commodified, and so mystified, relation to economies of bodily pleasure—is the condition of the normative "many."

Marx defines commodity fetishism as "a definite social relation between men, that assumes, in their eyes, the fantastic form of a relation between things"; the mystification consists in positing value as a fixed property of things rather than as a social relation among individuals. As with commodities, Marx adds in an important footnote, so too with people:

In a sort of way, it is with man as with commodities. Since he comes into the world neither with a looking glass in his hand, nor as a Fichtian philosopher, to whom "I am I" is sufficient, man first sees and recognizes himself in other men. Peter only establishes his own identity as a man by first comparing himself with Paul as being of like kind. And thereby Paul, just as he stands in his Pauline personality, becomes to Peter the type of the genus homo.[38]

Peter establishes his identity as a man differentially in relation to Paul; in the construction of social identity, as in structural linguistics, there are only differences without positive terms. "Peter" and "Paul" are purely relational terms, yet Peter experiences Paul, as Paul experiences himself, in the alleged fullness of his Pauline personality. Differential relations produce the illusion of identity as plenitude or internalized self-possession. The mystification, the origin of "the virtually unquestioned value attached to the expression of the self," consists in positing identity as an innate property of persons rather than as a social relation among people.

All this assumes, however, that Peter and Paul are adequate types of the genus homo. What if, as chance would have it, Paul turns out to be a defective type, a homosexual? How might this impinge on his relation to Peter? Marx insists that man does not come into the world with a looking-glass in his hand, yet a gay Paul suggests that at least some men do. Our culture routinely construes homosexuality as narcissism, which the muscled body, with its seemingly endless romance with the mirror, would only seem to substantiate. But does it follow that all muscleheads are necessarily Fichtians, fetishists of the transcendental "I"? Lacan argues that all men are "precipitated" by mirrors:

This jubilant assumption of his specular image by the child at the infans *stage, still sunk in his motor incapacity and nursling dependence, would seem to exhibit in an exemplary situation the symbolic matrix in which the I is precipitated in a primordial form, before it is objectified in the dialectic of identification with the other, and before language restores to it, in the universal, its function as subject.*

This form would have to be called the Ideal-I, if we wished to incorporate it into our usual register, in the sense that it will also be the source of secondary identifications, under which term I would place the functions of libidinal normalization. But the important point is that this form situates the agency of the ego, before its social determination, in a fictional direction, which will always remain irreducible for the individual alone.[39]

Lacan terms the mirror image "fictional" in the sense that it possesses a coherence and integrity that the infant, "still sunk in his motor incapacity and nursling dependence," utterly lacks. What seems no less fictional here, however, is Lacan's own attempt to situate the agency of the ego prior to its social determination, which it proleptically serves to justify. For if the mirror stage is the pre-symbolic, pre-ideological source of secondary identifications, which include the explicitly ideological work of libidinal normalization, then heterosexuality itself can only be pre- or extra-ideological. The argument is circular. The already-constituted subject retroactively posits a history, or prehistory, that is a proleptic apology for that subjectivity. Or, as Marx might say, the argument is self-defeating. The attempt to locate the "primordial" agency of the ego prior to its social determination merely perpetuates the identity fetishism it alleges to explode. Or, as the musclehead might say, the argument is irrelevant. A thesis that is an implicit apology for libidinal normalization is powerless to account for a perverse romance with the mirror.

Here Schwarzenegger is the superior theoretician:

You don't really see a muscle as part of you, in a way. You see it as a thing. You look at it as a thing and say well this thing has to be built a little longer. . . . And you look at it and it doesn't even seem to belong to you. Like a sculpture.[40]

The Lacanian mirror stage issues in an identification with a fictitious "Ideal-I," an image of perfect autonomy and self-mastery. The bodybuilder's mirror life ("it's not just a stage") is the pursuit of an Ideal-Thing. The mirror stage is a seduction into an impossible image of the body's coherence and integrity. The mirror life involves de-aggregation, the body-in-pieces. (One exercises the whole body, but working out involves only discrete body parts, which, to be worked effectively, must remain discrete. Thursday is, say, arms and shoulders; on Thursday one is, at least for a time, only arms and shoulders.) The mirror stage proleptically fuses identity and normative desire; the mirror life affords what Foucault terms, in another context, the pleasures of "desubjectivization," "desubjection":

I think it politically important that sexuality be able to function the way it functions in the saunas, where, without [having to submit to] the condition of being imprisoned in one's own identity, in one's own past, in one's own face, one can meet people who are to you what one is to them: nothing else but bodies with which combinations, fabrications of pleasure will be possible. These places afford an exceptional possibility of desubjectivization, of desubjection.[41]

As in the sauna, so too in the gym: a gay Paul does not have any interest in the rapt contemplation of his Pauline self, in the condition of being imprisoned in his "own face." If he squanders his time before the mirror, it is in a performative, constructive relation ("this thing has to be built a little longer") to the object (you "don't really see a muscle as part of you") he would become. And what seems a closed dyad is in fact a threesome or better: Paul's mirror life is always already structured by a desire to recruit Peters.

The logic of commodity fetishism ("A definite social relation between men that assumes, in their eyes, the fantastic form of a relation between things") presupposes an opposition between subjects and objects, persons and things, that Schwarzenegger, for one, finds ideologically untenable. (As does Althusser, and I suspect that Schwarzenegger is rather more Althusserian than Fichtian. The pre-Hollywood musclehead would have concurred with the Althusserian critique of the residual humanism of Marx's theory of commodity fetishism.) Žižek argues that commodity and identity fetishism are strictly incompatible. The two cannot, or at least do not, coexist in the same historical moment:

We cannot say that in societies in which production for the market predominates—ultimately, that is, in capitalist societies—"it is with man as with commodities." Precisely the opposite is true: commodity fetishism occurs in capitalist societies, but in capitalism relations between men are definitely not "fetishized": what we have here are relations between "free" people, each following his or her proper egoistic interest. The predominant and determining form of their interrelations is not domination and servitude but a contract between free people who are equal in the eyes of the law.[42]

Even if one were to accord the law, as opposed to the force of the norm, the significance it enjoys here, it is manifestly untrue that all "men" are equal before it. (Ask a gay man denied access to the deathbed of his lover what he thinks about equality before the law.) Indeed, there is no better evidence that identity fetishism is still too much with us than the specious universalism—the conflation of the privileges of the straight white male subject with the conditions of subjectivity itself—of Žižek's argument against it. In societies in which production for the market predominates, relations of domination and servitude are not acknowledged as such, and "human qualities" developed with an eye to the market are characteristically promoted under the rubric of "self-development" and the like. That is why, to return to an earlier example, Jenny Craig and company direct their normalizing energies toward the soul. To diet, to exercise, or to go under the knife is not to jockey for position in the meat or marriage markets; rather, it is to become ever more fully the woman you "really" are. That all the psychobabble issues in only one thing—a more marketable commodity, a fully naturalized object of male heterosexual desire—is but a happy coincidence. There is a straight as well as a perverse "implantation," and the trick is to make a legally and culturally compelled identity seem the full flowering of that most impoverished of all commodities: the soul of man under capitalism. It is not, then, strictly true that Miss Idaho has more to fear from subjectification than objectification. The one is functionally indistinguishable from the other.

The musclehead has nothing to fear. Here, for example, is Arnold striking poses, watching himself being watched in a mirror:

He walks over to one of the big mirrors and takes off his shirt. The gym goes even quieter than it was before, and everyone still in it stops whatever he is doing. . . . The men standing behind him watch in the mirror in the same, elated, adrenalized way you watch a fight as Arnold checks himself through five or six quick poses, his face now grinning and appraising wolfishly. They are all bodybuilders . . . and they have all seen Arnold pose before, yet they stare at the reflection like the ladies on Santa Monica Beach when they see a builder for the first time.[43]

The Fichtian "I am I" construes subjectivity as an effect of consciousness; Arnold remains pure spectacle. "I am I" is the mantra of bourgeois subjectivity. The musclehead responds with its phonetic perversion: "Pumping iron, nobody's going to be bigger than I am"—in effect, "I am Iron."[44] Arnold, the biggest of them all, is both the object of the gaze and the cynosure that structures the visual field, that interpellates others within it. All are bodybuilders; all are size queens (in all but the conventional sense of the term), and size is the only diacritical marker operable in this world of mirrors. There is an eleventh-hour attempt to recover the spectacle for the conventional diacritics of gender—"they stare at the reflection like the ladies on Santa Monica Beach"—but the comparison succeeds only in foregrounding its own incoherence.

Cross-gender desire assumes that relations between men and women are not fetishized; heterosexuality understands itself as a contract between "free" people, each pursuing his or her natural erotic and emotional interest. Even Freud naturalizes, all the more effectively for seeming to problematize, the logic by which gender comes to organize the visual field. Seeing is believing, and the evidence of sight issues in the commonsensical notion that "a human being is either a man or a woman." Freud problematizes the commonsensical by citing "cases in which the sexual characters are obscured, and in which it is consequently difficult to determine the sex" (141), but if it is not always easy to tell the boys from the girls, one has only to look harder, closer, better. To concede the occasional obscurity or ambiguity of the visual evidence of gender is not to challenge the grounding of gender difference in the self-evidence of perception itself. In life as in baseball, you can't tell the players without a program. The difference is that in life the program is insinuated within the body's "naturally given" imperatives.

The process by which "man first sees and recognizes himself in other men" is not, therefore, ideologically neutral. Bear in mind our suspicions about Paul. Should his gaze linger on Peter a moment longer than is strictly necessary—necessary, that is, to return to him an image of his own masculine intelligibility—our worst fears would be confirmed. The overly long or loving deployment of the gaze repositions the subject-who-looks as the object-who-is-known; caught looking, Paul is exposed as the pervert we always suspected him to be. But exactly how was he caught? Who was looking at Paul looking at Peter? And to what purpose? Because all gazes are potentially suspect—nothing is more thoroughly (self-)policed in our culture than the circulation of vision among men—prudence dictates an extension of the decorum of the public urinal to the public realm in general. Peter establishes his identity as a man by pretending not to look, by affecting not to compare. It is a non-man who will best return to Peter an image of his own masculine intelligibility.

Peter thus directs his gaze toward a woman, if only to reassure himself that there is nothing-much-to-see. Women want what they are in want of. The visual (non)evidence of the female body—the ideological construction of femininity as absence or castration—wholly defines the trajectory of normative desire. Gendered subjectivity comes to be experienced as the self-evident, irrefutable logic of perception itself, and "free" people, each pursuing his or her own erotic interests, contract to a relation of domination and servitude that is received as the logic of desire itself. It is, therefore, entirely possible, Žižek notwithstanding, to say that it is with men and women as it is with commodities. Heterosexuality is a social relation between people that constructs the very categories of subjectivity, the gendered individuals, that it alleges precede and subtend it. There are only differences without positive terms. The heterosexual mystification consists in positing gender identity as an innate property of persons rather than as a social relation, a thoroughly contingent structure of domination and servitude, between people.

The musclehead suffers from no such mystification. Recall, in this context, Schwarzenegger watching himself being watched by others. Desire positions the subject; it does not proceed from the nature of subjectivity itself; vision is eroticized, or, as Freud puts it, "the eye corresponds to an erotogenic zone" (169); the visual self-evidence of the erogenous zones does not itself dictate the logic of desire. Freud holds that the ego "is first and foremost a bodily ego"; the musclehead says always and forever.[45] The mirror stage translates an impossible image of the body's coherence and integrity into an ego-ideal. Misrecognition before the mirror is nothing but a losing sight of the specific materialities of the body, its imperfect organization and always threatened coherence, in favor of a vision of psychic mastery that proleptically defines the subject's relation to the world: "the morphological scheme established through the mirror stage constitutes precisely that reserve of *morphe* from which the contours of objects are produced; both objects and others come to appear only through the mediating grid of this projected or imaginary morphology."[46] Again, it's not just a stage: the presymbolic, pre-ideological source of secondary identifications, which include the explicitly ideological work of libidinal normalization, structures desire as phallic narcissism. Lacan speaks of the phallic erection of the subject. The first-person pronoun, the "I" that is itself "an orthographic erection," corresponds to "the statue in which man projects himself."[47] But the musclehead refuses the compensations of—the fool's bargain that is—phallic subjectivity. There is no misrecognition before the mirror, no losing sight of the body's burden of bulk and weight; if this or that "thing has to be built a little longer" (excluding, once again, the obvious), bigger it will be. Normative man becomes "Statue Man," as Mikkel Borch-Jacobsen terms him, through a stiffening or hardening of the ego.[48] Perverse man—and the bodybuilder is always a practicing pervert, whatever his "sexual orientation" happens to be—becomes Statue Man through a mad transformation of the flesh. The statue in which normative man projects himself stands guard on the border between self and other. Perverse man sculpts a body to meet the bodies that he can therefore meet.

Camille Paglia on political correctness:

What do I think started the reaction against "p.c."? I'm not sure what began this. I'm very superstitious. I just feel that something went full circle. It's like a Zeitgeist. The moment that we went from the Eighties to the Nineties, you know, the period of greed and materialism, the Gilded Age of Wall Street. Was it Malcolm Forbes who died on New Year's Eve? There was the fall of Trump, there was the fall of Leona Helmsley, and suddenly . . .[1]

Paglia's response is loony—Forbes, Trump, and Helmsley as the last bulwark of a crumbling liberal orthodoxy?—but she is not entirely to blame: the question is badly formulated. Nothing distinguishes political correctness from the reaction against it; on the contrary, p.c. has always existed, at least for gay men and women, only in the reaction to it or in the reactionary use of it. The "very superstitious" will note that Camille Paglia's initials are P.C. backwards, which cannot be unmeaningful: the lived politics of p.c. is an exact reversal of its P.R. Paglia's strategy is typical: invoke the hegemony of the new thought police and you have already eluded its grasp:

The abuse of language has got to stop. Throwing around words like racist *and* homophobic *and so on. Now,* homophobic *has a specific psychological meaning. It means someone who's obsessed with homosexuality, so that you go out and maybe kill or maim someone who is homosexual because of your own inner fear that you may be having homosexual impulses. It's a true phobia. We cannot allow the word* homophobic *to be constantly used for someone who says, "I don't like gay people" or "I think homosexuality is immoral, according to the Bible." We cannot be misusing this word. We can't condemn as* bigotry *everything that we don't agree with. Words like* bigotry *have got to go. Or you don't get enough money for AIDS: "Genocide!" When you use words like this—this is what they were shouting up at Kennebunkport when Bush was on vacation on Labor Day—"Genocide!" Now what does this do? I mean, you totally destroy the true meaning of genocide as it was authentically embodied under Hitler. (275–76)*

The charge of homophobia can be leveled only on the evidence of a gay limb or life, and only when motivated by a legally recognized and sanctioned defense: homosexual panic.[2] Everything shy of bashing belongs to the marketplace of ideas, which Paglia, good libertarian that she is, defends against proto-fascists of two varieties: gay activists (anyone who would disturb a presidential vacation, and on Labor Day no less, is clearly capable of anything) and p.c. academics (only the new thought police would refuse "I think homosexuality is immoral, according to the Bible" the intellectual consideration it deserves). The abuse of language must stop—remember when all those sad old queens first insisted on calling themselves "gay"?—in order for the abuse of perverts to proceed apace. The overtly homophobic ("I don't like gay people") does not qualify as such. It follows that the benign neglect of two or three U.S. administrations does not qualify as "genocide as it was authentically embodied under Hitler."

Paglia is not always so eager, however, to delimit the semantic and historical scope of her terminology:

There were anonymous posters put up recently all over New York, with Jodie Foster's picture: "Absolutely Queer." Absolutely queer? *I thought we got rid of absolutes. . . . Now we've got* gay *people talking about what is* absolute? *This is fascism! This is fascism! (276)*

Gay charges of genocide debase the true meaning of the term; gay activism itself, however, is "authentically" fascist. But "what does this do," as Paglia herself asks, other than attempt to embarrass gay activism into the silence that equals death? "Never again," but nothing in the injunction requires—indeed, everything argues against—the strategic deployment of the Holocaust, the Unthinkable, in order to foreclose the conditions under which genocide can be thought.

Now I too have certain reservations about the rhetoric of gay activism—hate is a family value, *the* family value; the best possible reason for joining the military is to get a date—but the charge of absolutism is not among them. And consider the illogic of Paglia's outrage: outing is the violation of a nonexistent right. *Bowers v. Hardwick* (1986) is conceptually incoherent, but unequivocal: the constitutional guarantee of the right to privacy does not extend to consensual acts of homosexual sodomy. (This is not to suggest that gay activism should direct itself toward a discourse of rights, least of all the right to privacy. A simple reversal of *Bowers v. Hardwick*, like the Clinton "compromise" on the issue of gays and lesbians in the military, would only legislate the closet, the parody form of bourgeois privacy.) Curiously, however, it is not the blanket refusal of a constitutional right, but the local violation of a nonexistent right, that routinely provokes liberal indignation. Randy Shilts speaks of Michelangelo Signorile, the man who posthumously outed Malcolm Forbes, as a "lavender fascist,"[3] and gay liberals routinely dismiss outing as a way of enforcing ideological conformity along illiberal lines. Like Paglia, Shilts translates victims of the death camps into their architects; like Paglia, the liberal critique of outing confuses solidarity, even in the midst of a pandemic, with the illiberal conformity demanded by heterosexism. No matter that gay men and women knew something of the "true meaning of genocide as it was authentically embodied under Hitler." There is no truth deeper than the psychosexual, and the psychosexual guarantees the political innocence of the heteronormative.

It is for this reason (or so I am pleased to imagine) that the pink triangle, perhaps the most conspicuous symbol of contemporary gay activism, inverts its Nazi prototype: today, the sexual politics of the Third Reich are received through a glass inversely.[4] A blithely counterfactual understanding of the sexual politics of fascism protects the regime of compulsory heterosexuality from the knowledge of its own genocidal past; in turn, the restriction of the "true meaning" of genocide to its "authentic" embodiment under Hitler shields heterosexuality from the knowledge of its own genocidal present. True, there are those who worry the erotic "fascination" that fascism continues to exert. Susan Sontag, for example:

Much of the imagery of far-out sex has been placed under the image of Nazism. Boots, leather chains, Iron Crosses on gleaming torsos, swastikas, along with meat hooks and heavy motorcycles, have become the secret and most lucrative paraphernalia of eroticism.

In the sex shops, the baths, the leather bars, the brothels, people are dragging out their gear. But why? Why has Nazi Germany, which was a sexually repressive society, become erotic? How could a regime which persecuted homosexuals become a gay turn-on?[5]

To answer a question that invites no answer: the imagery of kinky sex is placed under the sign of Nazism the better to mystify the banality—I mean the hetero-normativity—of our century's defining instance of evil. Fascism is not as erotically "fascinating" as Sontag might wish, although by worrying (and thus positing) its thoroughly deviant appeal, she need never acknowledge its continuity with other, less safely exoticized organizations of sexuality. Cock- or wedding-ring: when the former enjoys pride of place in the catalogue of fascist sexual paraphernalia, it merely titillates; when the latter is given its due prominence, it troubles.

And trouble it should: fascism understood itself as laboring in the cause of compulsory, state-sponsored heterosexuality, and my own argument is content to take it at its word. A thesis so seemingly modest in its ambitions obviously lacks the counterintuitive glamour of the position it struggles against, but it is a glamour that fascism itself renders suspect. Hitler, for one, routinely figured political apostasy as sexual deviancy, and any conflation of the politically "other" with the sexually perverse necessarily recalls, if not rehearses, the terms of a Nazi hermeneutic. Paglia seeks to preserve the integrity of the "authentically" fascist. The ubiquitous assumption that fascism was somehow a gay atrocity does precisely that.

The question Paglia asks of the shenanigans at Kennebunkport—"Now what does this do?"—is a good one. What does her selective commitment to the jargon of authenticity do? Why the resistance, which is by no means unique to her, to thinking power without the king, genocide without the Führer? Sedgwick argues that the question "what to do?" when faced with systematic oppression admits of no categorical response:

For someone to have an unmystified, angry view of large and genuinely systematic oppressions does not intrinsically or necessarily enjoin on that person any specific train of epistemological or narrative consequences. To know that the origin or spread of HIV realistically might have resulted from a state-assisted conspiracy—such knowledge is, it turns out, separable from the question of whether the energies of a given AIDS activist intellectual or group might be best used in the tracing and exposure of such a possible plot. They might, but then again, they might not. Though ethically very fraught, the choice is not self-evident; whether or not to undertake this highly compelling tracing-and-exposure project represents a strategic and local decision, not necessarily a categorical imperative.[6]

143

But if there is no categorical imperative to engage in the highly compelling project of trace-and-expose, there is a cultural one, especially in the context of a pandemic that continues to be construed in nineteenth-century, novelistic terms. Sedgwick begins by positing an "unmystified" subject, an individual already in possession of an "angry and large view of genuinely systematic oppressions," but who is not therefore or thereafter obliged to engage in a narrative search for origins. This seems to me, however, too optimistic by half. The cultural imperative to think in narrative terms, to engage in the project of trace-and-expose—witness the proliferation of conspiracy theories in recent years—is designed to guard against precisely what Sedgewick assumes: a demystified recognition of "genuinely *systematic* oppressions." Narrative typically figures structural injustice as individual villainy—recall Gaeten Dugas from *And the Band Played On*—and narrative conventions continue to delimit the scope of the politically thinkable. Political effects are acknowledged as such only if they can be traced to an initiating political agent. Genocide must be thought with the Führer or not at all.

The Freudian "hermeneutic of suspicion" obviously promotes the paranoid project of trace-and-expose, and for Freud, paranoia and homosexuality are like love and marriage: you can't have one without the other. Sedgwick argues that we can and should. At the very least, she contends, once-powerful narratives of demystification generated by gay paranoia are in danger of outliving their historical usefulness. "The liberal subject" went the way of disco. There is thus little purpose in continuing to expose the hidden violence of its genealogy:

Writing in 1988—that is, after two full terms of Reaganism in the United States—D. A. Miller proposes to follow Foucault in demystifying "the intensive and continuous 'pastoral' care that liberal society proposes to take of each and every one of its charges." As if! I'm a lot less worried about being pathologized by my shrink than about my vanishing mental health coverage—and that's given the great good luck of having health insurance at all. Since the beginning of the tax revolt, the government of the United States—and, increasingly, those of other so-called liberal democracies—has been positively rushing to divest itself of answerability for care to its charges (cf. "entitlement programs")—with no other institutions proposing to fill in the gap. (19)

Point well taken: the liberal-democratic state is considerably less liberal than the academic critique of it would suggest, but even the illiberal liberal state maintains a certain investment in "pastoral care." As does Sedgwick herself: her desire to "therapize" gays out of their paranoia is, to my mind, a particularly worrisome instance of it. (Again, I find myself in the uncomfortable position of disagreeing with a critic whom I greatly admire. At the very least, we owe to Sedgwick the clearest formulation of the issue at stake: the future of gay politics and the politics of paranoia may be functionally indistinguishable.) Sedgwick champions "reparative criticism," which she defines as a capacity for surprise, in opposition to the old paranoid project, which endlessly anticipates, and thus guarantees, the return of the same:

> To recognize in paranoia a distinctly rigid relation to temporality, at once anticipatory and retroactive, averse above all to surprise, is also to glimpse the lineaments of other possibilities. . . . [T]o read from a reparative position is to surrender the knowing, anxious paranoid determination that no horror, however apparently unthinkable, shall ever come to the reader as new: to a reparatively positioned reader, it can seem realistic and necessary to experience surprise. . . . Hope, often a fracturing, even a traumatic thing to experience, is among the energies by which the reparatively positioned reader tries to organize the fragments and part-objects she encounters or creates. Because she has room to realize that the future may be different from the present, it is also possible for her to entertain such profoundly painful, profoundly relieving, ethically crucial possibilities as that the past, in turn, could have happened differently from the way it actually did. (24–25)

But apparently even nonreparative critics (among whom I number myself) possess a capacity for surprise, for I find all this highly surprising. Granted, there is little that is new in the characterization of homosexuality (paranoid or otherwise) as the dispensation of the same, which is precisely what surprises. The return, albeit in different drag, of this all too familiar thematization of homosexuality as no-difference—especially in so distinguished and gay-affirmative a critic—suggests that a distinctly rigid relation to temporality or an aversion to difference is not exclusive to gay paranoia. In any case, we have every reason to remain paranoid *about* paranoia, or about still-powerful cultural narratives of trace-and-expose, particularly of the Freudian variety, which can expose only one thing. (It is, after all, the Freudian reading of fascism that is intent on ferreting out the hidden or repressed homosexual.) Yes, the past could have happened differently from the way it actually did, but it didn't, and all indications point to more of the same. The Nazis were neither the first nor the last to pursue a universal "cure" for homosexuality, and gay paranoia will seem anachronistic only when our culture's obsession with the etiology of perversion, which is always the dream of its prevention or cure, can be dismissed as the same.

i. To Lose Both Parents

Paglia's anxieties are needless: neither the academy nor the culture at large is in any danger of forgetting the connection between homosexuality and the "authentically" fascist. Consider, for example, the ease with which Scott Lively, the onetime membership director of the pro-family, antigay Oregon Citizens Alliance, intuits the connection:

I had known for a long time that it is axiomatic that when name-calling (as opposed to reasonable debate) happens, the names one calls others usually reflect the things one dislikes about oneself. I think it occurred to me that there was something awfully overstated about the Nazi-labelling campaign [by "homosexualist" opponents of the Oregon Citizens Alliance], even before I received a set of carefully-documented notes on prominent homosexuals in the Nazi Party.[7]

It takes one to know one, and for Lively as for Paglia, gay charges of fascism are easily refigured as the fascism of gayness or the gayness of fascism. To revivify the sexual politics of the Third Reich—and the Oregon Citizens Alliance can only envy Hitler his early triumphs, the banning of all pornography and homosexual rights movements—one has only to allude to the alleged homosexuality of much of the Nazi elite. Access to the documentary evidence—which assumes, erroneously, that "the question of homosexuality" admits of empirical verification or resolution—merely confirms a knowledge that Lively, like our culture at large, "always already" intuits.

Homophobia makes for stranger bedfellows than even the sexuality it deplores, and there are perhaps none stranger than Scott Lively and Julia Kristeva, the U.S. religious Right and high French feminism. But bedfellows they are, and Kristeva can hardly be accused of any "perverse denials of Biblical teaching":

And we know the role that the pervert—invincibly believing in the maternal phallus, obstinately refusing the existence of the other sex—has been able to play in anti-semitism and the totalitarian movements that embrace it. Let us remember the fascist or socialist homosexual community (and all homosexual communities for whom there is no "other race"), inevitably flanked by a community of Amazons who have forgotten the war of the sexes and identify with the paternal word and its serpent. The feminist movements are equally capable of such perverse denials of Biblical teaching.[8]

On the contrary: let us remember the dreary sameness with which the discourse of difference is now advanced, and the social-fascist heterosexual community (and all heterosexual communities for whom there is no other way of thinking otherness) whose murderous agenda it serves. Even etymologically, heterosexuality construes itself as the dispensation of difference, and here the ritual invocation of the "other race"—in effect, the erasure of the difference between the categories of sexuality and race—merely serves as a p.c. alibi for heterosexism as usual. (A strategy not lost on the U.S. Right. As the congressional debate on the issue of gays in the military evinced, the belated and selective championing of the cause of racial minorities easily mystifies a homophobic agenda.) Kristeva departs from Lively only in that she feels no need to maintain even the pretense of "reasonable argument." Lively's book, *The Pink Swastika: Homosexuality in the Nazi Party*, is replete with elaborate notes and bibliography. Kristeva merely appends a p.c. alibi to what everyone already knows ("And we know the role that the pervert . . ."), but which can thereafter be known with an even better political conscience.

Early critics of political correctness feared that it might restrict the scope of homophobic utterance. *Newsweek*, December 1990, sounded the alarm: Is an intellectual regime that (God forbid) requires students "to refrain from insulting homosexuals" the "New Enlightenment or the New McCarythism"? But in practice, political correctness never demanded anything quite so proto-fascist as the extension of basic civility to gays and lesbians. Far from restricting the scope of homophobic utterance, the New Enlightenment has afforded it a new impunity. Garden-variety homophobia always risks calling down upon itself the "specific psychological meaning of the term." To call a gay man a "cocksucker," for example, is unlikely to tell him anything he doesn't already know. It potentially reveals a great deal, however, about the individual who hurls the epithet. Hence, the strategic importance of a p.c. alibi: invoke it and you are spared the psychology. "I distrust male homosexuals": the truncated form of Gallop's statement is easily legible as bad repression. "I distrust male homosexuals because they choose men over women just as do our social and political institutions": the p.c. alibi transforms bad repression into good feminism. It is homosexuals, not homophobes, who have reason to fear the New Enlightenment.

Sedgwick cautions against the "currently respectable homophobic feminist-theory fantasy" that construes Nazism in the image of a band of homosexual brothers.[9] The point bears emphasizing, but the fantasy is neither new nor exclusively feminist. Certainly Lively is innocent of any feminist imaginings, yet his understanding of the sexual politics of Nazism is functionally indistinguishable from Kristeva's. True, the feminist version of the fantasy is now the most intellectually respectable, but here feminism merely rehearses a patriarchal tradition it alleges to critique. Janine Chasseguet-Smirgel, for example, advances the unremarkable thesis that

it is possible to conceive of reality as being made up of differences. Rather than to speak of the differences between the sexes and the generations as representing the only bedrock of reality, it would be more appropriate to think of reality as being entirely the result of differences.[10]

It is apparently impossible, however, to conceive of a refusal of difference or a failure to differentiate as other than homosexual. Chasseguet-Smirgel traces the psychology of fascism to the male pervert's lack of paternal identification, to anything that would check his desire to enter and plunder the maternal body. Fascism is thus a world of faggots without fathers.[11] Klaus Theweleit traces the psychology of fascism to the male pervert's lack of maternal identification, to his need to purge himself of the feminine qualities of warmth and sensuality. Fascism is thus a world of faggots without mothers.[12] To lose both parents, as Lady Bracknell observes, begins to look like carelessness, but in the case of the fascist pervert, it is wildly overdetermined. A fascism that is without mothers and/or fathers is a fascism for which neither bourgeois familialism nor heterosexual patriarchy bears any substantial responsibility, even as a revivified heterosexuality, a more effective interpellation into family values, remains the only effective guard against it.

Homosexuality is, then, fascism degree zero, the point at which ostensibly opposed readings of the politically monstrous forge common ground. Theweleit, for instance, explicitly defines his project against the work of Adorno, Horkheimer, and company, but only to extend, all the more effectively for seeming to critique, the psychologism into which Critical Theory degenerated. Adorno insisted that fascism is a persistent threat rather than a temporary aberration; Reich located that threat in the "sex-economic" system, as he termed it, of the bourgeois settlement.[13] Critical Theory promised an amalgamation of Freud, particularly the Freud of *Group Psychology and the Analysis of the Ego*, and Marx. At times, however, it issued in little more than an exculpatory and ahistorical psychologism:

In Oxford two sorts of students are distinguished, the tough guys and the intellectuals; the latter through this contrast alone, are almost automatically equated with the effeminate. There is much reason to believe that the ruling stratum, on its way to dictatorship, becomes polarized between these two extremes. Such disintegration is the secret of its integration, the joy of being united in the lack of joy. In the end the tough guys are the truly

effeminate ones, who need their victims in order not to admit that they are like them. To-
talitarianism and homosexuality belong together.[14]

Psychoanalytic readings of fascism derived from *Group Psychology* tend to emphasize identification with and idealization of paternal authority ("the tough guy"),
and hence the centrality of the leader to reactionary movements. Theweleit, by
contrast, focuses on the individual fascist's (or proto-fascist's) need to maintain
bodily cohesion, the better to protect against the threat of fusion or fragmentation
("the tough guy" battling the sissy within). But whatever the pathology fascism
happens to evince, homosexuality fits the bill. Thus, some 339 pages into the second volume of *Male Fantasies*, Theweleit broaches what he takes to be the deep
mystery at the heart of National Socialism: "We are now in a position to establish
why the fascists ultimately maintained the prohibition on homosexuality."[15] But
what Theweleit is pleased to term a mystery is little more than his (and our culture's) own mystification. Why, after all, wouldn't a regime committed to compulsory heterosexuality be given to the legal persecution and harassment of gays?
That is, the question is not why a regime that was de facto homosexual nevertheless maintained the de jure "prohibition" (to rehearse Theweleit's obscene euphemism) against it. Rather, the mystery is how our culture always finds itself in a position to think totalitarianism and homosexuality went together, go together, belong together.

And not our culture only: homosexuality is the essence of whatever sociopo-
litical order one happens to deem "other." In its insurgent phase, for example, Soviet communism was generally received as sexually progressive, and much tends
to be made of the fact that the Bolsheviks abolished czarist antihomosexual laws
some two months after storming the Winter Palace. But all czarist laws were abolished, and to assume that homosexuality was therefore legalized is to assume that
rape and murder were as well. (The logic of which Lively, for one, would readily
accept: legalize homosexuality and can rape and murder be far behind?) At best,
homosexuals were but the incidental beneficiaries of a generalized effacement of
all remnants of the *ancien régime;* more often than not, the extrajuridical repression of the 1920s was no less brutal for being without benefit of law.[16] In 1933 article 154a, which prescribed five years of hard labor for sex between men, appeared in the new Soviet penal code, thereby codifying the de facto repression of
the previous decade. (Stalin was no more adept at imagining what women did in
bed than the proverbial Queen Victoria.) *Pravda* heralded the new law as a "triumph of proletariat humanitarianism," the redeemed counterpart to the fascist

"legalization of homosexuality."[17] The Stalinist experiment in compulsory heterosexuality justified itself negatively against the example of fascism, even as the fascist "legalization of homosexuality" was assuming the most bizarrely counterintuitive of forms. Hitler was appointed chancellor on January 30, 1933; on February 23 of the same year, he banned pornography and all homosexual rights groups. (Another connection not lost on U.S. legislators, who routinely invoke antiporn laws in order to prohibit government funding of "sexually explicit"—that is, meaningful, useful—AIDS education material.) The murder of Roehm and the purging of the SA of homosexuals, real or imagined, occurred on June 28, 1934. In October of the same year, a special team to combat homosexuality and abortion was established within the criminal police force and the first wave of civilian arrests soon followed. Such was the fascist "legalization of homosexuality" against which the Stalinist experiment in compulsory heterosexuality justified itself.

All this will be readily admitted: the nonopposition between the fascist-dictatorial and the communist-dictatorial state is a central article of liberal faith; indeed, liberalism is only too eager to position itself between analogous totalitarianisms of the Right and the Left. Consider the blithe self-assurance of Churchill's characterization of the liberal settlement: "Democracy is the worst of all possible systems. The problem is that no other system is better." Apparently one has only to demonize as totalitarian any possible alternative to the worst of all possible systems in order to recuperate it as the best. From the perspective of all things sexual, however, the antithesis between the liberal-democratic state and totalitarianisms of the Right and Left is precarious at best. Himmler considered homosexuality a bourgeois vice, an "error of degenerate individualism."[18] The moral decadence of the Weimar Republic had issued in a virtual epidemic of perversion (Himmler estimated that fully 25 percent of the German population was tainted); the moral rejuvenation promised by the Third Reich would eradicate it. Yet even the laws that sent homosexuals to the camps—moral rejuvenation at its most efficient— did not originate with Himmler, and they long survived his demise (of which more presently). In his public directive to Roehm's successor as SA chief of staff, Hitler spoke of the need to ban all pornography and homophile organizations "in order not to offend the sensibilities of the people." Precisely the same justification, even the same phrasing, informed antigay legislation in both Wilheminian and Weimar Germany.[19] The fascist experiment in compulsory, state-sponsored heterosexuality, like the Stalinist, might have claimed any number of "liberal" precedents and analogues. The sexual politics of "the worst of all possible systems" are not transformed through comparison with the even-worse.

150

Today, moreover, the cry "This is fascism! This is fascism!" has an embarrassing array of possible referents, although the Gran Fury poster of Jodie Foster (*pace* Camille Paglia) is not among them. "I thought we got rid of absolutes," Paglia contends, but the Freudianism to which she pays homage suggests otherwise: "Absolutely Queer" plays against (among other things) the first category of aberration, "absolute inversion," specified in *Three Essays on the Theory of Sexuality*. The allusion is apparently lost on Paglia, yet her position remains broadly, if crudely, Freudian. Not that this should surprise: some version of Freudianism, however vulgarized, invariably informs the conflation of male homosexuality and the "authentically fascist." By the same token, however, some version of Freudianism, albeit not acknowledged as such, invariably informs the Nazi conflation of male homosexuality and political apostasy. We no longer speak of the fascist "legalization of homosexuality," but only because *Pravda*'s homophobic disinformation has given way to Theweleit's homophobic speculation. The former is sublimely indifferent to the documentable evidence. The latter finds sustenance in making that evidence betray its "latent" content.

ii. There Are No Bad Heterosexuals

Absolute inverts fail absolutely: "Persons of the opposite sex are never the object of their sexual desire, but leave them cold, or even arouse sexual aversion in them. As a consequence of this aversion, they are incapable, if they are men, of carrying out the sexual act."[20] Curiously, however, Freud admits of no absolute successes, no unimpeachable heterosexuals: "By studying sexual excitations other than those that are manifestly displayed, it [psychoanalysis] has found that all human beings are capable of making a homosexual object-choice and have in fact made one in their unconscious" (145 n. 1). Why the asymmetry? Why do some of us fail so spectacularly while others succeed only precariously?

Sedgwick maintains that homosexuality—and hence sexuality as such—is a fundamentally incoherent concept:

Most moderately to well-educated Western people in this century seem to share a similar understanding of homosexual definition, independent of whether they themselves are gay or straight, homophobic or antihomophobic. That understanding is close to what Proust's probably was, what for that matter mine is and probably yours. That is to say, it is organized around a radical and irreducible incoherence. It holds the minoritizing view that there is a distinct population of persons who "really are" gay; at

151

the same time, it holds the universalizing views that sexual desire is an unpredictably powerful solvent of stable identities; that apparently heterosexual persons and object choices are strongly marked by same-sex influences and desires, and vice versa for apparently homosexual ones.[21]

True enough, although the incoherence *between* universalizing and minoritizing definitions is already anticipated by an incoherence (or at least asymmetry) *within* the universalizing premise. All heterosexuals are capable of making a homosexual object choice and have in fact already made one in their unconscious. Absolute inverts do not, however, return the favor. All heterosexual behavior is potentially explicable as, attributable to, latent homosexual desire. Latent heterosexuality, outside the psychoanalytic promise of cure or the religious promise of conversion, is a culturally unintelligible term. The universalizing premise isn't quite: "the unpredictably powerful solvent of sexual identities" is powerless before the minoritizing presence—already, as it were, within the universalizing premise—of absolute inverts.

Sedgwick's point is broadly compelling: universalizing and minoritizing premises tend to cohabit uneasily within modern sexual definition. There is, however, a fairly strict division of labor between the two, and it is the universalizing premise that commands the theoretical field. The work of Karl Ulrichs and Magnus Hirschfield, leading proponents of minoritizing, "third sex" understandings of homosexual definition, now belongs to the history of sexology. Freudianism, by contrast, has come to infiltrate virtually every aspect of Western life. The historic success of psychoanalysis could not easily have been predicted—Freud himself thought that there were well-nigh insurmountable obstacles to any general acceptance of his work—and if its good fortune no longer strikes us as unlikely, it is only because we are now so thoroughly naturalized in its conventions. But unlikely it is. To put the matter bluntly: genocidal ambitions, then as now, logically presuppose a minoritizing view of the expendable population, and homosexuality, then as now, is routinely thought under the genocidal rubric of prevention, cure, or eradication.

Consider, however, yet another Freudian asymmetry:

In my experience anyone who is in any way, whether socially or ethically, abnormal mentally is invariably abnormal also in his sexual life. But many people are abnormal in their sexual life who in every other respect approximate to the average, and have, along with the rest, passed through the process of human cultural development, in which sexuality remains the weak spot. (149)

There are, to be sure, some good homosexuals, although the "rarest and most perfect" among them—Freud's primary example is Leonardo—effectively sublimate their sexuality out of existence.[22] By definition, however, there can be no bad heterosexuals. Examine the latent "sexual excitations" and proclivities of the socially or ethically abnormal and you invariably find a repressed or practicing pervert. Ernest Hemingway once accused Gertrude Stein of a menopausal reversal of Freud's sexual chauvinism:

> Last time I saw her she told me she had heard an incident, some fag story which proved me conclusively to be very queer indeed. I said You knew me for four or five years and you believe that? . . . I never cared a damn about what she did in or out of bed and I liked her very damned much and she liked me. But when the menopause hit her she got awfully damned patriotic about sex. The first stage was that nobody was any good that wasn't that way. The second was that anybody that was that way was good. The third was that anybody that was any good must be that way. Patriotism is a hell of a vice.[23]

But if it is indeed a vice to claim a virtue based on what you do (or don't do) in bed, it is the vice of the virtue that is heterosexuality. Freud's "patriotism" is less extreme than Stein's: anyone who is any good may or may not be "that way," but there is no ambiguity about the bad. The connection between social and sexual abnormality is causal, not casual, and homosexuality, not sexuality as such, remains the weak spot in the process of human cultural development. To his credit, Freud was committed to the repeal of paragraph 175 of the German legal code, the antisodomy statute, and his opposition to "separating off" homosexuals from the rest of humankind was clearly principled. Yet however admirable the motives, the refusal to ghettoize homosexuals psychoanalytically in no way prevented (or prevents) their incarceration and/or eradication politically. What Freud terms the "bedrock" of universal bisexuality enjoys no explanatory power whatsoever; far from destabilizing sexual identity, the universalizing premise merely holds in reserve the possibility of trotting out, when convenient or expedient, the charge of homosexuality, which is uniquely privileged with explanatory power. Hemingway is at least half right: sexual patriotism is a hell of a hetero vice.

Nazi antihomosexual laws, although directed against individuals who "really were" gay, also tended toward universalizing, psychologizing premises. Before 1935, the only punishable offense under paragraph 175 of the German penal code was sodomy. The introduction of paragraph 175A, however, expanded the category of punishable acts to include kissing and touching, and after 1936, when the rules governing the introduction of evidence into court were effectively abolished, sentencing depended less on the severity of the alleged act than on "the psychological type" to which the offender was said to belong:

The definitions of homosexuality [in the Third Reich] went far beyond the performance of sexual acts. Himmler built upon the ever-widening nineteenth-century definition of homosexuality, which had stressed the contrast between homosexuality and manliness, sickness and health, and thus extended the performance of a sexual act into a judgement upon all aspects of the homosexual's personality.[24]

The ever-widening nineteenth-century definition of homosexuality—the transition, however incomplete or equivocal, from a taxonomy of deeds to a discourse of psychological types—was to find its logical fulfillment in Freud. Not that the Third Reich embraced Freudianism. Himmler, the regime's leading arbiter of sexual orthodoxy, was relentlessly psychologizing in his approach to homosexuality, yet Nazism remained officially opposed to the emerging discipline of psychoanalysis, which it construed as a distinctly Jewish and/or homosexual aberration. The Berlin Psychoanalytic Institute (1920), the first of its kind in the world, had been in the vanguard of psychoanalytic activity. Hitler's rise to power, however, resulted in a crippling exodus of Jewish staff and students, and by 1936 the institute ceased to function as an independent entity. In 1938 the annexation of Austria sent Freud himself into exile and psychoanalysis was officially declared "un-German." Despite the hostility of the new regime, however, psychotherapy (if not psychoanalysis proper) flourished, even fattened, under the Third Reich.[25] The Jewish origins of the discipline may have proved troublesome, but ideological purity never blinded the party to the pragmatic uses to which the new science (or a properly vulgarized, Nazified version thereof) could be put. Franz Wirz, Hitler's chief administrator for university affairs, frankly acknowledged the intellectual opportunism of the regime: "We all know that the Wasserman reaction was discovered by a Jew. But no one in Germany would be so foolish as to no longer make use of this reaction."[26] And no fool they, psychotherapists sympathetic to the new order, or those simply intent on professional survival, established the German Institute for Psychological Research and Psychotherapy (1936) under the directorship of Matthias Heinrich Göring, a cousin to the prominent Nazi of the same name. The Göring Institute, as it came to be known, was the first such institute to receive public funding for the teaching, practice, and promulgation of psychotherapy. The new German psychotherapy was intellectually impoverished; as an institutional and professional entity, however, it enjoyed a hitherto unrivaled prestige.[27]

It was a prestige that extended to psychosexual explanation in general: the institutional fattening of psychotherapy under the Third Reich was but a specific manifestation of the full coming-into-being of a broader cultural logic that was to make (homo)sexuality the explanation for everything in need of explanation. Unlike Stalin, Hitler never accused individuals from his own party or ranks of explicitly political crimes against the state;[28] rather, political apostasy was figured as sexual deviancy. In the case of Roehm, the political threat, which may have included socialist agitation for a second revolution, and the sexual proclivity, which included sex with men, happened to correspond. More often than not, however, the two were yoked together by violence. In *The Order of the Day*, Thomas Mann confesses to the "private suspicion that the élan of the [German] march on Vienna had a secret spring: it was directed at the venerable Freud, the real and actual enemy, the philosopher and revealer of the neuroses, the great disillusioner."[29] It is my suspicion, however, that National Socialism was considerably less mystified on the subject of the politics of sexuality or the sexuality of politics than is our current understanding of it. The Nazi conflation of political apostasy and sexual deviancy reverberated with what Žižek terms "totalitarian laughter," cynical distance, irony.[30] That Roehm "really did" have sex with men is hardly irrelevant. By the same token, however, it is hardly the point. For a Nazi of any prominence to be denounced as homosexual was to be judged politically expendable, which is as good a definition of homosexuality as any. The charge had only to be feared, not believed.

Totalitarian laughter is not, of course, intended for everyone. Pastor Adolph Sellman, a member of the influential West German Morality League, a precursor of the Oregon Citizens Alliance, was doubtless earnest in his praise for Hitler's return to family values. "At a stroke," he rhapsodized, "things changed in Germany. All filth and trash vanished from the public domain."[31] What the good pastor apparently never heard was this:

I [Hitler] abominate prudishness and moral prying. . . . What has it to do with our struggle? These are the outworn notions of reactionary old women . . . who can only visualize national rejuvenation in terms of virtuous customs and austerity. "League of Virtue" and "Christian-German Table-Companions," "replacing the material loss of the nation with spiritual gains"—and all the rest of that tawdry patriotic mumbo-jumbo. Our uprising has nothing to do with bourgeois virtues.[32]

The West German Morality League reserved special praise for Hitler's antiporn and antigay laws—there is no easier way to capture the hearts and souls of the religious

Right—yet homosexuality was not primarily a moral category in the Third Reich. Again, Roehm's sexuality proved incompatible with national moral rejuvenation only when he proved a threat to Hitler's personal power. For the Nazis, the connection between political apostasy and sexual deviance was strategic; for us, it is ontological. Such is the precise measure of our distance from a Nazi hermeneutic. We have come to accept the truth value of a connection that fascism itself forges, in both senses of the word, with a murderous smile.

The manifest content of the sexual politics of the Third Reich is, and always was, perfectly clear. Nazism, to repeat a phrase that bears repeating, was a crime of compulsory, state-sponsored heterosexuality. As early as 1928, a party official responded to a questionnaire by Adolf Brand, a gay rights activist, as follows:

Those who are considering love between men or between women are our enemies. Anything that emasculates our people and that makes it fair game for our enemies we reject, because we know that life is a struggle and that it is insanity to believe that all human beings will one day embrace each other as brothers. . . . We reject all immorality, especially love between men, because it deprives us of our last chance to free our people from the chains of slavery which are keeping it fettered today.[33]

But if all this is clear enough, it also clearly protests too much: so virulent a homophobia inevitably betrays the latent perversion lurking beneath its surface. Nazism was ethically "abnormal"; it follows that its adherents were sexually "aberrant." Berlin's Sexual Research Institute was one of the first victims of official Nazi terror, and for reasons that might, at least at first, seem perfectly obvious. Its founder, Magnus Hirschfield, was a prominent Jew, leftist, and pervert. Nazism was manifestly opposed to all three, but again, manifest content can hardly account for the deep truth of the (homo)sexual. Hence, explanations of the type provided by Ludwig Lenz, a gynecologist who escaped the terror of May 6, 1933, with his life:

Why was it then, since we were completely non-party, that our purely scientific Institute was the first victim which fell to the new regime? . . . What explanation is there for the fact that the trades union buildings of the socialists, the communist clubs, and the synagogues were only destroyed at a much later date and never so thoroughly as our pacific Institute? Whence this hatred, and, what was even more strange, this haste and thoroughness?

The answer to this is simple and straightforward enough—we knew too much.

It would be against medical principles to provide a list of the Nazi leaders and their perversions. One thing, however, is certain—not ten percent of those men who, in 1933, took the fate of Germany into their hands were sexually normal.[34]

The statistics remain historically constant—"one in ten," as we now say—though the preponderance of hetero over homo is apparently reversible at will. When the regime of compulsory heterosexuality turns overtly genocidal, you can bet the farm that not one in ten is sexually normal. Lenz intends no irony. The simple and straightforward answer is the patently counterintuitive one: "the real and actual enemy" was not Jews, leftists, or perverts, but the repressed homosexuality of Nazism itself. Barbara Ehrenreich contends that "as a theory of fascism" the first volume of Theweleit's *Male Fantasies* "sets forth the jarring—and ultimately horrifying—proposition that the fascist is not doing 'something else,' but doing what he wants to do. . . . Theweleit insists that we see and not 'read' violence."[35] This seems to me exactly wrong: a theory of the psychosexual etiology of National Socialism that makes only passing mention of anti-Semitism necessarily understands the Holocaust, the murder of some six million Jews, as doing "something else," as directed against "something else."[36] Would, however, that Theweleit's thesis were as Ehrenreich has it. A fascist thug who is not engaged in displacement is not sexually "something other" than what he professes to be, what he is legally required to be. Crimes committed in the name of compulsory heterosexuality would thus be crimes of compulsory heterosexuality.

Sedgwick cautions against the hermeneutic violence that purports to know the sexual subject better than it knows itself:

The authority to describe and name . . . [anyone's] sexual desire is a terribly consequential seizure. In this century, in which sexuality has been made expressive of the essence of both identity and knowledge, it may represent the most intimate violence possible. . . . The safer proceeding would be to give as much credence as one finds it conceivable to give to self-reports of sexual difference—weighing one's credence, when it is necessary to weigh it at all, in favor of the less normative and therefore riskier, costlier self-reports.[37]

The ambition is admirable, but the recommended "proceeding" seems to me dubious. "Riskier" self-reports are routinely credited, even if they are no less risky for that: the statement "I'm gay" (at least if the speaker is male) is more likely to be met with "I always knew" than "I don't believe it." It is claims to normativity that characteristically strain credulity. Lively, for one, is unwilling to take the would-be heterosexual at their word. "Was Hitler a Homosexual?" (82) he asks (and in asking answers). Even in his own lifetime, Hitler's sexuality was subject to speculation, which is to say, his heterosexual credentials were less than impeccable. (He was, after all, a bachelor well into his thirties and beyond.) The psychological profile commissioned by the U.S. government during the war diagnosed repressed homosexuality, and what psychology divined physiology ultimately confirmed: the 1945 autopsy revealed a "sexual malformation," an undescended left testicle.[38] The physiology is in dispute, but not the poetics it bodies forth. A once popular ditty:

> Hitler has only got one ball
> Göring has two but they are small
> Himmler's are rather similar
> And Goebbels has no balls at all.

Clearly these were not real men at all. The standard biographies speak of Hitler's fascination with pornography and erotic art, an imagination excited by rape, prostitution, and syphilis; the more salacious among them rehearse the rumor that he turned tricks as a young man in Vienna. None of this is necessarily damning in itself and even sexual entrepreneurship is recuperable as "just a phase." Factor in the ethical abnormality, however, and the regime of compulsory heterosexuality need never acknowledge this thing of darkness as its own.

Evidence of Hitler's sexual indiscretions was said to be in the hands of Mussolini, but then *The Protocols of the Elders of Zion* was once said to be documentary evidence, and the de facto homosexuality of National Socialism hardly requires documentary support or documentable evidence. Documents do, of course, survive:

1. In order to keep the SS and Police clean of vermin with homosexual inclinations, the Führer has resolved by a decree of 15 November 1941 that a member of the SS or Police who commits sex offenses with another man or lets himself be abused for sex offenses shall be punished with death, *regardless of his age. In less serious cases penal servitude or imprisonment of not less than six months may be imposed.*
2. The Führer's decree is not being published, because that might give rise to misunderstandings.[39]

Himmler's confidential circular of November 1941, a redaction of the "Führer's Decree Relating to the Maintenance of Purity in the S.S. and Police," was not published for fear of acknowledging, especially in the wake of the purging of the SA, that the official instruments of the party were tainted by homosexual vermin. By his own 1937 accounting, Himmler had succeeded in ferreting out no more than one homosexual a month, a far less impressive record than his contemporary counterparts in the U.S. military.[40] But if the numbers proved disappointing, it wasn't for lack of trying. The intensity of Himmler's homophobia was exemplary, and the more intense the homophobia the more compelling the evidence of homosexual panic, and hence of latent homosexual desires: "Himmler's struggle over his sexuality as a young man is relevant—his effort at 'iron' self-control, his prudishness, and his extreme conventionality. Himmler seems to have feared his own sexuality."[41] If Hitler's heterosexual credentials were less than impeccable, Himmler's were more, which is to say, they too were less. "Homophobia has a specific psychological meaning. It means someone who's obsessed with homosexuality, so maybe you go out and maybe you kill or maim someone who is homosexual because of your own inner fears that you may be having homosexual impulses." Scratch a homophobe, find a homosexual.

A phobia is a sickness, and in a post-Kantian ethical system it is not possible—with at least one exception—to be both sick and blameworthy with respect to the same defect.[42] Hence, homophobia, like claustrophobia or agoraphobia, is construed as a regrettable, rather than a legally actionable or morally reprehensible, disorder. The term "heterosexism," however, is isomorphic with "racism," and "racial panic," unlike its psychosexual analogue, is not a legally sanctioned defense. (Had the Nuremberg trials recognized the murder of gays as a crime, homosexual panic, not heterosexism, would doubtless have been the defense.) Universalizing understandings of homosexuality are psychologizing, and the psychology of deviance is derived from the template of male/female difference. Minoritizing understandings, by contrast, tend to replicate models of racial difference.[43] In matters sexual, the Third Reich favored universalizing, psychologizing premises; in matters racial, it was officially committed to a minoritizing, biologizing view. Robert Jay Lifton terms Nazism a "biocracy," but here too a certain conceptual incoherence obtained.[44] When occasion required, biologism deferred to a radical constructivism. "I decide who is a Jew," Himmler is alleged to have boasted, and again, Himmler's definitional decisions (or speech acts) had only to be feared, not believed. Yet if neither race nor sexuality is reducible to the biological, the conceptual incoherence at the heart of modern sexual definition and the opportunity for mystification it affords remain unique. This is not, I hasten to add, to engage in the one-downmanship that makes for hierarchies of oppression. Rather, it is to suggest, following Foucault, why (homo)sexuality enjoys virtually unlimited explanatory powers.

Consider the various indignities that Jews and gays continue to suffer in the contemporary reception of the Third Reich. Hannah Arendt comes perilously close to suggesting that Jews somehow invited (or at least facilitated) the Holocaust, and Theweleit renders anti-Judaism and anti-Semitism more or less incidental to the rise of National Socialism. These are gross indignities. Yet alone among the victims of the Holocaust—and homosexuals are alone in never having been officially recognized as such—the men in pink triangles are refigured as its perpetrators. Žižek argues that ideology flourishes, rather than flounders, on the discrepancy between it and the "facts":

An ideology is really "holding us" only when we do not feel any opposition between it and reality—that is, when the ideology succeeds in determining the mode of our everyday experience of reality itself. How then would our poor German, if he were a good anti-Semite, react to this gap between the ideological figure of the Jew (schemer, wire-puller, exploiting our brave men and so on) and the common everyday experience of his good neighbour, Mr. Stern? His answer would be to turn this gap, this discrepancy itself, into an argument for anti-Semitism: "You see how dangerous they really are? It is difficult to recognize their real nature. They hide it behind the mask of everyday appearance—and it is exactly this hiding of one's real nature, this duplicity, that is a basic feature of Jewish nature." An ideology really succeeds when even the facts which at first sight contradict it start to function as arguments in its favor.[45]

There is a point beyond which, however, even the most ingenious of anti-Semites cannot negotiate the discrepancy between the "facts" and the ideology that holds him, and when the tension proves intolerable, the facts are jettisoned. Our good anti-Semite is thus reduced to the patently counter-factual gesture of Holocaust denial. There is no point, however, beyond which even the most plodding of homophobes cannot negotiate an analogous discrepancy. Lively, for example, readily concedes the historical reality of the Holocaust. It did in fact happen (despite, apparently, the best efforts of the Christian West), and a handful of gays and lesbians may even have found their way into the death camps. But facts that might be expected to trouble the ideology of compulsory heterosexuality—the liberal-democratic and the fascist-dictatorial state cohere in a shared sexual politics—merely serve as an argument for a more thoroughgoing commitment to it. Homosexuality and totalitarianism went together, go together; eradicate the former and the latter is no longer a threat. Arendt argues that the very concept of "factuality" presupposes the "continued existence" of the "nontotalitarian" world:

The decision regarding success and failure under totalitarian circumstances is very largely a matter of organized and terrorized public opinion. In a totally fictitious world [a totalitarian world], failures need not be recorded, admitted, and remembered. Factuality itself depends for its continued existence upon the existence of the nontotalitarian world.[46]

But the "nontotalitarian" reception of the sexual politics of the Third Reich suggests otherwise: the "facts" can always be made to offer up their latent—read: exculpatory—(homo)sexual content. In an erotic economy in which the only "absolute" is inversion, heterosexuality is necessarily regulative, not constitutive. Even for those who understand themselves as such, who know themselves as such, normativity remains a consummation devoutly to be wished. The Freudian construction of heterosexuality corresponds to, is underwritten by, literally nothing, with the crucial exception of ethical normality. Yet if psychoanalysis thus evacuates heterosexuality of its existential density and specificity—you can't prove that you are one by what you do or don't do in bed—it also provides it with its most effective line of defense: when ethical and sexual normativity are coextensive, there can be no bad heterosexuals. The knowledge that Lively considers "axiomatic" is crudely Freudian: projection motivates the "awfully overstated," the clearly overdetermined, "homosexualist" campaign of labeling homophobes Nazis. Lively never acknowledges his debt to the godless Freud, but the omission is less an act of intellectual dishonesty than it is testimony to the ubiquity of a mode of "knowingness" that, released from its disciplinary moorings, need never justify itself as such. Althusser maintains that ideology imposes "obviousnesses as obviousnesses."[47] Freudianism is perhaps unique in insinuating the counterintuitive as the axiomatic. The naive may think the "homosexualist" campaign of Nazi-labeling to be motivated by the manifest continuity between the agenda of the Oregon Citizens Alliance and the early triumphs of the Nazi Party. Those adept at negotiating the intricacies of psychosexual motivation—and in our culture, who isn't?—know better. Scratch a Nazi, find a faggot.

iii. Talk Grows of the Government Being Out to Get Blacks (Or, In Defense of Paranoia)

It has been some time since AIDS has been afforded the status of a crisis, much less a holocaust, and the heated diction of "genocide" and the like, once the staples of a certain activist discourse, now seems little more than anachronistic. The ease with which the "disease of gayness" has come to be normalized presupposes a

161

culture in which the lives of gay men and women continue to be construed as expendable. "It would be unjustifiable to assert," Freud cautions in *Three Essays on the Theory of Sexuality*, that recent inquiries into the organic determinants of homoeroticism will "put the theory of inversion on a new basis, and it would be hasty to expect them to offer a universal means of 'curing' homosexuality" (147 n. 1). But a dream deferred is not necessarily a dream abandoned—witness the recent inquiries into the hormonal determinants of homosexuality—and there is no lack of haste in Freud's own discourse, which moves from questions of etiology to "cure" with grim alacrity. The "final solution" to the problem of homosexuality is no less final for being thought under the gentlemanly decorum of "prevention," "conversion," or "cure."

The Nazis were not the first to dream of a universal means of curing homosexuality nor the last to plot its eradication. The laws that sent homosexuals to the camps, although sharpened under Hitler, did not originate with him, and they long survived his demise. Postwar Germany, reluctantly bowing to U.S. pressure, granted restitution to various categories of ex-inmates, Jews and politicals among them. Not so homosexuals. A gay man who had been sentenced to, say, eight years in prison and who had served five of those eight years in a camp still had to complete, after the so-called liberation, three years of his sentence.[48] Homosexuality remained both a criminal offense in postwar Germany and an insurmountable barrier to emigration to most other countries. (Hence, the paucity of firsthand accounts from gay ex-inmates. To speak one's perversion was to risk imprisonment and/or deportation.) As Richard Plant observes, for homosexuals, "the Third Reich did not fully end with its defeat."[49] Fascism was in fact an innovation, our century's only unique contribution to political philosophy.[50] Its sexual politics, however, was an exacerbated version of heterosexism as usual.

In the curiously neglected final chapter of the first volume of *The History of Sexuality*, Foucault argues that although genocide remains "the dream of modern powers," it is not genocide as it is "classically" or conventionally understood. The latter involves the "recent return of the ancient right to kill"; its symbol is the sword and it presupposes a modality of power that reveals itself in all its "murderous splendor." Genocide in its distinctly modern form, however, "is situated and exercised at the level of life, the species, the race, and the large-scale phenomena of the population."[51] Foucault does acknowledge the grimly obvious: "wars were never so bloody as they have been since the nineteenth century, and all things being equal, never before did regimes visit such holocausts on their own populations" (136–37). Yet however much this "formidable power of death" is still with us, it now presents itself as but the "counterpart of a power that exerts a positive influence on life, that endeavors to administer, optimize, and multiply it, subjecting it to precise controls and comprehensive regulations" (137). The "ancient right to *take* life or *let* live" is superseded by the modern "power to *foster* life or *disallow* it" (138):

Since the classical age the West has undergone a very profound transformation of these mechanisms of power. "Deduction" has tended to be no longer the major form of power but merely one element among others, working to incite, reinforce, control, monitor, optimize, and organize the forces under it: a power bent on generating forces, making them grow, and ordering them, rather than one dedicated to impeding them, making them submit, or destroying them. There has been a parallel shift in the right of death, or at least a tendency to align itself with the exigencies of a life-administering power and to define itself accordingly. This death that was based on the right of the sovereign is now manifested as simply the reverse of the social body to ensure, maintain, or develop its life. (136)

The power that refrains from overt destruction does not hesitate to exclude certain lives from "the realm of utility and value," to "disallow" them, in the complete form of Foucault's chillingly accurate phrase, even "to the point of death" (138). Systematic "disallowal" does not qualify as genocide as it was "authentically embodied under Hitler," and Paglia would doubtless dismiss Foucault's reconceptualization of the term as yet another perverse contamination of semantic integrity, yet another instance of gay resistance to the ideology of "authenticity." But what Paglia is pleased to term the "authentic" is itself patently strategic. The ethics of any use of the term "genocide" is best adjudicated by its efficacy—by the number of undead, by the lives unlost—and Paglia's insistence on the "authentic" meaning merely facilitates the perpetuation of genocide in different, less murderously obvious, modalities.

Paglia is not alone, of course, in her selective commitment to the jargon of authenticity. Nor are gays the only victims of it. "Talk Grows of the Government Being Out to Get Blacks," an October 29, 1990, *New York Times* survey, is equally intent on preserving "the true meaning of genocide as it was authentically embodied under Hitler." The *Times* is clearly unsympathetic to the talk—which focuses on the charge, among others, that "AIDS was invented by racist conspirators to kill blacks"—even as it entertains the possibility that racism, real or imagined, impinges on the cultural reception (although never the construction) of the pandemic. (Given the official 1990 statistics—12 percent of the nation's population accounted for 30 percent of its 500,000 AIDS cases—it could hardly do otherwise.)[52] The Tuskegee syphilis study, "in which the government withheld treatment from some 399 black men from 1932 to 1972 in order to observe the progress of the disease," is a disturbing precedent, and it is duly noted. Yet if Tuskegee provides compelling evidence of the government once having been out to get blacks through the administration of disease, it implicitly invalidates all the current talk, which cannot point to a specific government atrocity in order to substantiate its claims. And even if it could, the *Times* admits of only one "authentic" standard: "Dr. Poussaint said that the number of blacks who entertained the theory of AIDS as biological warfare was dismaying. 'What do they think?' he said, 'that there's a Nazi regime?'" But what does the good Dr. Poussaint think? That the liberal-democratic state has only to invoke the specter of its demonic other in order to forestall each and every critique of it? That genocide must be thought with the Führer or not at all?

The Third Reich was unique in first thinking genocide through eugenics— "only in Nazi Germany was sterilization a forerunner of mass murder"—and early German eugenicists envied the greater scope and freedom enjoyed by their U.S. and British counterparts.[53] In 1923 Fritz Lenz, a German physician who was later to become a leading ideologue of "racial hygiene," complained that Germany had nothing to rival the eugenics institutes in England and the United States, and nothing to equal the U.S. laws prohibiting marriage for the mentally defective or between people of different races. (At a time when the Weimar constitution prohibited "the infliction of bodily alterations on human beings," some twenty-five U.S. states had enacted laws allowing for the compulsory sterilization of the criminally insane and the genetically inferior.) The "next round in the thousand year fight for the Nordic race," Lenz predicted, "will probably be fought in America."[54] Germany soon surpassed the United States in the realization of its biomedical vision: in a three-year period, Nazi authorities sterilized some 220,000 people, almost ten times the number sterilized during the same period in the United States. But all was not lost. The *Journal of the American Medical Association* took comfort in noting that the rules of the game were specific to each country. Domestic considerations necessitated a "more gradual evolution of practice and principles" regarding sterilization—the liberal-democratic tortoise and fascist-dictatorial hare— rather than an outright repudiation of the Nazi agenda.[55] The history of Dr. Poussiant's own profession argues against him: it is entirely possible to pursue a Nazi biomedical vision within a liberal-democratic state. There are domestic precedents enough for thinking power without the king, genocide without the Führer.

The *Times* would have us think psychologically:

Until his brother became yet another black man to die of AIDS, Keith Brown never imagined that a disease so devastating would hit so close to home. Searching for an explanation, he found himself drawn to one his brother had long embraced but that Mr. Brown used to reject: that AIDS was invented by racist conspirators to kill blacks.

Given its genesis, who could begrudge Mr. Brown the extravagance of his opinions? But who, by the same token, need take them seriously? In an article in which nothing eludes the ideology of "human interest," even the force of the Tuskegee syphilis study is rendered psychological: "Mr. Brown said his parents recently told him that a distant relative was among the Tuskegee blacks who went untreated. 'When I heard that it blew my mind,' he said." What, then, does the *Times* see as "The Ramifications," as the final subheading of the article puts it, of all this psychologically self-destructive talk?

Simply this: government conspiracies are not killing blacks; conspiracy theories themselves are. Or, in the rather more circumspect locution of the *Times*: "While there is no precise way to measure the impact of conspiracy theories, many public health-care workers fear the discussion is inhibiting the fight against AIDS and drugs." Black paranoia is without any basis in fact, but it is not therefore inefficacious: "Talk of white plots may harm not only the physical health of black America but the spiritual health as well." Physical health, because conspiracy theories "make people wary of using condoms to avoid the disease, of early testing to detect it, and of using drugs to treat it." And spiritual health, because conspiracy theories provide yet another excuse for blacks not to assume responsibility for themselves, and as everyone knows, they are already much too adept at exploiting racism—that unhappy historical curiosity—in order to explain their contemporary lot. The talk must, therefore, cease. It is both insulting to whites—it flies in the face of our many pastoral efforts to safeguard the well-being of our colored brethren—and dangerous to blacks.

Conspiracy theories, like the devil himself, can assume almost limitless forms, but the *Times* is invested in promoting only one. Consider the three "rumors" that form the basis of the poll:

1. Some people say the Government deliberately singles out and investigates black elected officials in order to discredit them in a way it doesn't do with white officials.

2. Some people say the Government deliberately makes sure that drugs are easily available in poor black neighborhoods in order to harm black people.

3. Some people say the virus which causes AIDS was deliberately created in a laboratory in order to infect black people.

To what should come as no one's surprise, blacks chose "true" or "might possibly be true" ("almost certainly not true" was the only other permitted response; respondents were thus free to identify themselves as either naive or paranoid) with greater frequency than whites. The charges are various, but all three cohere in a shared structural assumption: behind every political effect there must be an initiating and (at least in theory) an identifiable political agent. Sedgwick construes the highly compelling game of trace-and-expose as a paranoid response to the powers that be; in the *Times*, however, it is a narrativizing injunction imposed by those powers. And short of winning the game, of exposing the wizard behind the curtain, there can be no "authentic" claim to oppression. Recall Sedgwick's contention that there is no "categorical imperative" to play the game:

To know that the origin or spread of HIV realistically might have resulted from a state-assisted conspiracy—such knowledge is, it turns out, separable from the question of whether the energies of a given AIDS activist intellectual or group might be best used in the tracing and exposure of such a possible plot. They might, but then again, they might not.

But again, if there is no categorical imperative, there is a cultural one, and the *Times* is fully complicit in it. One must know with absolute certainty who the guilty party is—such knowledge, it turns out, is the only damning evidence that can be brought against the state. In the guise of attempting to save blacks from themselves, the *Times* is actually in the business of construing "black talk"—always understood to be a monolithic whole—in what it takes to be its most easily discreditable form. (Yes, this is to suggest that our culture is invested in the dissemination of specific forms of paranoia. And yes, this is something to be paranoid about.) The medical misinformation (strictly speaking, a virus does not "cause" AIDS) is continuous with the larger mystification: political effects are not always bound to initiating political agents; sometimes the buck stops nowhere. Foucault cautions us against the game of trace-and-expose:

Power relations are both intentional and nonsubjective. If in fact they are intelligible, this is not because they are the effect of another instance that "explains" them, but rather because they are imbued, through and through, with calculation: there is no power that is exercised without a series of aims and objectives. But this does not mean that it results from the choice or decision of an individual subject; let us not look for the headquarters that presides over its rationality; neither the caste which governs, nor the groups which control the state apparatus, nor those who make the most important economic decisions direct the entire network of power that functions in a society. (94–95)

But the *Times* would have us play the game, the better to foreclose any attempt to think power without the king, genocide without the Führer.

Jean Baudrillard argues that political referendums no longer belong to "the realm of representation":

They [the masses] don't express themselves, they are surveyed. They don't reflect upon themselves, they are tested. The referendum (and the media are a constant referendum of directed questions and answers) has been substituted for the political referent. Now polls, tests, the referendum, media are devices which no longer belong to the realm of representation, but to one of simulation. They no longer have a referent in view, but a model.[56]

The "organized and terrorized public opinion" of the fascist-dictatorial state becomes the organized and fictitious public opinion of the liberal-democratic. (It is now commonplace to regret government by public opinion poll, as if our political institutions had suddenly become too democratic, too responsive to "the voice of the people." But the problem is exactly the opposite. The technocrats of public opinion literally pay lip service to that voice by ventriloquizing it.) The *Times* effectively produces the "talk" it alleges to record, and the talk it produces is restricted to genocide in its explicitly legal sense. Raphael Lemkin, the jurist who coined the term, defined it as "the criminal intent to destroy or to cripple permanently a human group," and his definition was more or less adopted by the UN Convention on the Prevention and Punishment of the Crime of Genocide (1948).[57] (In Baudrillard's terms, the *Times* survey belongs to the order of the "model" rather than the "referent," but the model nevertheless requires a referent, an originating and intending agent, if the talk is to be considered credible. It is not enough to suspect that the origin or spread of HIV *realistically might* have resulted from a state-sponsored conspiracy; one must be able to name the conspirators.) Apologists for the "authentic" meaning of the term argue that the criterion of intentionality lends genocide its analytical power and legal enforceability, but there is in fact no effective mechanism for punishment in the thus misnamed UN Convention on the Prevention and Punishment of the Crime of Genocide, and the analytical force of a category that more or less requires its perpetrators to declare their criminal intentionality is dubious at best.[58] In a study of the genocide of the aboriginal peoples of Australia, Tony Barta, following Marx, attempts to establish sets of relationships structuring historical reality as the proper object of historical inquiry, rather than the intentions and actions of individuals.[59] The recognition that genocide can be but the incidental by-product of business-as-usual represents a significant advance over the UN Convention, which binds genocide to a quasi-personified understanding of the operations of state policy and power, yet an exclusive focus on "relations of destruction" may be itself too lurid, too murderously obvious. Again, the power that refrains from overt destruction does not hesitate to exclude certain lives from the realm of utility and value, and systematic relations of disallowal, even to "the point of death," are all the more effectively genocidal for never being named as such.

Nothing, it turns out, is too crudely obvious for the *Times*, although it in no way follows that a crudely conspiratorial construction or understanding of racism is easily dismissable. Consider two more "rumors"—I take them from Henry Louis Gates's *Thirteen Ways of Looking at a Black Man*—that once enjoyed a certain currency in the black community:

1. Some people say that the soft drink Tropical Fantasy is manufactured by the KKK and contains a special ingredient designed to sterilize black men.
2. Some people say that members of the Los Angeles Police Department fantasize about a bonfire of black bodies and boast about planting evidence in order to frame black suspects.[60]

Gates terms such talk "counternarrative," stories that "encode regnant anxieties," rumors that flourish where "official" news proves untrustworthy (186). Counternarrative is meant to challenge all the news deemed fit to print or believe, yet it nevertheless remains bound, if only through the logic of binary opposition, to the politics of narrative explanation itself. And it is precisely narrative explanation, counter or otherwise, that our culture is invested in promoting.

Gates on counternarrative:

People arrive at an understanding of themselves and the world through narratives—narratives purveyed by schoolteachers, newscasters, "authorities," and all the other authors of our common sense. Counternarratives are, in turn, the means by which groups contest that dominant reality and the fretwork of assumptions that support it. Sometimes delusion lies that way; sometimes not. There's a sense in which much of black history is simply counternarrative that has been documented and legitimized, by slow, hard-won scholarship. (186–87)

Much of this seems to me compelling, and I would emphasize that frequently delusion does not that way lie. But what counternarrative seems powerless to contest, the promise implicit in the term notwithstanding, is the fretwork of assumptions that underwrite narrative itself. Consider, finally, two more rumors of my own devising:

1. Some people say that government's benign efforts to promote abstinence and/or safer sexual practices in minority communities (but not, of course, safer drug use, which remains beyond the political pale) have been met with inexplicable resistance on the part of the very communities most at risk.
2. Some people say—in fact, the *Times* quotes one Mark Russell as saying—that the government deliberately created the AIDS crisis in response to changing economic conditions. The postindustrial economic order that renders cheap black labor superfluous also renders black lives expendable.

The latter proposition obviously contests the official wisdom that the former promotes, and only an empty formalism would conflate the two. But by the same token, only a politics indifferent to the implications of form would fail to note the structural logic in which the two cohere. Counternarrative, talk of the government being out to get blacks, registers a profound degree of alienation from the dominant order. It does so, however, while simultaneously imagining the anonymous injustices and structural violence of that order in the comforting mode of human agency and intentionality. History, to invert Althusser, remains a process with a subject and a telos.

"Talk of the Government Being Out to Get Blacks" is in the business of teaching marginalized people the modes of thinking appropriate to their place, and pedagogical efforts of this kind routinely invoke the category of "the good minority." In the conservative imagination, there is never more than one at a time, and the *Times* is no exception. Sexually unspecified (and so presumptively straight) blacks are implicitly enjoined to mimic the example of sexually specified (and so gay) whites: "AIDS conspiracy theories once circulated among white homosexuals too, though gay groups rarely speak of them now." Perverts do not generally fare well in competitions for good minority status and the few victories they do garner tend to be pyrrhic. Certainly good minority status comes at too high a price in the pages of the *Times*. Better to be bad, in fact, than to acquiescence in the silence that equals death; better Lively's understanding of the politics of homosexuality than the *Times'*:

It is significant that "gays" and lesbians are prominent in the "multi-cultural" hierarchy. In political circles "multi-culturalism" and "diversity" have become synonymous with "gay rights." The authors contend that it is primarily the homosexualist movement, not ethnic minority groups, which has advanced the multi-cultural/diversity agenda. . . . There is an obvious benefit for homosexualists in creating a society of "separate but equal" groups with divergent values and practices. By establishing cultural distinctiveness as the criteria [sic] for being a minority group, homosexualists foster the perception that their behavior-based identity equates to ethnic heritage for the purposes of civil rights laws.[61]

Respect for cultural distinctiveness might seem outrageous enough, but it is not all that we have to fear from the "homosexualist brotherhood": the new multicultural thought police are but the vanguard of a highly organized "homo-fascist" conspiracy (143) that is out to get the family, the government, and the church. (Would that it were so.) The *Times* assumes—and it is an assumption every bit as extravagant as the talk it alleges to deplore—that white homosexuals are full participants in the privileges of white masculinity. Lively assumes—and it is the better assumption—that homosexuals threaten the heteronormative reproduction of the same with difference. The *Times* invokes homosexuals as the good minority; Lively thinks them bad to the bone. Both take as axiomatic, however, what is in fact oxymoronic: gay power.

There is nothing new, of course, in the attribution of preternatural powers and influence to the politically and socially disenfranchised. Where Lively speaks of a "homo-fascist" brotherhood, for example, his precursors spoke of an international conspiracy of Jews. Delusions of persecution assume historically variable forms, but the structuring pathology, Freud argues, is always the same:

We are in point of fact driven by experience to attribute to homosexual wishful phantasies an intimate (perhaps an invariable) relation to this particular form of disease [paranoia]. Distrusting my own experience on the subject, I have during the last few years joined with my friends [Jung and Ferenczi] . . . in investigating upon this single point a number of cases of paranoid disorder which have come under observation. The patients whose histories provided the material for this enquiry included both men and women, and varied in race, occupation, and social standing. Yet we were astonished to find that in all of these cases a defence against a homosexual wish was clearly recognizable at the very center of the conflict which underlay the disease, and that it was in an attempt to master an unconsciously reinforced current of homosexuality that they had all of them come to grief.[62]

Turnabout is proverbial fair play, and if gay charges of fascism can be troped as the fascism of gayness, delusions of homosexual persecution—and Lively's, for one, are intense—can be troped as homosexual wish-fantasy. But again, the victory would be pyrrhic. Lively as fellow traveler can be no one's idea of a good time and to consider him as such is necessarily to concede all to the universalist premise. In "Some Neurotic Mechanisms in Jealousy, Paranoia, and Homosexuality," Freud speaks of "the delusions of reference" from which the paranoid suffer:

They . . . cannot regard anything in others as indifferent, and they . . . take up the minute indications which these other, unknown people present them, and use them in their delusions of reference. The meaning of their delusion of reference is that they expect from all strangers something like love.[63]

"Everything means intensely and it means me." So says the paranoid. "Everything about paranoia means obliquely and it means homosexuality." So says the head-doctor. But where, exactly, does the "delusion of reference" lie? With the hermeneutic narcissism of the disorder? Or with the hermeneutic reductivism of its diagnosis? And what of gay paranoia? If everything, or at least everything politically and ethically aberrant, is made to mean homosexuality, isn't gay paranoia simple good sense? Freud concedes that the "sexual etiology" of the disorder is "by no means obvious"; "especially among males, social humiliations and slights" would seem a more likely cause.[64] And so it would, among women as well as men. But explanations of the "more likely" kind hold little charm for psychoanalysis. Its intellectual glamor has always been predicated on a scrupulous avoidance of the obvious, a frank embrace of the counterintuitive, and the ferreting out of (homo)sexual etiologies has always been its pastime of choice.

But what of psychoanalysis itself? Is it too subject to the game of trace-and-expose? Freud himself entertains the possibility: "the delusions of paranoiacs have an unpalatable external similarity and internal kinship to the systems of our philosophers," very much including Freud's own "system."[65] What seems to me unpalatable, however, is a hermeneutic that always and everywhere suspects only one thing. Freud's reading of paranoia is easily deconstructed: if a defense *against* a homosexual wish—as opposed, presumably, to a wish for more homosexual contacts—is the informing pathology, paranoia necessarily illuminates the operations of homophobia, not the practices of homosexuality.[66] Yet if this is blindingly obvious, it is also cold comfort. The homophobia that is at the heart of the lived politics of heteronormativity is construed as a pathology of repressed homosexuality, and the explanatory power attributed to perversion is, if anything, augmented.

Imagine what a Freudian might do with "Talk Grows of the Government Being Out to Get Blacks." Oddly enough, there is no talk of black homosexuality in all the talk of the government being out to get blacks. Sexual perversion is mentioned only once and only in reference to those white boys who long ago abandoned their paranoid fantasies. Surely this must signify, if ever so obliquely: having relaxed into the perversion that paranoia is designed to guard against, white homosexuals are released from the absurd delusion that the government is out to get them. Complicity with the status quo is effectively indistinguishable from psychosexual health, but we are not therefore to assume that homosexuality, white or otherwise, functions as a positive ideal. Freud opposes the pervert to the neurotic, not the normative, but even for Freud, a neurotic heterosexual may well be preferable to a practicing pervert. Happily, however, the alternatives are not so stark. By examining the latent etiology of their own talk, by translating ostensibly social "slights and humiliations" back into their psychosexual determinates, blacks might be spared both the paranoia and the perversion.

The absurdity of all this will be readily apparent: a strictly Freudian reading of "Talk Grows of the Government Being Out to Get Blacks" would necessarily diagnose repressed homosexuality, but the diagnosis enjoys neither cultural currency nor academic respectability. The same cannot be said, however, of the psychoanalytic construction of white racism. "The Negrophobic man is a repressed homosexual": this is, once again, Fanon on the psychology of racism, but it might be virtually anyone on anything he or she happens to find ethically or politically distasteful.[67] Granted, Fanon's reading of the psychosexual determinates of racism is not "strictly" Freudian. Freud posits an "intimate," perhaps "invariable," connection between paranoia and homosexuality that supersedes considerations of gender, "race, occupation, and social standing." Fanon complicates, but does not thereby overthrow, the psychoanalytic hierarchy:

Let me observe at once that I had no opportunity to establish the overt presence of homosexuality in Martinique. This must be viewed as the absence of the Oedipus complex in the Antilles. . . . We should not overlook, however, the existence of what are called there "men dressed like women" or "godmothers." Generally they wear shirts and skirts. But I am convinced that they lead normal sex lives. They can take a punch like any "he-man" and they are not impervious to the allures of women. . . . In Europe, on the other hand, I have known several Martinicans who became homosexuals, always passive. But this was by no means a neurotic homosexuality: For them it was a means to a livelihood, as pimping is for others.[68]

For Fanon, the absence of any talk of black homosexuality in all the talk of the government being out to get blacks would be easily explicable. Black homosexuality exists only as a residual effect of colonialism, and even then only as a practical necessity, never as an erotic proclivity or pleasure. In effect, heterosexuality is anticolonialism, which is to say, anticolonialism serves as yet another p.c. alibi for heterosexism as usual. Fanon departs from Freud on any number of issues. The ability to take a punch like any "he-man" seems evidence of a kinkier sex life than Freud condones; the category of "neurotic homosexuality" is distinctly un-Freudian (although truth be told, some of us manage to be both); and the father of psychoanalysis never lived anywhere that Oedipus was not. Yet however significant the differences, Fanon on white racism proves as comforting to the regime of compulsory heterosexuality as Lively on Nazism, Irigaray on patriarchy, or Freud on sexuality. The conventional celebration of "the venerable Freud" as "the great disillusioner" exactly reverses his historical function: psychoanalysis guarantees the political innocence of the regime of compulsory heterosexuality.

Notes

Notes to Chapter 1

1. Michel Foucault, *The History of Sexuality,* vol. 1, trans. Robert Hurley (New York: Vintage, 1978), 37; hereafter cited parenthetically by page number.

2. Eve Kosofsky Sedgwick, *Between Men: English Literature and Male Homosocial Desire* (New York: Columbia University Press, 1985), 88–89.

3. On the relation among connotation, denotation, and homosexuality, see D. A. Miller, "Anal Rope," *Representations* 32 (fall 1990): 114–33.

4. I take this comparison from Jacques Donzelot, *The Policing of Families,* trans. Robert Hurley (New York: Pantheon, 1979), 170.

5. Marjorie Garber, *Vice Versa: Bisexuality and the Eroticism of Everyday Life* (New York: Simon and Schuster, 1995), 18.

6. Sigmund Freud, "Introductory Lectures," in *The Standard Edition of the Complete Psychological Works of Sigmund Freud,* trans. James Strachey, 24 vols. (London: Hogarth Press, 1953–74), 16:308; Sigmund Freud, *Three Essays on the Theory of Sexuality,* in *The Standard Edition,* 7:145 n. 1.

7. David M. Halperin, *Saint Foucault: Towards a Gay Hagiography* (New York: Oxford University Press, 1995), 33–34.

8. Garber, *Vice Versa,* 65–66.

9. Lee Edelman, *Homographesis: Essays in Gay Literary and Cultural Theory* (New York: Routledge, 1994), 201.

10. Sedgwick, *Between Men,* 88–89.

11. I take this example from D. A. Miller, *The Novel and the Police* (Berkeley: University of California Press, 1988), 182–83.

12. Janet E. Halley, "'Like Race' Arguments," in *What's Left of Theory? New Work on the Politics of Literary Theory,* ed. Judith Butler, John Guillory, and Kendall Thomas (New York: Routledge, 2000), 60. Ann Pellegrini kindly directed me toward this argument.

13. Sigmund Freud, *New Introductory Lectures on Psycho-Analysis,* in *The Standard Edition,* 22:141.

14. Luce Irigaray, *The Sex Which Is Not One,* trans. Catherine Porter with Carolyn Burke (Ithaca: Cornell University Press, 1983), 172.

15. Edelman, *Homographesis,* 6–7.

16. Sigmund Freud, *Group Psychology and the Analysis of the Ego,* in *The Standard Edition,* 18:141; hereafter cited parenthetically by page number. *Group Psychology* also contains a much-cited discussion of the "artificial"—and tellingly, all-female—dynamics of a girls' boarding school.

17. Sigmund Freud, *On Narcissism: An Introduction,* in *The Standard Edition,* 14:69–102.

18. D. A. Miller, *The Novel and the Police,* x.

19. Freud thought it possible, in some limited circumstances, to develop the blighted germs of heterosexual tendencies that are present in every homosexual. In practice, however, he tended to focus primarily on "contingent" homosexuals, those not too "pronounced" in their deviance.

20. Barbara Johnson, *A World of Difference* (Baltimore: Johns Hopkins University Press, 1987), 12.

21. James Joyce, *Ulysses,* rev. ed. (New York: Vintage, 1986), 170.

22. David Pence, as quoted in Cindy Patton, "Tremble, Hetero Swine!" in *Fear of a Queer Planet: Queer Politics and Social Theory,* ed. Michael Warner (Minneapolis: University of Minnesota Press, 1993), 152.

23. On the repercussions of the Supreme Court decision for thinking the relation between race and sexuality, see Halley, "'Like Race' Arguments," 50–69.

24. Frantz Fanon, *Black Skin, White Masks,* trans. Charles Lam Markmann (New York: Grove, 1967), 156; hereafter cited parenthetically by page number. My reading of Fanon is indebted to Edelman, *Homographesis,* 66–67.

25. See, for example, Michael Warner's introduction to *Fear of a Queer Planet,* vii–xxxi.

26. See Janet R. Jakobsen, *Working Alliances and the Politics of Difference: Diversity and Feminist Ethics* (Bloomington: Indiana University Press, 1998), 128–35.

27. Sigmund Freud, "Dora: An Analysis of a Case of Hysteria," in *The Standard Edition,* 7:16–17.

28. Sigmund Freud, "Creative Writers and Day-Dreaming," in *The Standard Edition,* 9:146–47.

29. Eve Kosofsky Sedgwick, *Epistemology of the Closet* (Berkeley: University of California Press, 1990), 48.

30. Patton, "Tremble, Hetero Swine!" 147–48.

31. Roland Barthes, *Mythologies,* trans. Annette Lavers (St. Albans: Paladin, 1976), 112.

32. On the opposition between the two, see Foucault, *The History of Sexuality,* 53–73.

Notes to Chapter 2

1. Oscar Wilde, *The Picture of Dorian Gray,* in *The Complete Works of Oscar Wilde* (New

NOTES TO CHAPTER 2

York: Harper and Row, 1989), 34. All references to Wilde's work are to this edition and are hereafter cited parenthetically by page number.

2. Michel Foucault, *The History of Sexuality,* vol. 1, trans. Robert Hurley (New York: Vintage, 1978), 43.

3. H. Montgomery Hyde, *The Trials of Oscar Wilde* (London: William Hodge, 1948), 114, 229. Alan Sinfield argues that *"The Picture of Dorian Gray* invokes the queer image, to some readers, at least, *despite at no point representing it." The Wilde Century: Effeminacy, Oscar Wilde and the Queer Moment* (New York: Columbia University Press, 1994), 103. Neil Bartlett notes that Dorian is "proved guilty of adultery, debauchery, lechery, greed, vanity, murder, and opium addiction. Only one of his vices is hidden, only one sin cannot be named." *Who Was That Man?* (London: Serpent's Tail, 1988), 93–94.

4. Walter Benjamin, "The Work of Art in the Age of Mechanical Reproduction," in *Illuminations,* ed. Hannah Arendt, trans. Harry Zohn (New York: Schocken, 1969), 237; hereafter cited parenthetically by page number.

5. Benjamin might also be said to be innocent of Benjamin's myth of technological progress and determination. At the very least, there is a deep ambivalence in his attitude toward the art of the motion picture.

6. Late-nineteenth-century drama was far from moribund. Sarah Bernhardt made her debut on the English stage in 1879; the plays of Ibsen were introduced a decade later; and the 1890s are generally celebrated as the decade of Shaw and Wilde. But if not moribund, the art of the theater was nevertheless residual. In an age when the novel reigns supreme, as Bakhtin puts it, all other genres are more or less "novelized," a phenomenon to which Shaw and the "Ibsenism" he championed bear testimony. Bakhtin never considers the alternative possibility, the "theatricalization" of the novel, suggestively explored by Joseph Litvak in *Caught in the Act: Theatricality in the Nineteenth-Century English Novel* (Berkeley: University of California Press, 1992).

7. Gotthold Ephram Lessing, *Laokoön and How the Ancients Represented Death,* trans. E. C. Beasley (London: G. Bell and Sons, 1914), 91; hereafter cited parenthetically by page number.

8. D. A. Miller, "The Late Jane Austen," *Raritan* 10, no. 1 (summer 1990): 57.

9. See the chapter entitled "The Perverse Implantation" in *The History of Sexuality,* 36–50.

10. Wilkie Collins, *The Woman in White,* ed. Harvey Peter Sucksmith (New York: Oxford University Press, 1973), 299.

11. As quoted in T. J. Spencer, "The Decline of Hamlet," in *Hamlet: Stratford-upon-Avon Studies 5* (New York: St. Martin's, 1964), 192–93. Hamlet is placed in the company of

Goethe's *Die Leiden des jungen Werthers* (1774), Byron's *Laura* (1814), Étienne de Senancour's *Obermann* (1804), and Chateaubriand's *René* (1802).

12. *Hamlet*, 2. 232–42, in *The Complete Works*, original Spelling Edition, ed. Stanley Wells and Gary Taylor (Oxford: Clarendon, 1986); all subsequent references are to this edition.

13. Harold Bloom, *Ruin the Sacred Truths: Poetry and Belief from the Bible to the Present* (Cambridge: Harvard University Press, 1989), 85.

14. Michel Foucault, *Discipline and Punish: The Birth of the Prison*, trans. Alan Sheridan (New York: Vintage, 1979), 193.

15. Francis Barker, *The Tremulous Private Body: Essays on Subjection* (London: Methuen, 1984), 35.

16. Robert Weimann, "Representation and Performance: The Uses of Authority in Shakespeare's Theater," *PMLA* 107, no. 3 (May 1992): 499.

17. Georg Wilhelm Friedrich Hegel, *Introductory Lectures on Aesthetics*, trans. Bernard Bosanquet (Harmondsworth: Penguin, 1993), 23; hereafter cited parenthetically by page number.

18. Johann Wolfgang von Goethe, *Wilhelm Meister's Apprenticeship*, trans. Thomas Carlyle (New York: Collier, 1962), 287–88; hereafter cited parenthetically by page number.

19. The villainous Count Fosco in *The Woman in White* reverses the process, which is itself evidence of his villainy:

> *Mind, they say, rules the world. But what rules the mind? The body. The body (follow me closely here) lies at the mercy of the most omnipotent of all potentates—the Chemist. Give me—Fosco—chemistry; and when Shakespeare has conceived Hamlet, and sits down to execute the conception—with a few grains of powder dropped into his daily food, I will reduce the mind, by the actions of his body, till his pen pours out the most abject drivel that has ever degraded paper.*

Collins, *The Woman in White*, 560.

20. The most common explanation for the Queen's reference to Hamlet's scandalous physique—at least among critics who accept that "fat" means "fat"—is patently antitheatrical: Gertrude's remark is an unfortunate concession to the body of the actor who initiated the role; it in no way impinges on Hamlet "himself." Steeven, following Roberts, speculates that the same actor who played Henry VIII played Hamlet; in his *Memoirs of the Principal Actors in the Plays of Shakespeare*, Collier argues for Burbage. Rather than accept what Weimann terms "consequential" fissures between actors and their roles, the body of the performing agent and the body to be performed, criticism attempts to recover a pure textuality unsullied by the accidents of performance.

21. Barker, *The Tremulous Private Body*, 39.

22. M. M. Bakhtin, *The Dialogic Imagination: Four Essays*, trans. Caryl Emerson and Michael Holquist (Austin: University of Texas Press, 1981), 5–6.

23. On bourgeois ex-nomination, see Roland Barthes, *Mythologies*, trans. Annette Lavers (St. Albans: Paladin, 1976), 137–38.

24. Raymond Williams, *Problems in Materialism and Culture* (New York: Schocken, 1981), 84.

25. Joel Fineman, "The Significance of Literature: *The Importance of Being Earnest*," *October* 15 (1981) 79.

26. It is worth noting that many plays in the 1890s, including highly successful ones, were not always published. To the extent that the "literary" presupposes a culture of the book, late-nineteenth-century drama does not fully qualify as such.

27. Christopher Craft, "Alias Bunbury: Desire and Termination in *The Importance of Being Earnest*," *Representations* 31 (summer 1990): 24.

28. Wilde writes at a time when Stanislavski, an important agent of the novelization or "psychologization" of the theater, was on the historical horizon. *The Importance of Being Earnest* demands, however, an altogether different "method" of acting. In New York, Wilde studied with Steele McKay, a disciple of François Delsartre, the founder of a system of voice training for actors that had been popular in France as early as 1839. McKay extended the Delsartrian method to include a highly codified regime of gestures and poses, a structure of signification that, as Wilde says in a different context, "stops bravely at the surface." McKay taught Wilde using *Hamlet*.

29. Sigmund Freud, *Moses and Monotheism*, in *The Standard Edition of the Complete Psychological Works of Sigmund Freud*, trans. James Strachey, 24 vols. (London: Hogarth, 1953–74), 23:114.

30.

> "The power of Christianity has been in the immense emotion it has excited," he [Matthew Arnold] says; not realizing at all that this is a counsel to get all the emotional kick out of Christianity one can, without the bother of believing it; without reading the future to foresee Marius the Epicurean, *and finally* De Profundis.

T. S. Eliot, "Arnold and Pater," in *Selected Essays*, rev. ed. (London: Faber and Faber, 1951), 434–35.

31. On the "squeam-inducing" power of the text, see Eve Kosofsky Sedgwick, *Epistemology of the Closet* (Berkeley: University of California Press, 1990), 148.

32. Karl Marx, "Private Property and Communism," in *Early Writings*, trans. T. B. Bottomore (New York: McGraw-Hill, 1964), 159–60.

33. Walter Benjamin, "The Storyteller," in *Illuminations*, 108.

34. Robert Sherard, *The Life of Oscar Wilde* (London: Methuen, 1906), 246–47.

35. J. K. Huysmans, *Against Nature*, trans. Robert Baldick (Harmondsworth: Penguin, 1959), 119.

36. On this theme, see Walter J. Ong, S.J., *Interfaces of the Word: Studies in the Evolution of Consciousness and Culture* (Ithaca: Cornell University Press, 1977), 121–46.

37. Friedrich Nietzsche, *Ecce Homo*, trans. R. J. Hollingdale (New York: Penguin, 1979), 126.

38. This is not to suggest that the olfactory, at least as currently constructed, eludes the diacritics of gender. In the eighteenth and early nineteenth centuries, the same perfumes were conventionally worn by both men and women; it was not until the late nineteenth century that certain scents—particularly floral blends—were deemed exclusively female. "Woodsy" colognes, such as pine or cedar, were considered acceptable for men, although the olfactory ideal of bourgeois masculinity tended to be the smell of clean skin combined with tobacco. See Constance Classen, David Howes, and Anthony Synnott, *Aroma: The Cultural History of Smell* (New York: Routledge, 1994), 83–84. Only recently has a limited number of perfumes been marketed as gender neutral.

39. Sigmund Freud, *Civilization and Its Discontents*, in *The Standard Edition*, 21:99–100 n. 1.

40. Max Nordau, *Degeneration* (New York: D. Appleton, 1895), 503.

41. Classen, Howes, and Synnott define "osmologies" as "classificatory systems based on smell," of which they provide several examples. See *Aroma*, 95–122.

42. D. A. Miller, *The Novel and the Police* (Berkeley: University of California Press, 1988), 25.

43. See Lee Edelman, *Homographesis: Essays in Gay Literary and Cultural Theory* (New York: Routledge, 1994), 15.

44. Jürgen Habermas, *The Structural Transformation of the Public Sphere: An Inquiry into a Category of Bourgeois Society*, trans. Thomas Berger (Cambridge: MIT Press, 1989), 49.

45. Jacques Derrida, "The Purveyor of Truth," *Yale French Studies*, no. 52 (1975): 107.

46. Jonathan Crary, *Techniques of the Observer: On Vision and Modernity in the Nineteenth Century* (Cambridge: MIT Press, 1990), 150 et passim.

47. As quoted in *Oscar Wilde: Art and Morality. A Record of the Discussion Which Followed the Publication of Dorian Gray* (New York: Haskell House, 1971), 33.

48. Max Horkheimer and Theodor W. Adorno, *Dialectic of Enlightenment*, trans. John Cumming (New York: Continuum, 1993), 184.

49. Eve Kosofsky Sedgwick, *Tendencies* (Durham: Duke University Press, 1993), 57.

50. See Edelman, *Homographesis*, passim.

51. Maurice Blanchot, *The Gaze of Orpheus*, trans. Lydia Davis (Barrytown, NY: Station Hill, 1981), 75.

52. Stanley Cavell, *The World Viewed: Reflections on the Ontology of Film* (New York: Viking, 1971), 90, 94; hereafter cited parenthetically by page number.

53. Steven Shaviro, *The Cinematic Body* (Minneapolis: University of Minnesota Press, 1993), 32, 31.

54. Sedgwick, *Epistemology of the Closet*, 172.

55. Another example of the same logic: AIDS is not a "supernatural" visitation on the perverse, a pamphlet from the InterVarsity Christian Fellowship assures us, but the "natural" consequence of an unnatural use of the body. "If you use something in a way it wasn't intended to be used, it breaks." Andreas Tapia, *The AIDS Crisis: The Facts and Myths about a Modern Plague* (Downer's Grove, IL: InterVarsity Press, 1988), 13.

56. Frank Harris, *Oscar Wilde* (New York: Carroll and Graf, 1992), 290.

57. Kaja Silverman, *The Acoustic Mirror: The Female Voice in Psychoanalysis and Cinema* (Bloomington: Indiana University Press, 1988), 49.

58. As quoted in Diana Fuss, *Identification Papers* (New York: Routledge, 1995), 90.

59. Robert B. Ray, *A Certain Tendency of the Hollywood Cinema, 1930–1980* (Princeton: Princeton University Press, 1985), 32.

60. "There is, of course, absolutely no characterization and all the people speak equally strained Oscar." As quoted in Jonathan L. Freeman, *Professions of Taste: Henry James, British Aestheticism, and Commodity Culture* (Stanford: Stanford University Press, 1990), 173. James's critique of Wilde exactly reverses Wilde's critique of Shakespeare.

61.

> *Magician and surgeon compare to painter and cameraman. The painter maintains in his work a natural distance from reality, the cameraman penetrates deeply into its web. There is a tremendous difference between the pictures they obtain. That of the painter is a total one, that of the cameraman consists of multiple fragments which are assembled under a new law.*

Benjamin, "The Work of Art in the Age of Mechanical Reproduction," 233–34. On the imbrication of the vocabulary of surgical pathology and film, see Fuss, *Identification Papers*, 90–91.

62. Richard Ellmann, *Oscar Wilde* (Markham, Ontario: Viking, 1987), 549.

63. Ellmann, *Oscar Wilde*, 549.

Notes to Chapter 3

1. As quoted in Richard Meyer, "Rock Hudson's Body," in *Inside/Out: Lesbian Theories, Gay Theories*, ed. Diana Fuss (New York: Routledge, 1991), 274.

2. D. A. Miller, "Sontag's Urbanity," *October* 49 (summer 1989): 95.

3. Paula Treichler, "AIDS, Homophobia, and Biomedical Discourse: An Epidemic of Signification," in *AIDS: Cultural Analysis/Cultural Activism*, ed. Douglas Crimp (Cambridge: MIT Press, 1988), 32; Thomas Yingling, "AIDS in America: Postmodern Governance, Identity, and Experience," in Fuss, *Inside/Out*, 291–92.

4. Cindy Patton, *Inventing AIDS* (New York: Routledge, 1990), 128.

5. Susan Sontag, "AIDS and Its Metaphors," in *Illness as Metaphor and AIDS and Its Metaphors* (New York: Doubleday, 1989), 110; hereafter cited parenthetically by page number.

6. Andrew Sullivan, "The Marriage Moment," *Advocate,* January 20, 1998, 61–63.

7. Gabriel Rotello, "The 'Risk' in a Cure for AIDS," *New York Times,* July 14, 1996, 17.

8. Michael Warner, *The Trouble with Normal: Sex, Politics, and the Ethics of Queer Life* (New York: Free Press, 1999), 51, 61–80. See also Douglas Crimp on the "normalization" of AIDS/HIV:

> *If, for the first eight years of the epidemic—the terms of Ronald Reagan's presidency—indifference took the form of callously ignoring the crisis, under George Bush, AIDS was "normalized" as just one item in a long list of supposedly intractable social problems.*
>
> *How often do we hear the list recited—poverty, crime, drugs, homelessness, and AIDS.*
>
> *AIDS is no longer an emergency. It's merely a permanent disaster.*

Douglas Crimp, "Right On, Girlfriend!" in *Fear of a Queer Planet: Queer Politics and Social Theory,* ed. Michael Warner (Minneapolis: University of Minnesota Press, 1993), 304.

9. William Eskridge, *The Case for Same-Sex Marriage: From Sexual Liberty to Civilized Commitment* (New York: Free Press, 1996), 58, 74.

10. Sigmund Freud, *Three Essays on the Theory of Sexuality,* in *The Standard Edition of the Complete Psychological Works of Sigmund Freud,* trans. James Strachey, 24 vols. (London: Hogarth Press, 1953–74), 7:197; hereafter cited by page number in the text as *TE*.

11. Sigmund Freud, "Dora: An Analysis of a Case of Hysteria," in *The Standard Edition,* 7:16–17; hereafter cited by page number in the text as D.

12. Leo Bersani, *The Freudian Body: Psychoanalysis and Art* (New York: Columbia University Press, 1986), 32. On Freud's tendency to identify psychosexual health with narrative or the ability to narrate, see Steven Marcus, *Freud and the Culture of Psychoanalysis* (New York: Norton, 1984), 60–61.

13. Bersani, *The Freudian Body,* 32.

14. A point made by David M. Halperin in *Saint Foucault: Towards a Gay Hagiography* (New York: Oxford University Press, 1995), 47.

15. Bersani, *The Freudian Body,* 33.

16. Leo Bersani, "Is the Rectum a Grave?" in Crimp, *AIDS: Cultural Analysis/Cultural Activism,* 211.

17. Simon Watney, *Policing Desire: Pornography, AIDS, and the Media* (Minneapolis: University of Minnesota Press, 1987), 33–34.

18. Paul de Man, "The Epistemology of Metaphor," in *On Metaphor*, ed. Sheldon Sacks (Chicago: University of Chicago Press, 1979), 21–22.

19. Peter Brooks, *Reading for the Plot: Design and Intention in Narrative* (New York: Knopf, 1984), 91.

20. E. M. Forster, *Aspects of the Novel* (London: Edward Arnold, 1927), 113.

21. "Dismisses" is not, perhaps, altogether fair: Rotello views safer sexual practices as a practical good, but as an inadequate or partial response to an epidemic that demands a broader (or is it deeper?) transformation of identity. I say epidemic, as opposed to pandemic, because Rotello insists that AIDS is, at least in a Western context, largely a homosexual (or at least nonheterosexual) phenomenon. See Gabriel Rotello, *Sexual Ecology: AIDS and the Destiny of Gay Men* (New York: Penguin, 1997), 91–117 et passim; hereafter cited parenthetically by page number.

22. Warner, *The Trouble with Normal*, 29.

23. Warner, *The Trouble with Normal*, 99.

24. Sigmund Freud, *On Narcissism: An Introduction*, in *The Standard Edition*, 14:85.

25. E. J. Graff, "Retying the Knot," in *Same-Sex Marriage: Pro and Con*, ed. Andrew Sullivan (New York: Vintage, 1997), 136.

26. Jacques Lacan, "Du Trieb de Freud et du désir du psychanalyste," in *Ecrits* (Paris: Seuil, 1966), 851–54.

27. Michel Foucault, *The History of Sexuality*, vol. 1, trans. Robert Hurley (New York: Vintage, 1978), 113.

28. Jacques Donzelot, *The Policing of Families*, trans. Robert Hurley (New York: Pantheon, 1979), 230–31.

29. John Weir, *The Irreversible Decline of Eddie Socket* (New York: Harper, 1991), 166.

30. Ethan Mordden, *Buddies* (New York: St. Martin's, 1986), xi.

31. Fredric Jameson, "Seriality in Modern Literature," *Bucknell Review* 18 (1970): 68.

32. Sigmund Freud, *Beyond the Pleasure Principle*, in *The Standard Edition*, 18:36.

33. Andrew Sullivan argues that gays and lesbians have always been, as it were, citizens of that "predisturbance order":

> The family is prior to the liberal state. . . . Heterosexuals would not conceive of such rights as things to be won, but as things that predate modern political discussion. But it says something about the unique status of homosexuals in our culture that we now have to be political in order to be prepolitical.

Andrew Sullivan, *Virtually Normal* (New York: Knopf, 1995), 186.

34. Jane Gallop, *The Daughter's Seduction: Feminism and Psychoanalysis* (London: Macmillan, 1982), 127–28; hereafter cited parenthetically by page number.

35. Michael Warner, "Homo-Narcissism; or, Heterosexuality," in *Engendering Men: The Question of Male Feminist Criticism*, ed. Joseph A. Boone and Michael Cadden (New York: Routledge, 1990), 202.

36. Randy Shilts, *And the Band Played On: Politics, People, and the AIDS Epidemic* (New York: St. Martin's, 1987), 198; hereafter cited parenthetically by page number.

37. A point well argued by Douglas Crimp in "How to Have Promiscuity in an Epidemic," in *AIDS: Cultural Analysis/Cultural Activism*, 245.

38. I make no pretense of doing justice to the complexities of Auden's poem; in what follows, I am concerned only with the meanings it has been made to bear in light of Kramer's play.

39. Jean Laplanche, *Life and Death in Psychoanalysis*, trans. Jeffrey Mehlman (Baltimore: Johns Hopkins University Press, 1976), 14.

40. Paul Monette, *Afterlife* (New York: Avon, 1990), 5; hereafter cited parenthetically by page number.

41. Sigmund Freud, "'Civilized' Sexual Morality," in *The Standard Edition*, 9:200.

42. Larry Kramer, *The Normal Heart* (New York: New American Library, 1985), 61, 85.

43. Paul Monette, *Halfway Home* (New York: Avon, 1991), 262; hereafter cited parenthetically by page number.

Notes to Chapter 4

1. D. A. Miller, *The Novel and the Police* (Berkeley: University of California Press, 1988), x.

2. In *Essential Works of Socialism*, ed. Irving Howe (New Haven: Yale University Press, 1976), 46.

3. White quoted in Melody D. Davis, *The Male Nude in Contemporary Photography* (Philadelphia: Temple University Press, 1991), 75.

4. Jean Baudrillard, *For a Critique of the Political Economy of the Sign*, trans. Charles Levin (St. Louis: Telos Press, 1981), 102–11. Much of this paragraph is a direct paraphrase of Baudrillard, although for reasons that I specify below, his account of the determination of value in the modern art market seems to me partial.

5.

Here we find something like a truth of modern art: it is no longer the literality of the world, but the literality of the gestural elaboration of creation—spots, lines, dribbles. At the same

time, that which was representation—redoubling the world in space—becomes repetition— an indefinable redoubling of the act in time.
Baudrillard, *For a Critique*, 106.

6. See Jacques Derrida, "Signature Event Context," in *Margins of Philosophy*, trans. Alan Bass (Chicago: University of Chicago Press, 1979), 307–30.

7. Susan Sontag, *On Photography* (New York: Farrar, Straus and Giroux, 1977), 20–21.

8. Philip Fisher, "Jasper Johns: Strategies for Making and Effacing Art," *Critical Inquiry* 16, no. 2 (winter 1990): 315.

9. Fisher, "Jasper Johns," 317–18.

10. As quoted in Richard Meyer, "Robert Mapplethorpe and the Discipline of Photography," in *The Lesbian and Gay Studies Reader*, ed. Henry Abelove, Michèle Aina Barale, and David M. Halperin (New York: Routledge, 1993), 373.

11. As quoted in Meyer, "Robert Mapplethorpe and the Discipline of Photography," 374.

12. Plato, *The Republic*, in *The Dialogues of Plato*, trans. Benjamin Jowett, 4th ed. (Oxford: Clarendon, 1953).

13. Immanuel Kant, *Critique of Judgement*, trans. Werner S. Pluhar (Indianapolis: Hackett, 1987), 45.

14. The NEA budget does not represent the entirety of U.S. government support for the arts; hence, the figures I give, which do not take into account the specific structures of funding in any given nation, distort the picture to the disadvantage of the United States.

15. Kobena Mercer, "Skin Head Sex Thing: Racial Difference and the Homoerotic Imaginary," in *How Do I Look? Queer Film and Video*, ed. Bad Object-Choices (Seattle: Bay Press, 1991), 170; hereafter cited parenthetically by page number.

16. Kobena Mercer, "Imagining the Black Man's Sex," in *Photography/Politics: Two*, ed. Paul Holland, Jo Spence, and Simon Watney (London: Methuen, 1987), 61–69.

17. Davis, *The Male Nude in Contemporary Photography*, 75; Kay Larson, as paraphrased in Davis, 71.

18. D. A. Miller, *Bringing Out Roland Barthes* (Berkeley: University of California Press, 1992), 36.

19. Frantz Fanon, *Black Skin, White Masks*, trans. Charles Lam Markmann (New York: Grove, 1967), 116, 111.

20. On the suit as the "phallic" extension of the penis, see Miller, *Bringing Out Roland Barthes*, 28–29.

21. Charles Bernheimer, "Penile Reference in Phallic Theory," *differences* 4, no. 1 (spring 1992): 121.

22. Bourdieu empirically "measures" aesthetic taste by asking subjects to respond to a series of photographs. He finds that there is a direct "correlation between educational capital and the propensity or at least the aspiration to appreciate a work of art 'independently of its content,' as the culturally most ambitious [of his] respondents put it." On the other hand, subjects with little cultural capital (inferior educations, no family "heritage") evaluate as "good" only photographs whose representational content they deem worthy of representation (the beautiful or the good). See Pierre Bourdieu, *Distinction: A Social Critique of the Judgement of Taste*, trans. Richard Nice (Cambridge: Harvard University Press, 1984), 53 et passim; hereafter cited parenthetically by page number.

23. Bourdieu speaks of the "essential hypocrisy (seen, for example, in the opposition between pornography and eroticism) [that] masks the interest in function by the primacy given to form," *Distinction*, 200.

24. See D. A. Miller's discussion of the novel reading subject: "Our most intense identification with characters [in novels] never blinds us to our ontological privilege over them: they will never be reading about *us*." *The Novel and the Police*, 162.

25. William H. Masters and Virginia E. Johnson, *Crisis: Heterosexual Behavior in the Age of AIDS*, as quoted in Cindy Patton, *Inventing AIDS* (New York: Routledge, 1990), 48–49.

26. Sigmund Freud, "An Autobiographical Sketch," in *The Standard Edition of the Complete Psychological Works of Sigmund Freud*, trans. James Strachey, 24 vols. (London: Hogarth Press, 1953–74), 20:28.

27. On the relation between the modern "disciplines" of knowledge and our disciplinary regime of the norm, see Jürgen Habermas, *The Philosophical Discourse of Modernity: Twelve Lectures*, trans. Frederick G. Lawrence (Cambridge: MIT Press, 1987), 245–46. A photographic purchase on the world is, in a sense, the logical corollary of this nonparticipatory technology of power. As Sontag argues, "Whatever the moral claims made on behalf of photography, its main effect is to convert the world into a department store or museum-without-walls, in which every subject is deprecated into an article of consumption, promoted into an item for aesthetic appreciation." *On Photography*, 110. And a personal observation: I am no longer content with the reason I have always provided myself for my reluctance to be photographed. Although I still maintain that I am better looking than the photographic evidence allows, it now seems to me that I elude the camera in order to maintain the illusion that I am not routinely the object of a nonparticipatory observation and knowledge.

28. Michel Foucault, *Discipline and Punish: The Birth of the Prison*, trans. Alan Sheridan (New York: Vintage, 1979), 202.

29. Leo Bersani, "Is the Rectum a Grave?" in *AIDS: Cultural Analysis/Cultural Activism*, ed. Douglas Crimp (Cambridge: MIT Press, 1988), 222; hereafter cited parenthetically by page number.

30. Eve Kosofsky Sedgwick, *Epistemology of the Closet* (Berkeley: University of California Press, 1990), 31.

31. Sigmund Freud, *Three Essays on the Theory of Sexuality,* in *The Standard Edition,* 7:187 n. 1.

32. Francis Barker, *The Tremulous Private Body: Essays on Subjection* (London: Methuen, 1984), 45.

33. Barker, *The Tremulous Private Body,* 48.

34. Barker, *The Tremulous Private Body,* 46–47.

35. *Areopagitica,* in *John Milton: Complete Poems and Major Prose,* ed. Merritt Y. Hughes (New York: Macmillan, 1985), 727.

Notes to Chapter 5

1. John Berger, *Ways of Seeing* (New York: Penguin, 1977), 47. Berger's precise formulation is *"men act* and *women appear"*; for reasons I trust my chapter makes clear, I have substituted "do" for "act." To the extent that "act" carries with it suggestions of theatricality or performativity, "real men" are at pains to distance themselves from it.

2. On Schwarzenegger's sexually dubious past, see Wendy Leigh, *Arnold: An Unauthorized Biography* (Chicago: Congden Press, 1990), 50–51, 60–65.

3. Laura Mulvey, "Visual Pleasure and Narrative Cinema," in *The Sexual Subject: A Screen Reader in Sexuality* (New York: Routledge, 1992), 28.

4. Sigmund Freud, *Three Essays on the Theory of Sexuality,* in *The Standard Edition of the Complete Psychological Works of Sigmund Freud,* trans. James Strachey, 24 vols. (London: Hogarth Press, 1953–74), 7:145 n. 1; hereafter cited parenthetically by page number.

5. The term "male beauty contests" was meant to distinguish bodybuilding from the "legitimate" sport of weight lifting, a topic I return to below. See F. Valentine Hooven III, *Beefcake: The Muscle Magazine of America, 1950–1979* (Benedikt Taschen, Köln, 1995), 22.

6. Michel Foucault, "Sade, sergent du sexe," *Cinématographe* 16 (December 1975–January 1978): 3–5; as quoted in David M. Halperin, *Saint Foucault: Towards a Gay Hagiography* (New York: Oxford University Press, 1995), 96.

7. See, for example, David Halperin's reading of bodybuilding as an instance of "ascesis" in Foucault's sense of the word; *Saint Foucault,* 115–19.

8. Samuel Wilson Fussell, *Muscles: Confessions of an Unlikely Bodybuilder* (New York: Avon, 1991), p, 37.

9. Fussell's English professor mother thinks that bulk and the ability to write a book are incompatible:

> *"That's development, Mother. These men [the bodybuilders in* Pumping Iron*] are engaged in the pure pursuit of physical development."*
>
> *"Yes, and meanwhile they are functionally illiterate. One of them can't even speak."*
>
> *"That's Lou Ferrigno, Mother, and it's not his fault. He's deaf."*
>
> *"We'll you're not deaf, so why do you want to do this to yourself? And the bully with the gap between his teeth. Who is the punk? He's a moron."*
>
> *"That's Arnold Schwarzenegger. He writes books."*
>
> *"Not without a ghost writer, he doesn't."*

Fussell, *Muscles*, 60.

10. *A Memoir of the Reverend Sydney Smith*, as quoted in Roy Porter, "Barely Touching: A Social Perspective on Mind and Body," in *The Languages of Psyche: Mind and Body in Enlightenment Thought*, ed. G. S. Rousseau (Berkeley: University of California Press, 1990), 80.

11. Sigmund Freud, "Dora: An Analysis of a Case of Hysteria," in *The Standard Edition*, 7:40.

12. Jacques Lacan, "The Function and Field of Speech and Language in Psychoanalysis," in *Ecrits*, trans. Alan Sheridan (New York: Norton, 1977), 92.

13. Here, for example, is part of a letter written by Paul to HIV: "I have tried to love you as best I can, but sometimes I really have difficulty doing so. Please, let's be friends and make up." HIV responds: "Okay. Love, HIV." Marianne Williamson, *A Return to Love: Reflections on the Principles of A Course in Miracles* (New York: HarperCollins, 1992), 213.

14. Slavoj Žižek, *For They Know Not What They Do: Enjoyment as a Political Factor* (London: Verso, 1991), 143.

15. Žižek argues, following Lacan, that

> the fundamental experience of man qua *being-of-language* is that his desire is impeded, constitutively dissatisfied: he *"doesn't know what he really wants."* What the hysterical *"conversion"* accomplishes is precisely an inversion of this impediment: by means of it, the impeded desire converts into a desire for impediment; *the unsatisfied desire converts into a desire for unsatisfaction.*

For They Know Not, 143–44. The hysterical symptom is not, then, the mere exemplification of an "Idea," but an index of "the imperfection proper to the Idea itself"; if a desire cannot be satisfied, it is because the subject always desired unsatisfaction. But if hysteria thus subverts the subject's self-knowledge, the conversion into "a desire for unsatisfaction" hardly threatens an economic order in which desire must never come to rest on an adequate object. Consumer capitalism presupposes that there is always something other, different, better, more.

16. Susan Sontag, "AIDS and Its Metaphors," in *Illness as Metaphor and AIDS and Its Metaphors* (New York: Doubleday, 1989), 127–28; hereafter cited parenthetically by page number.

17. Marcia Ian argues that a "male bodybuilder's body ideally has no interior. It is to contain no space, but be solid, lean meat. The term 'musclehead,' a colloquial and non-pejorative synonym for 'serious lifter,' even suggests that his head be equally dense." She intends this as criticism. See Marcia Ian, "When Is a Body Not a Body? When It Is a Building," in *Stud: Architectures of Masculinity*, ed. Joel Sanders (Princeton: Princeton Architectural Press, 1996), 191.

18. Jean-Paul Sartre, *Being and Nothingness*, trans. Hazel E. Barnes (New York: Washington Square Press, 1956), 302.

19. Jacques Lacan, *The Four Fundamental Concepts of Psychoanalysis*, trans. Alan Sheridan (New York: Norton, 1978), 95–96.

20. As quoted in Alan M. Klein, *Little Big Men: Bodybuilding Subculture and Gender Construction* (Albany: State University of New York Press, 1993), 184–85.

21. Lee Edelman, *Homographesis: Essays in Gay Literary and Cultural Theory* (New York: Routledge, 1994), 204–5.

22. Anthony Trollope, *Phineas Redux* (New York: Oxford University Press, 1983), 252.

23. On the obscenity charges brought against Macfadden, see Greg Mullins, "Nudes, Prudes, and Pygmies: The Desirability of Disavowal in *Physical Culture*," *Discourse* 5, no. 1 (fall 1992): 27–48.

24. Kenneth R. Dutton, *The Perfectible Body: The Western Ideal of Male Physical Development* (New York: Continuum, 1995), 287.

25. D. A. Miller, *Bringing Out Roland Barthes* (Berkeley: University of California Press, 1992), 41.

26. As quoted in Ian, "When Is a Body Not a Body?" 193.

27. Ann Pellegrini, *Performance Anxieties: Staging Psychoanalysis, Staging Race* (New York: Routledge, 1997), 164–70; see also Christine Holmund, "Visible Difference and Flex Appeal: The Body, Sex, Sexuality, and Race in the *Pumping Iron* Films," *Cinema Journal* 28, no. 4 (summer 1989): 38–51.

28. Gilles Deleuze and Felix Guattari, *Anti-Oedipus: Capitalism and Schizophrenia*, trans. Robert Hurley, Mark Seem, and Helen R. Lane (Minneapolis: University of Minnesota Press, 1983), 270.

29. As quoted in Hooven, *Beefcake*, 109.

30. As quoted in Charles Gaines and George Butler, *Pumping Iron*, rev. ed. (New York: Simon and Schuster, 1981), 93.

31. See Melody D. Davis, *The Male Nude in Contemporary Photography* (Philadelphia: Temple University Press, 1991), 18.

32. Gaines and Butler, *Pumping Iron*, 174.

33. Mark Merlis, *American Studies* (New York: Penguin, 1994), 37.

34. Because of their too-intimate association with the physique pictorials of the 1950s and 1960s, "posing pouches" are now banned from competitive bodybuilding, although the regulation "trunks" that have substituted for them are hardly more substantial. In recent years, they have tended to be cut higher in the rear, the better to expose the contestant's gluteal striation, the visible separation of muscle bands in the gluteus maximus or large muscles of the buttocks. See Dutton, *The Perfectible Body*, 260, 311.

35. On the jock strap, near kin of the posing pouch, Pronger writes, "there are two sides to the jock strap, symbolizing the homoerotic paradox: the pouch at the front as the shrine of masculinity, joined to the straps at the back, which frame its mythic violation." See the commentary to figure 5 in Brian Pronger, *The Arena of Masculinity: Sports, Homosexuality, and the Meaning of Sex* (New York: St. Martin's, 1990). What Pronger calls the "homoerotic paradox" I would call the heterosexual dichotomy.

36. See D. A. Miller on the difference between "being" and "having" a dick:

> *The entitled man, or the boy aspirant to entitlement, is less inclined to contour his genitals in briefs than to make them invisible in boxer shorts. A twice obnoxious preference, it now seems to me: on the one hand, a presumptuous discourse of procreative sexuality, testicular "freedom" always being sanctioned by its beneficial effect on the production of fertile sperm; on the other, an immodest practice of hiding the penis, which disappears into a cool rectangularity that (already anticipating the* suit *that is such underwear's "logical" and ethical extension) only apotheosizes it as the phallus. In boxer shorts, a man no longer has a dick; he becomes one.*

Miller, *Bringing Out Roland Barthes*, 28–29.

37. Jean Baudrillard, "Virtuelle Katastrophen," as quoted in Douglas Crimp, "Portraits of People with AIDS," in *Discourses of Sexuality: From Aristotle to AIDS*, ed. Domna C. Stanton (Ann Arbor: University of Michigan Press, 1992), 387–88.

38. Karl Marx, *Capital: A Critique of Political Economy*, ed. Fredrick Engels, trans. Samuel Moore and Edward Aveling, 3 vols. (New York: International Publishers, 1967), 1:52.

39. Jacques Lacan, "The Mirror Stage," in *Ecrits*, 2.

40. Arnold Schwarzenegger, *Encyclopedia of Modern Bodybuilding* (New York: Simon and Schuster, 1985), 52.

41. Michel Foucault, "Le gai savoir," as quoted in Halperin, *Saint Foucault,* 94.

42. Slavoj Žižek, *The Sublime Object of Ideology* (London: Verso, 1989), 25.

43. Leigh, *Arnold: An Unauthorized Biography*, 52.

44. Jonathan Goldberg notes the phonetic equation of "iron" and "I am" in the chorus of the film *Pumping Iron*; see "Recalling Totalities: The Mirrored Stages of Arnold Schwarzenegger," *differences* 4, no. 1 (spring 1992): 177.

45. Sigmund Freud, *The Ego and the Id*, in *The Standard Edition*, 19:26.

46. Judith Butler, "The Lesbian Phallus and the Morphological Imaginary," *differences* 4, no. 1 (spring 1992): 147.

47. Lacan, "The Mirror Stage," 2. Diana Fuss speaks of the Lacanian "I" as "that orthographic architectural column"; see her *Identification Papers* (New York: Routledge, 1995), 48.

48. Mikkel Borch-Jacobsen, *Lacan: The Absolute Master*, trans. Douglas Brick (Stanford: Stanford University Press, 1991), 65.

Notes to Chapter 6

1. Camille Paglia, "The M.I.T. Lecture: Crisis in the American Universities," in *Sex, Art, and American Culture* (New York: Vintage, 1992), 287; hereafter cited parenthetically by page number.

2. See Eve Kosofsky Sedgwick, *Epistemology of the Closet* (Berkeley: University of California Press, 1990), 19–21.

3. As quoted in Neil Miller, *Out of the Past: Gay and Lesbian History from 1869 to the Present* (New York: Vintage, 1995), 460.

4. My focus is primarily on National Socialism, which, strictly speaking, should be distinguished from fascism proper. Although I have elsewhere insisted on the importance of the distinction—see Paul Morrison, *The Poetics of Fascism: Ezra Pound, T. S. Eliot, Paul de Man* (New York: Oxford University Press, 1996)—I use the terms Nazism, National Socialism, and fascism more or less interchangeably here. I am concerned with the contemporary reception of reactionary political movements, in which distinctions between and among movements tend to be moot.

5. Susan Sontag, "Fascinating Fascism," in *A Susan Sontag Reader* (New York: Vintage, 1983), 323.

6. Eve Kosofsky Sedgwick, "Paranoid Reading and Reparative Reading: Or, You're So Paranoid, You Probably Think This Introduction Is about You," in *Novel Gazing: Queer Readings in Fiction*, ed. Eve Kosofsky Sedgwick (Durham: Duke University Press, 1997), 4; hereafter cited parenthetically by page number.

7. Scott Lively and Kevin Abrams, *The Pink Swastika: Homosexuality in the Nazi Party* (Kreizer, OR: Founders Publishing Corporation, 1995), x.

8. Julia Kristeva, *About Chinese Women*, trans. Anita Barrows (New York: Urizen Books, 1977), 23.

9. Eve Kosofsky Sedgwick, "Privilege of Unknowing: Diderot's *The Nun*," in *Tendencies* (Durham: Duke University Press, 1993), 49 n. 14.

10. Janine Chasseguet-Smirgel, *Sexuality and Mind: The Role of the Father and the Mother in the Psyche* (New York: New York University Press, 1986), 82.

11. Chasseguet-Smirgel, *Sexuality and Mind*, 81–93.

12. Klaus Theweleit, *Male Fantasies*, vol. 2, trans. Erica Carter and Chris Turner (Minneapolis: University of Minnesota Press, 1989).

13. See Wilhem Reich, *The Mass Psychology of Fascism*, rev. ed., trans. Vincent R. Carfagno (New York: Farrar, Straus and Giroux, 1970).

14. Theodor W. Adorno, *Minima Moralia: Reflections from Damaged Life*, trans. E. F. N. Jephcott (London: Verso, 1974), 46.

15. Theweleit, *Male Fantasies*, 339.

16. See Simon Karlinsky, "Russia's Gay Literature and Culture: The Impact of the October Revolution," in *Hidden from History: Reclaiming the Gay and Lesbian Past*, ed. Martin Duberman, Martha Vicinus, and George Chauncey, Jr. (New York: Meridian, 1990), 355. My entire paragraph is indebted to Karlinsky's article, which is a corrective to the section on Russia in John Lauritsen and David Thorstad's *The Early Homosexual Rights Movement: 1864–1935* (New York: Times Change Press, 1974), which did much to promote the notion that the early Bolsheviks were sexual radicals.

17. Karlinsky, "Russia's Gay Literature and Culture," 361.

18. As quoted in George L. Mosse, *Nationalism and Sexuality: Respectability and Abnormal Sexuality in Modern Europe* (New York: Howard Fertig, 1985), 165.

19. As quoted in Mosse, *Nationalism and Sexuality*, 159.

20. Sigmund Freud, *Three Essays on the Theory of Sexuality,* in *The Standard Edition of the Complete Psychological Works of Sigmund Freud*, trans. James Strachey, 24 vols. (London: Hogarth Press, 1953–74), 7:136; hereafter cited parenthetically by page number.

21. Sedgwick, *Epistemology of the Closet*, 85.

22. Sigmund Freud, *Leonardo da Vinci and a Memory from His Childhood,* in *The Standard Edition*, 11:80.

23. Ernest Hemingway, *Selected Letters, 1917–1961*, ed. Carlos Baker (New York: Scribner's, 1981), 387–88.

24. Mosse, *Nationalism and Sexuality*, 166. On the relation between sentencing and the "psychological type" of an allegedly gay defendant, see Richard Plant, *The Pink Triangle: The Nazi War against Homosexuals* (New York: Henry Holt, 1986), 111–12.

25. See Geoffrey Cocks, *Psychotherapy in the Third Reich: The Göring Institute* (New York: Oxford University Press, 1985), 3.

26. As quoted in Cocks, *Psychotherapy in the Third Reich*, 5.

27. Hitherto unrivaled, and, according to Geoffrey Cocks, still unrivaled: "The particular conditions that prevailed in 1933 allowed . . . psychotherapists to achieve an institutional status and capacity for practice that has been unrivalled in Germany before or since." Cocks, *Psychotherapy in the Third Reich*, 3.

28. Theweleit, *Male Fantasies*, 337.

29. Thomas Mann, *The Order of the Day* (1935), as quoted in Chassequet-Smirgel, *Sexuality and Mind*, 145.

30. Žižek rejects the conventional wisdom that locates "the source of totalitarianism" in "a dogmatic attachment to the official world: the lack of laughter, of ironic detachment." On the contrary, "cynical distance, laughter, irony, are, so to speak, part of the [totalitarian] game." Slavoj Žižek, *The Sublime Object of Ideology* (London: Verso, 1989), 27–28.

31. As quoted in Hans Peter Bleuel, *Sex and Society in Nazi Germany*, ed. Heinrich Fraenkel, trans. J. Maxwell Brownjohn (New York: Lippincott, 1973), 5.

32. As quoted in Bleuel, *Sex and Society*, 4.

33. As quoted in Erwin J. Haeberle, "Swastika, Pink Triangle, and Yellow Star: The Destruction of Sexology and the Persecution of Homosexuals in Nazi Germany," in Duberman, Vicinus, and Chauncey, *Hidden from History*, 374.

34. Ludwig L. Lenz, *The Memoirs of a Sexologist,* as quoted in Haeberle, "Swastika, Pink Triangle, and Yellow Star," 369.

35. Barbara Ehrenreich, foreword to Theweleit, *Male Fantasies*, xi.

36. Theweleit's work focuses on the Freikorps, a miscellaneous group of proto-fascists, not the Nazis proper. His work never adequately addresses, however, how the misogyny of the former translates into the anti-Semitism of the latter. The effect, if not the intention, is to render anti-Semitism largely irrelevant to the rise of National Socialism.

37. Sedgwick, *Epistemology of the Closet*, 26.

38. Walter C. Langer, *The Mind of Adolf Hitler: The Secret Wartime Report* (New York: Basic Books, 1972), 173–75.

39. As quoted in Günter Grau, *Hidden Holocaust? Gay and Lesbian Persecution in Germany, 1933–45*, trans. Patrick Camiller (New York: Cassell, 1995), 198.

40. "We are still getting one case of homosexuality a month in the SS. Over the year

193

[1937] there were roughly eight to ten cases in the SS as a whole." Himmler, speaking on February 18, 1937, to SS-Gruppenführers at Bad Tölz; quoted in Grau, *Hidden Holocaust?* 196.

41. Mosse, *Nationalism and Sexuality*, 164. Lively is blunter: "Himmler may have been a homosexual." *The Pink Swastika*, 112.

42. As David Halperin notes, homosexuality is the exception:

> As constructed by homophobic discourse, "the homosexual" is indeed an impossibly—and, it now appears, fatally—contradictory creature. For "the homosexual" is simultaneously (1) a social misfit, (2) an unnatural monster or freak, (3) a moral failure, and (4) a sexual pervert. Now it is of course impossible, under a post-Kantian system of ethics at least, for anyone to be all of those things at the same time—to be, for example, both sick and blameworthy in respect of the same defect—but no matter: such attributes may be mutually incompatible in logical terms, but they turn out to be perfectly compatible in practical, that is to say political, terms.

David M. Halperin, *Saint Foucault: Towards a Gay Hagiography* (New York: Oxford University Press, 1995), 46.

43. See Lee Edelman, *Homographesis: Essays in Gay Literary and Cultural Theory* (New York: Routledge, 1994), 199.

44. Robert J. Lifton, *The Nazi Doctors: Medical Killing and the Psychology of Genocide* (New York: Basic Books, 1986), 17.

45. Žižek, *The Sublime Object of Ideology*, 49.

46. Hannah Arendt, *The Origins of Totalitarianism*, rev. ed. (New York: Harcourt Brace Jovanovich, 1979), 388.

47. Louis Althusser, *Lenin and Philosophy and Other Essays*, trans. Ben Brewster (New York: Monthly Review Press, 1971), 172.

48. Plant, *The Pink Triangle*, 181.

49. Plant, *The Pink Triangle*, 181.

50. A. James Gregor, *Italian Fascism and Developmental Dictatorship* (Princeton: Princeton University Press, 1979), 33.

51. Michel Foucault, *The History of Sexuality,* vol. 1, trans. Robert Hurley (New York: Vintage, 1978), 137; hereafter cited parenthetically by page number.

52. The 1998 statistics are even grimmer: blacks make up 13 percent of the population but account for 57 percent of new HIV infections.

53. Lifton, *The Nazi Doctors,* 22.

54. Lifton, *The Nazi Doctors,* 22–23. Hirshman and Larson note that "although eugenics eventually was to be identified with the nastiest of nativist and fascist social movements, it first arose in England and the United States among reform-minded elites, intellectuals, and professionals. These Progressives, socialists, and free love advocates, including many women radicals, were key players in the eugenics movement." Linda R. Hirshman and Jane E. Larson, *Hard Bargains: The Politics of Sex* (New York: Oxford University Press, 1998), 170.

55. As quoted in Lifton, *The Nazi Doctors*, 24.

56. Jean Baudrillard, *In the Shadow of the Silent Majority* (New York: Semiotext(e), 1983), 20.

57. As quoted in George J. Anderopoulos, "Introduction: The Calculus of Genocide," in *Genocide: Conceptual and Historical Dimensions*, ed. George J. Anderopoulus (Philadelphia: University of Pennsylvania Press, 1994), 1.

58. In 1998 the United Nations finally established a permanent court to carry on the legal tradition initiated by the Nuremberg tribunal. The United States voted against the measure.

59. Tony Barta, "Relations of Genocide: Land and Lives in the Colonization of Australia," in *Genocide and the Modern Age*, ed. Isidor Wallimann and Michael Dobkowski (Westport, CT: Greenwood, 1987), 247.

60. See Henry Louis Gates, Jr., *Thirteen Ways of Looking at a Black Man* (New York: Random House, 1997), 105–6; hereafter cited parenthetically by page number.

61. Lively, *The Pink Swastika*, 180.

62. Sigmund Freud, "Psycho-analytic Notes on an Autobiographical Account of a Case of Paranoia (Dementia Paranoides)," in *The Standard Edition*, 12:59.

63. Sigmund Freud, "Some Neurotic Mechanisms in Jealousy, Paranoia and Homosexuality," in *The Standard Edition*, 18:226.

64. Freud, "Psycho-analytic Notes on an Autobiographical Account of a Case of Paranoia," 60.

65. Sigmund Freud, "Preface to Reik's *Ritual: Psycho-analytic Studies*," in *The Standard Edition*, 17:261.

66. This is argued by Guy Hocquenghem in *Homosexual Desire*, trans. Daniella Dangoor (Durham: Duke University Press, 1993).

67. Frantz Fanon, *Black Skin, White Masks*, trans. Charles Lam Markmann (New York: Grove, 1967), 156.

68. Fanon, *Black Skin, White Masks*, 180 n. 44. Mark Haile notes that the hetero/homo binary is powerless to account for the sexual experiences of many U.S. blacks:

> There is a construction of sexuality far more elaborate than mere "straight" or "gay," especially in the black community. . . . [The] field of sexual identities for black lesbian and gay men . . . is identical to neither the white lesbian and gay community in America, nor the framework of sexual orientation as has been studied on the African continent. If HIV

prevention is to be effective in communities of color, the complexity of black sexual identi-
fications needs to be acknowledged. How, for example, does one best reach a non-gay iden-
tified black man who nevertheless has sex with men?

But as Haile is also careful to note, none of this justifies denying the reality of black gay
and lesbian experience. See Mark Haile, "It Can Happen to Anybody, Even Me, Magic
Johnson," *BLK* 3, no. 9 (1991): 20–25.

Index

Adorno, Theodor W., 148–19, 192n. 14
AIDS: and activism, 56–58, 66–67, 74, 105, 141–44, 161; and anal sex, 64–65, 105–7, 130; changing demographics, 55–56; and conspiracy theories, 143–44, 163–67, 169; cultural construction of, 15, 43, 65, 76, 78–79, 116, 118; as death wish, 55–57, 62, 64–65, 67–68, 75, 89; and the economic system, 132–33; and education, 150; and ersatz heterosexuality/virtual normality, 56–57, 74, 77–78, 80, 105; and genocide, 55, 141, 161–62; and Rock Hudson, 54–55; and Mapplethorpe, 84–85, 87–89; and the marriage plot, 56–58, 63, 67–68, 78, 80; medical definition of, 55; and metaphor, 64, 68; and narrative, 15, 55–58, 62–68, 72–73, 76–77, 80, 144; and newer therapies, 56–57, 65; and *The Picture of Dorian Gray*, 15, 43, 55, 58, 61, 63, 66, 84, 89; and promiscuity, 57, 62–65, 67, 76, 79–80, 105, 107, 132–33; and race, 163–64, 194n. 52; as "truth" of homosexuality, 15, 85, 88–89, 161–62; writing love letters to, 118
Allbright, Ivan, 46
allegory, 125
Althusser, Louis, 136, 161, 169
America, Miss, 117
America, Mr., 125, 130
American Studies (Merlis), 130
Anderopoulos, George J., 195n. 57
antisemitism, 146, 157, 160–61, 193n. 36
Arendt, Hannah, 67, 160–61
Aristotle, 23, 25–26, 31–32, 66
art market, 82, 85–87, 98
Atlas, Charles, 119–21, 123–25, 129

Auden, W. H., 76–77
Austen, Jane, 70, 107

Bakhtin, M. M., 28–30, 52, 72
Bally Total Fitness, 129
Barker, Francis, 23, 27, 110–11, 178n. 15
Barta, Tony, 168
Barthes, Roland, 14, 179n. 23
Bartlett, Neil, 177n. 3
Bataille, Georges, 79
Baudelaire, Charles, 46
Baudrillard, Jean, 85–86, 132–33, 167, 184–85n. 4
beauty pageants, 113, 115–17, 121
Benjamin, Walter, 18–19, 36–37, 46–48, 52, 177n. 5
Berger, John, 13
Berlin Sexual Institute, 156
Bernhardt, Sarah, 177n. 6
Bernheimer, Charles, 93
Bersani, Leo, 59, 62, 104–8, 182n. 13
Bildungsroman, 17, 25, 27, 56, 59, 72–73
bisexuality, 4–5, 7–9, 12, 153
Blanchot, Maurice, 46
Bleul, Peter, 193n. 32
Bloom, Harold, 22–23
bodybuilding: as *ars erotica*, 15, 116; and beauty pageants, 113, 116, 121; and class, 117; vs. exercise/weight lifting, 116, 127; and gender, 114–15, 126–28, 137–38; and the mirror stage, 135–37, 139; and narrative, 15, 114; and the nineteenth-century novel, 25; and the phallic, 130, 132; and race, 127–28; and sexual orientation, 114, 117; and spectacle, 114–17, 128; and sport, 116–17
Bond, James, 6

ABOUT THE AUTHOR

Paul Morrison is an associate professor of English at Brandeis University. He is the author of *The Poetics of Fascism: Ezra Pound, T. S. Eliot, Paul de Man.*